When Women Kill

SUNY Series in Violence

David Luckenbill, Editor

When Women Kill

Coramae Richey Mann

STATE UNIVERSITY OF NEW YORK PRESS

Published by
State University of New York Press, Albany

Quotation from P. J. Hanke and A. J. Shields (1992), "Sentencing Variations of
Women Convicted of Homicide in Alabama: 1929–1985," paper presented at the
annual meeting of the American Society of Criminology, is reprinted with
permission of the authors. Selections from Scott Decker (1993), "Exploring
Victim-Offender Relationships in Homicide: The Role of Individual and Event
Characteristics," *Justice Quarterly* 10 (4): 585–612, is reprinted with permission of
the author.

For information address State University of New York Press,
State University Plaza, Albany,
NY 12246

Production by Laura Starrett
Marketing by Terry Abad Swierzowski

Library of Congress Cataloging in Publication Date
Mann, Coramae Richey, 1931–
    When women kill / Coramae Richey Mann.
        p.   cm.—(SUNY series in violence)
    Includes bibliographical references and index.
    ISBN 0-7914-2811-7 (hc).—ISBN 0-7914-2812-5
    1. Women murderers—United States.   I. Title.   II. Series.
HV6046.M363   1996
364.1'523'082—dc20   95-15374
                                                              CIP

10   9   8   7   6   5   4   3   2

Contents

List of Tables

List of Figures

Acknowledgments

This book is based upon homicide research undertaken in six U.S. cities. Without the splendid cooperation of the police administrators in those cities, neither the research project nor this book would have been possible. For that reason, I am deeply indebted to Fred Rice, former Chief of Police of Chicago, Illinois; George Napper, at that time Director of Public Safety, Atlanta, Georgia; former New York City Police Commissioner, Benjamin Ward; then Baltimore Commissioner of Police, Bishop Robinson; former Houston, Texas Police Chief Lee Brown; and prior Los Angeles Chief of Police, Daryl Gates.

I gratefully acknowledge the imaginative graphics prepared by Gina Lake of the Department of Criminal Justice at Indiana Universty. Jane Lyle of the Indiana University Press came through for me by casting her brilliant editorial eyes upon the final manuscript draft in thoughtful critique. I am grateful also to the three anonymous reviewers who helped to guide this effort and to David Luckenbill, who kept me inspired throughout.

And once again, my father, Edward Grant Richey, stood by me patiently over the many months it took to put together *When Women Kill*. He never complained when I retreated to my basement office to write, or dashed to the library for a citation, or to the computing center to pick up printouts of data analyses. Many times he took those trips with me; thus I consider him an integral part of this book and dedicate it to him.

Chapter 1

Introduction

Velma Margie Bullard Barfield, a fifty-year-old grandmother, was put to death by the state of North Carolina in November in November of 1984 for allegedly poisoning a number of people who were close to her, including her mother. As the last female homicide offender executed in the United States, Barfield will undoubtedly be remembered as a poisoner. Similarly, the name of Lucretia Borgia is considered synonymous with the appellation "woman poisoner." Alleged poisoning was the crime of nineteenth-century America, and "murder by poison was particularly feared because there was no way to see it coming or to defend against it"; poisoning was also "associated with women" (Jones, 1980: 103). In fact, throughout history, women who kill have been viewed as distancing themselves from their victims through the application of measured doses of poison over lengthy periods of time—a murder method often considered devious, cunning, and deceitful.

In his book *The Criminality of Women* (1950), Otto Pollak advanced a theory of female criminality that emphasized women's "deceitfulness" and claimed, "In general, it can be concluded that homicide committed by women can be called secret murder and that the general observations about the highly masked character of female crime are well substantiated by the modus operandi of the woman who kills" (p. 19). Such a view has been paralleled in literature, where a nexus has often been asserted between the female animal in the wild and the human female. The poet Rudyard Kipling, for example, claimed that "the female of the species is more deadly than the male," while the German philosopher Fredrich Nietzsche declared that "in revenge and in love woman is more barbarous than man." In her view of the literature on women who killed their mates from 1895 to 1970, Rasche (1990: 48) describes such views as the "deadlier species" model and notes that "traditionally, woman has been viewed in Western culture as a different species of creature from man." Homicide arrest statistics suggest that, antithetical to the musings of male literary writers, women are *not* the deadliest of the species. Quite the contrary: in male-male and female-female recorded homicides, "*the differ-ence between the sexes is immense, and it is universal.* There is no known human society in which the level of lethal violence among women even begins to approach that among men" (Daly and Wilson, 1988: 146). Nor is there "evidence that women in modern America are approaching the level of violent conflict prevailing among men. Indeed there is no evidence that the women in *any* society have *ever* approached the level of violent conflict prevailing among men in the same society" (ibid., p. 149). Very few Americans associate violence with females, and an even lesser number are able to visualize women as significant contributors to the public conception of violence as a national problem, much less adopt a serious view of women as cunning murderers.

Yet, American society reflects a culture that was built on violence. Americans appear to idolize and sensationalize violence in the print media, movies, our television "soaps," "cop" shows, and other television programming. At this writing, the current public fascination with every nuance of former football megastar O. J. Simpson's murder trial is a barometer of the degree of violence addiction endemic in this country. Since violence is so pervasive in our society, it is logical to assume that women have not remained uncontaminated by it. Further, as the re-nowned violence researcher Murray Straus (1989a) observes, "Female assaults grow out of the same cultural and structural roots as male vio-lence."

In an effort to bring us closer to an understanding of female homicide offenders and concomitantly provide a better perception of the crime of homicide, this book examines female perpetrators who were apprehended for killing other humans. The impetus for this study was a long-standing interest in women criminals and a curiosity that crystallized as the result of a 1984 invitation from Margaret Heckler, then Secretary of the U.S. Department of Health and Human Services, to undertake a review of the major homicide research concerning black women who kill. Despite exhaustive scrutiny of the literature, little was uncovered in that probe for data (Mann, 1986). In light of the increasing rate of violence nationwide, the paucity of information on this specific female offending group, and the fact that young persons of color are the most frequent murder offenders and victims, it became obvious that additional knowledge about female criminal homicide offenders was needed.

This volume is based on the findings of a field study undertaken in 1985 and 1986 in six United States cities with homicide rates equal to or higher than the national rates for the years 1979 and 1983. In addition to time limitations, financial constraints, and data access problems, an attempt was made to designate cities that were proportionately representa-tive of cleared homicide cases by region for 1979 and 1983 according to the FBI Uniform Crime Reports. The optimal study would have included male killers, but again, time and fiscal constraints precluded such a comparison study which would have required additional male sampling. However, while the inclusion of male subjects would have been desirable, their omission can be justified on the grounds that the principal topic of interest was the rarely studied female homicide offender and the primary thrust of the research was to obtain as complete a picture as possible of each homicide event and of its major actors—the female offender and her victim.

Because of the exploratory nature of the study, no preconceived hypotheses were generated for testing, and by definition the qualitative approach used is limited largely to descriptive measures. Nonetheless, the aforementioned intensive review of the literature on female homicide offenders suggested potential research directions and stimulated a number of research questions. Previous investigative research experience demonstrated that additional questions normally arise after the data are analyzed; this effort was no exception. The study is configured by the following research questions: (1) Is the "subculture of violence" theory applicable to African American female homicide offenders? (2) Is there any validity to the "southern subculture of violence" as applied to women killers? (3) Is an economic theory of crime applicable to women who commit homicide? (4) How significant is the role played by drugs (alcohol and narcotics) in female-perpetrated homicides? (5) Can victim precipitation and/or the "battered woman syndrome" predict female criminal homicide? (6) Are ecological factors—season/weather, time, day of week— influential in murders committed by females? (7) Are minority women who murder treated more punitively by the criminal justice system than nonminority women? (8) Does race of the victim influence the sentencing process? (9) Are there city/regional differences in the criminal court processing of women who kill?

Race and ethnicity are paramount considerations in the study of murder because of the disproportionate number of instances in which both the victims of an offense and those arrested for its commission, are racial/ethnic minorities. Women of color are no exception to the race/ homicide nexus, particularly African American women. Even though the UCR Supplemental Homicide Reports (SHR) provide some details on the characteristics of offenders and their victims, they do not yield other specifics of interest on female offenders or certain nuances of the crime indicated in the commission of homicide. This study was undertaken to close some of these information gaps.

DEFINITIONS

The terms *homicide* and *murder* are frequently used interchangeably in the research literature. the Uniform Crime Reports (UCR) record arrests involving the taking of another's life as *murder and nonnegligent manslaughter*. Daly and Wilson (1988: 14) refer to homicides as "those interpersonal assaults and other acts directed against another person (for example, poisonings) that occur outside the context of warfare, and that prove fatal." However, Wilbanks' (1982): 153) differentiation of the terms is appropriate for our purposes:

> *Homicide*, the more inclusive term, refers to the killing of one human being by another. This term covers both criminal and noncriminal (justifiable and excusable) homicides. *Murder* is a criminal homicide that involves both intent and premeditation. Some states distinguish between *first-degree* (generally requiring both intent and premeditation) and *second-degree* murder (requiring intent but not premeditation). *Manslaughter* is a type of criminal homicide, but is not considered murder. Other types of criminal homicide that are not considered murder are vehicular homicide and negligent homicide.

Although the more exact and preferred nomenclature is *criminal homicide*, depending upon the reference cited in this work, any of these terms may be used.

Female, the generic term for a woman or girl as distinguished from a man or boy, and *woman* are also frequently used interchangeably. Whereas many adolescent females commit criminal homicide, the majority (80.2 percent) of females arrested for this crime are women (U.S. Department of Justice, 1993: 231). For this reason and for consistency, the term *woman* is the preferred term used throughout the book.

FEMALE FAMILY VIOLENCE AND OTHER ASSAULTS

In a recent commentary, McNeely and I (1990) argued that domestic violence is a human issue, not just a gender issue. Our reasoning was based on the facts that "(a) women are more prone than men to engage in severely violent acts; (b) each year more men than women are victimized by their intimates; and (c) between 1975 and 1985 violence by men against women decreased, whereas violence by women against men increased" (p. 130). Leaving the Pandora's box of extent and seriousness of injury inflicted closed for the time being, let us examine the basis of these statements. Murray Straus and his colleagues at the Family Violence Research Program of the Family Research Laboratory at the University of New Hampshire undertook a profound examination of violence in the family in the 1970s. The resultant 1975 National Family Violence Survey (NFVS) discovered that wives assault their husbands at about the same rate that husbands assault their wives (Straus, Gelles, and Steinmetz, 1980). Any violence between spouses yielded annual incidence rates of

12 per 100 couples for both husbands and wives, but the rates of *severe* violence by the wife were 5 per 100 (2,700,000 assaults) compared to 4 per 100 (2,200,000 assaults) for husbands (Straus, 1986: Table II). Also, McLeod's (1984) examination of 6,200 domestic assault cases reported that weapons were involved in 82 percent of male victimizations by females but, conversely, only 25 percent of female victimizations by males involved weapons. In her studies, Steinmetz (1978: 503) found the average violence scores of wives (4.04, 7.82, 7.00, respectively) to be higher than those of the husbands (3.52, 6.00, 6.60, respectively), and also that women's assaultive acts were more frequent. Repeated public surveys in Canada also indicate that wives assault their husbands as often as or more frequently than husbands assault their wives (Christensen, n.d.).

Straus used a much larger nationally representative sample in a replication of his 1975 national survey (6,002 couples compared to the initial survey of 2,143 couples), and again he found women to report physical assaults on their husbands at about the same high rate as the reported assaults on wives by husbands (Straus, 1989b). From 1975 to 1985 the rates of both husband-wife overall violence and severe violence decreased. Whereas wife-husband severe violence rates also decreased, their overall violence rate increased. Although the differences were not statistically significant,[1] Straus found that in minor assaults on their partners, the women's rate slightly exceeded the men's (77 v. 69 per 1,000), but for severe assaults men slightly exceeded the women (49 v. 44 per 1,000).

There is also ample evidence suggesting that men underreport violent encounters with women and, conversely, the possibility that females overreport violence against them (Mann, 1989). Rape universally connotes an assault on a woman by a man, yet women do rape men, usually in gang rapes. In personal interviews with male rape victims, Sarrel and Masters (1982) found posttrauma reactions in all eleven cases of adult males who were sexually molested by females. All of the men experienced symptoms of physical and psychological trauma and described varying levels of "fright, panic, and confusion at the time they were molested" (p. 126). According to sex therapists Masters and Johnson (cited in Sarrel and Masters, 1982), the vast majority of such cases are never reported. Men are disinclined to report rape by other males, so:

> How much more reluctant then would be the man who is the victim of sexual assault by gunslinging or knife-wielding women? Would such a man choose to test the credulity of the police or even his closest friends? "I was raped by two women last night" may not fall in the same category as "I was taken aboard a UFO by little green men," but the inherent implausibility of the claim might restrain even a braggart (Rosenfeld, 1983: 28).

Child and elderly abuse are two other forms of family violence perpetrated by females which have only recently been brought to light. In their treatise on family violence issues, Thibault and Rossier (1992) cite figures from a 1986 national study by the American Human Association which show that 60.7 percent of the caretakers reported for child maltreatment were females and that females accounted for 56.8 percent of major physical child abuse cases and 57.3 percent of child fatalities.[2] These percentages reflect an impressive increase since 1978 when an American Humane Society report on 100,000 cases of child abuse found that only 45 percent of the abusers were women (Mann, 1984a: 24).

Physical mistreatment of the elderly by their adult offspring has been alluded to as "a new plague." Estimates of the annual number of victims of this "hidden family problem" range from 500,000 to 1 million (Pierce and Trotta, 1986: 103). Data from six Florida counties reported by Giordano (1982) indicate that the average victim of multiple abuse was a white female who, if unmarried, was typically abused by her daughter. More recently, Pierce and Trotta (1986: 102) observe that since women are almost always the primary caregivers to the elderly, they are most likely to be the typical abusers. Most often the abusive female relative is a daughter, followed by a granddaughter.

Characteristically, the reason this type of abuse is considered a "hidden" family problem is that such incidents are seldom reported to the authorities. Men will rarely call the police when they are abused by their wives or female lovers; elderly parents are reluctant to bring their daughters or granddaughters to the attention of law enforcement; and because of their age, immaturity, and dependency, infants and small children cannot or will not tell on their mothers.

An endless list of plausible causal factors could be generated to explain female violence directed against family members. Particularly notable would be the internal and external stresses associated with the roles of wife and caregiver. But what about nonfamilial violence perpetrated by women? An examination of the most recent available FBI Uniform Crime Reports (UCR) reveals some rather astonishing statistics involving female arrests for assault. In 1992, for example, 64,359 females were arrested for aggravated assault, a number that constituted 14.8 percent of all persons arrested for this violent index crime (U.S. Department of Justice, 1993: 234). Aggravated assault ranked tenth among the crimes for which females were arrested (2.9 percent). Even more illuminating is the fact that 156,584 females were arrested in 1992 for other (nonfelony) assaults (17.2 percent of total arrests for this offense), which made arrests for these crimes the fourth most frequent arrest offense of females (6.9 percent). Arrest trends from 1988 to 1992 show a 46.6 percent increase in female arrests for other assaults over this time period, compared to a 26.3 percent increase for males (ibid., p. 224). Over this five-year time span, the percentage increases for aggravated assault were also substantially higher for females (37.4 percent) than for males (24.3 percent). In light of the previous discussion about the reluctance or inability of family members to report violence committed by a wife, child, or mother, we can assume that many such arrests are extrafamilial.

Data collected from the top three states that arrest and imprison women—California, Florida, and New York[3]—indicate similar rankings of violent crimes committed by women.[4] There were 10,141 California women arrested for felony assault in 1990, ranking this offense third among female felony arrests (after drugs and thefts) and eighth among all offenses for which women were arrested in that state. That same year, aggravated assault was the second most frequent index crime for which women were arrested in Florida (N = 5,110). Among all female arrests in Florida in 1990, aggravated assault was the fourth most frequent offense. In 1990 in New York State assault ranked first in the felony category and accounted for 14.7 percent of all female felony arrests (N = 3,891); together, misdemeanor and felony assaults totaled 8.1 percent of the 1990 arrests of New York State women (N = 7,703) and were fourth in arrest ranking.

Both the national distributions and the rankings of female arrests for assault in California, Florida, and New York State suggest not only that women are committing an impressive number of assaultive crimes, but also that such arrests are increasing at a faster rate than those of men. In the rank ordering of the frequency of female arrests, assaults clearly occupy a prominent place among the crimes females commit. Furthermore, there is a very thin line between assaults and homicide. It has been pointed out, for instance, that "evidence regarding the escalatory character of interactions that culminate in criminal homicide was provided first by Wolfgang in his rich descriptions of the moves and counter moves in what he styled *victim-precipitated* criminal homicide" (Wilson, 1993: 44). Also, Block's (1987) seventeen-year study of homicides in Chicago found that 69 percent were initiated by assaultive behavior such as arguments, brawls, or fights.

FEMALE CRIMINAL HOMICIDE OFFENDERS

In an early monograph, *The Contemporary Woman and Crime* (1975), Rita Simon examined longitudinal national data concerning the involvement of women in crime and the types of crime with which they were charged. She reported an average rate of change of −0.05 for female violent crimes over the period 1953–1972 with a 1972 percentage of 11.0 (p. 39), concluding, "A popular impression that in recent years women have been committing crimes of violence at a much higher rate than they have in the past is disputed by the facts shown." Undoubtedly the same statement is applicable two decades later, since females were arrested for 12.5 percent of all index violent crimes in 1992 (U.S. Department of Justice, 1993: 234). Finally, Simon's examination revealed that females were arrested for 15.6 percent of all criminal homicides in 1972, for a modest average rate of change of 0.08 over their percentage of 14.1 in 1953. On the basis of this finding, Simon deduced, "For criminal homicide the percentage of males and females have remained remarkably stable over the past 20 years and the average rate of change is practically nil" (p. 41).

Compared to males, female arrests for homicide are not striking. In 1979, one of the years included in the study reported in this volume, there were 18,264 total arrests for murder and nonnegligent manslaughter (U.S. Department of Justice, 1980: 199).[5] At that time, 13.7 percent of those arrested were females and such arrests constituted only 0.2 percent of all offenses for which females were charged. By 1983, the other year for which data were reported, female arrests for murder still accounted for only 0.2 percent of female total arrests and 13.3 percent of all murder arrests—again far less than the male proportion (U.S. Department of Justice, 1984: 186).[6] Almost a decade later, the most recent available UCR data indicate that females represented only 9.7 percent of persons arrested for the 19,491 murders in 1992, an appreciable decrease from 1983 (U.S. Department of Justice, 1993: 234). Total arrest trends indicate a decrease of 9.6 percent in female arrests for murder from 1988 to 1992, and by 1992 such arrests dropped to only 0.1 percent of all female arrests (U.S. Department of Justice, 1993: 224).

Returning to our examination of state-level exemplars rather than national homicide statistics, we find that in California and Florida, murder accounted for only 0.1 percent of all female arrests in 1990. Equally modest figures were found for New York State, which matched the 1990 national figure of 0.2 percent.[7]

In sum, up to this point our analysis indicates that, at least according to official statistics, three salient facts seem evident: (1) compared to males, females are not arrested in appreciable numbers for murder; (2) arrests for murder constitute a very small proportion of the crimes for which females are arrested; and (3) there has not been a significant increase in the number of females arrested for murder as a percentage of all such arrests for at least four decades.

PREVIOUS RESEARCH ON WOMEN MURDERERS

The following discussion of existing studies of women murderers is limited to generic descriptions, since the detailed findings of these research efforts are interspersed appropriately throughout the book. Another limitation to this review of prior research is that it includes only female offender-based studies or those that substantially discuss female offenders as an identifiable subgroup within a larger data set.[8] The earlier studies are presented in chronological sequence and ordered in time periods by decade.

One of the most prolific authors on homicide research, William Wilbanks (1982: 155), describes the five most commonly used data bases viewed as "the foundation for descriptive and theoretical studies of female involvement in homicide": (1) the Uniform Crime Reports (UCR); (2) the National Center for Health Statistics (NCHS); (3) city studies; (4) prison studies; and (5) "anecdotal studies." His excellent description of these resources, including their positive and negative features, is briefly discussed next (ibid., pp. 155–160).

Uniform Crime Reports (UCR)

In our previous examination of female violence and homicide offending, we relied almost exclusively on Uniform Crime Report statistics to describe the phenomenon. UCR arrest figures derived from local police jurisdictions across the nation are reported to the Federal Bureau of Investigation which publishes them annually. The UCR murder and nonnegligent manslaughter data are useful for longitudinal studies and for computing female homicide rates. Also, information on age is easily obtained. A serious drawback of UCR homicide statistics is that data are not available on gender *and* race. To remedy this oversight, FBI supplementary homicide data tapes are accessible to researchers.

National Center for Health Statistics (NCHS)

Data from the NCHS are also referred to as vital statistics. Collected from death certificates, this information provides useful victimization data and circumstances of the homicide such as choice of weapon, victim demographics (for example, age, sex, race, weight), the number of wounds, and the time of death. A major disadvantage of NCHS data is that they are victim-based and yield little material on offenders.

Prison Studies

A great deal of detail concerning individual homicides can be garnered through the use of prison data, which rely on information from prison records and/or interviews of inmates. Nonetheless, Wilbanks (1982: 158) points to serious biases in this type of sample, "Obviously it is not representative of all offenders in a particular jurisdiction; those not caught, charged, convicted, or sentenced to prison are not included. Furthermore, a sample of offenders present at a particular time is likely to overrepresent serious (long term) offenders, since those with shorter sentences are less likely to be "caught" at the time the sample is drawn."

Prison studies that rely on inmate interviews for details of murders have limitations similar to those for data gathered from the respondents in victimization surveys—forgetting, inaccurate or incomplete recall, lying, differential respondent productivity, and reliance on the skills and effects of the interviewers (Mann, 1993).

"Anecdotal" Studies

Instead of using sampling procedures, this type of data base relies on cases collected from various sources such as media accounts and offender autobiographies. Wilbanks is highly critical of data gleaned from such sources because "the cases reported are not representative of any group of offenders and may merely reflect the bias of the author" (ibid.).

City Studies

This type of jurisdictional research provided the data base used in the present study. City studies commonly rely on information from death certificates and/or police reports, thereby providing richer detail. The in-depth examination of police and homicide files, for example, provides a splendid source of information on the nuances of a homicide: time, place, weapon used, use of alcohol and narcotics by the offender and victim, the possible motive, the victim-offender relationship, prior arrests, previous violent offenses of the offender (and often the victim as well), the criminal justice processing of the offender, and the final case disposition. The disadvantages of using city data include the problems of generalizing to other jurisdictions and the serious obstacle of missing data.

A quick perusal of Table 1.1, which includes the identified studies of female criminal homicide offenders from 1958 to 1992 by data bases, demonstrates the preponderance of prison and city studies in such research. The table lists homicide studies of women offenders by the names of the researchers, the study years and year reported, the location of the study, the number of cases, the type of study (data base),[9] the percentage of African Americans in the studies, the mean age of the offenders, the percentage found to have prior records, and the victim/offender relationship (family/intimate, acquaintance/friend, stranger, or unknown).

Beginning with Wolfgang's seminal study of homicide reported in 1958, a total of twenty-five empirical studies[10] focusing on female homicide offenders are identified. Three of the studies describe national rates of and/or general trends in male and female homicide (Shin, Jedlicka, and Lee, 1977; Wilbanks, 1982; 1983a), whereas the remaining research efforts are city or prison studies. Among the cities included are Philadelphia, Baltimore, Detroit, St. Louis, Atlanta, Pittsburgh, Houston, Tusca-

Table 1.1

Selected Characteristics of Empirical Studies of Female Criminal Homicide Offenders, 1958–1992.

Researcher(s)	Year Reported	Location/ (Data base)	Study Period	Number of Cases	% African American	Mean Age	% Prior Record	Firearm Used	Victim/Offender Relationship Family/ Intimate	Acq/ Friend	Stranger	Unk
					1958–1967							
Wolfgang	1958	Philadelphia (Police)	1948–52	108	85.2	32.6	51.6	22.5	67.4	21.8	3.3	7.7
Pokorny	1965	Houston (Police)	1958–61	99	70.7	—	—	56.0	50.1	33.4	2.4	14.1
					1968–1977							
Cole, Fisher, & Cole	1968	California (Prison)	1965	111	43.2	37.0	67.0	(W) 37.0 (AA) 31.0	67.0	—	33.0	—
Ward, Jackson, & Ward	1969	Minnesota (Prison)	1963–66; 1968	179	25.0[1]	—	20.0	34.0	54.0[1]	18.0	8.0	20.0
Suval & Brisson	1974	North Carolina (Prison)	1969–1971	87	80.5	30.0[2]	27.2	—	—	—	—	—
Rosenblatt & Greenwood	1974	Canada (Prison; Mental Hospital)	1970–71	24	—	35.0[3]	16.7	50.0	87.5	8.3	—	4.2
Raskó	1976	Hungary (Police; Court)	"WWII end to recent times,"	125	—	—	—	—	75.5	13.6	10.7	—
Gibbs, Silverman, & Vega	1977	Florida (Prison)	1977	43	60.5	33.0	—	78.7[4]	55.9[4]	24.4[4]	19.8[4]	—

Table 1.1 (Continued)

Researcher(s)	Year Reported	Location/ (Data base)	Study Period	Number of Cases	% African American	Mean Age	% Prior Record	Firearm Used	Victim/Offender Relationship			
									Family/ Intimate	Acq/ Friend	Stranger	Unk
			1978–1987									
Totman	1978	California (Prison)	July–Dec., 1969	50	26.0	32.9[4]	77.8[4]	61.0	100.0	—	—	—
Biggers	1979	Florida (Prison)	2 years	32	—	35.0	—	—	78.0	—	12.5	9.4
McClain	1981	Detroit, St. Louis, Atlanta, Pittsburgh, Houston, Los Angeles	1975	119	100.0 (selected)	32.8	—	72.6	—	—	—	—
Wilbanks	1983a	Dade County; Miami, FL (Police)	1980	47	59.6	—	—	59.2	70.2	19.2	8.5	2.1
	1983b	UCR (National)	1980	2412	—	—	—	57.5	59.6	27.9	6.5	6.1
Bunch, Foley, & Urbina	1983	Florida (Prison)	—	90	52.5	29.3	—	—	*Only 33.3% knew victims well.*			
Weisheit	1984	Illinois (Prison)	I 1940–66 II 1981; 1983	460	73.0	I 32.8 II 27.3	—	44.0	57.0	29.0	11.0	3.0
Kowalski, Shields & Wilson	1985	Alabama (Prison)	1929–71	455	87.7	33.0	45.6	38.6	63.8	29.2	7.1	—
Formby	1986	Tuscaloosa County, AL (Prison)	1970–79	14	64.0	40.0	—	57.0	64.0	29.0	7.0	—
Block	1986	Baltimore, MD (State's Atty.)	1974–84	258	89.5	30.9	—	40.5	—	—	—	—

Study	Year	Location	Years	N								
Hewitt & Rivers	1986	Delaware County, Muncie, IN (Court and Police)	1960–84	11	64.0	39.9	—	—	75.0	25.0	—	—
Goetting	1987	Detroit (Police)	1982–83	56	96.4	34.1	51.4	55.4	100.0	—	—	—
Silverman & Kennedy	1987	Canada (National)	1961–83	948	1.5[2]	—	—	26.0	64.0	29.0 (incl. other family)	7.0	—
Mann	1987	Atlanta, Baltimore, Chicago, Houston, Los Angeles, New York City (Police)	1979; 1983	296	77.7	30.9	54.4	46.6	64.4	27.3	7.4	1.0

1988–1992

Study	Year	Location	Years	N								
Arnold, Goldstein, Brownstein, & Ryan	1988	New York City (Police)	Mar. 1–Oct. 31, 1988	21	71.0	30.0	—	33.0	62.0	5.0	14.0	19.0
Winn, Haugen & Jurik	1988	Maricopa County, Phoenix, AZ (Court)	1979–84	50	26.0	—	60.0	59.0 (all cases)	65.0	—	13.0	—
Hazlett & Tomlinson	1988	Alabama, Illinois, Texas (State Data)	1980–84	4432	71.8	33.0	—	59.5	73.5	20.8	5.3	0.7
Hanke & Shields	1992	Alabama (Prison)	1929–85	746	78.8	33.0	(Mis) 65.4 (Fel) 97.2	48.8	52.7	32.9	14.4	—

1. 1963 & 1968 samples combined.
2. Estimated from data.
3. Hospital cases only.
4. Averaged.

loosa (Alabama), Chicago, New York City, and Los Angeles. Previous state female homicide studies were reported from California (2), Florida, (2), Illinois, Minnesota, New York, and North Carolina. Three studies from other countries are included for cross-cultural comparisons: two in Canada (Rosenblatt and Greenland, 1974; Silverman and Kennedy, 1987) and one in Hungary (Raskó, 1976).

Studies from 1958 to 1967

The first decade in our schematic is limited to the time-honored Marvin Wolfgang study.[11] Wolfgang (1958) established the city as "an ideal laboratory" for the analysis of homicide in his classic "question-driven" investigation of patterns of criminal homicide derived from 588 cases collected in Philadelphia from 1948 through 1952 (Cheatwood, 1991: 4). Although the data in the present study of female homicide offenders do not exactly replicate those from the Wolfgang study, there are many similarities, and the Wolfgang "model" and findings are cited extensively throughout this volume.

The Wolfgang Philadelphia study used police records to compile material on the "age, sex, race, as well as criminal histories of victims and offenders in homicide events; alcohol use of victims; the relationship of victim and offender using an eleven-part classification scheme; the relationship of other felonies to homicide, and patterns of weapon use" (Zahn, 1991: 17). These variables, as well as some additional ones, are included in the study reported here. Further, "two influential but controversial concepts that grew out of the research—victim precipitation and the subculture of violence" (Block and Block, 1991)—are important components in the conceptual development of the current study. In the first instance, the knotty problem of *victim precipitation* is especially germane to women homicide offenders because of the extraordinary reliance on self-defense as a justification for murder. Wolfgang (1958) created the term based on his finding of multiple instances of victims who instigated their own deaths through hostile movements, insults, insinuations, or physical actions against their eventual perpetrators:

> The term *victim-precipitated* is applied to those criminal homicides in which the victim is a direct, positive precipitator in the crime. The role of the victim is characterized by his having been the first in the homicide drama to use physical force directed against his subsequent slayer. The victim-precipitated cases are those in which the victim was the first to show and use a deadly weapon, to strike a blow in an altercation—in short, the first to commence the interplay of resort to physical violence (Wolfgang, 1958: 252).

Wolfgang's second abstraction—*the subculture of violence*—has garnered little empirical support (Hawkins, 1986). This theory, which is applied almost exclusively to African Americans but also, more recently, to Hispanic Americans, suggests that value systems prescribing violence, including homicide, are peculiar to lower-class, urban areas and constitute an integral part of criminogenic conduct norms handed down through generations. The applicability of the subculture of violence perspective to African American females has received little research attention. An attempt to remedy that empirical oversight is made in this volume.

In a "partial replication" of Wolfgang's Philadelphia study, Pokorny (1965) reported on 438 homicide cases, 99 of which involved female offenders, which took place in Houston, Texas between March 15, 1958 and December 31, 1961. Pokorny found that there were many similarities between the two cities, "Criminal homicide occurs most often between members of the same race; that the persons involved tend to be relatives or friends rather than strangers; that males are more frequently involved, both as offenders and victims; and that the most likely hours are between 8:00 p.m. and 2:00 a.m. The persons involved typically live at the same address or within a mile or two of each other (ibid., p. 487)."

Studies from 1968 to 1977

Empirical studies of female homicide offenders over the next ten years, including the Canadian study by Rosenblatt and Greenland (1974), focused almost exclusively on imprisoned women murderers (Cole, Fisher, and Cole, 1968; Ward, Jackson, and Ward, 1969; Suval and Brisson, 1974; Gibbs, Silverman, and Vega, 1977). These studies produced details on the victim, the murder, the motive for the murder, social and demographic characteristics of the offender, and the criminal histories of the incarcerated women.

Although the thrust of Raskó's (1976) research was the victims of female killers in Hungary, the use of police and court records for her data base enabled Raskó to extract information on the victim-offender relationship, the mode of attack, and the role of alcohol in the homicides.

Using national homicide rates from 1940 to 1974, Shin, Jedlicka, and Lee (1977) provide another research exception to the female prison studies of this decade. Shin et al. centered their examination on homicide among African Americans and included gender and age differences by race.

Studies from 1978 to 1987

While prison studies of women homicide offenders continued to be popular in the late 1970s and 1980s (Totman, 1978; Biggers, 1979; Bunch, Foley, and Urbina, 1983; Weisheit, 1984), a number of researchers used a city (Wilbanks, 1983a; Zimring, Mukherjee, and Van Winkle, 1983; Block, 1986; Formby, 1986; Goetting, 1987; Hewitt and Rivers,

1986)—or, more important, more than one city—for their data bases (McClain, 1981; 1982; Mann, 1988). The increasingly recognized national problem of drug abuse among women generated studies on the influence of drugs on female homicide commission (Abel and Zeidenberg, 1986).

During this decade, Wilbanks (1983b) reported national homicide rates among females in the United States. Across our northern border, Silverman and Kennedy (1987) used national data that focused on Canadian females who had committed manslaughter over a twenty-three-year period or infanticide over a ten-year period.

These were exciting times for researchers interested in female crime and delinquency, a topic that had been virtually ignored until the 1970s. Notably, Freda Adler's classic treatise on female criminality, *Sisters in Crime*, was published in 1975, and Jane Totman produced her fascinating monograph based on California prison case file reviews and interviews, *The Murderess: A Psychosocial Study of Criminal Homicide* (1978).

Those researchers who studied female homicide offenders in the 1980s began to speculate, some even to theorize, about the etiology of female violence. As researchers specialized in specific aspects of homicides by female offenders, several themes appeared. In the prison studies, where a variety of test data were available, the possible influence of offender characteristics such as *intelligence* was introduced. The *psychology* of women murderers was extrapolated from various psychological and personality instruments routinely administered in prisons. Level of education and other *social characteristics* such as employment status, marital status, and family background began to appear as items of interest relative to women who kill. A *sex-role perspective* was interjected as causative by some researchers (Bunch, Foley, and Urbina, 1983; Kowalski, Shields, and Wilson, 1985). *Race* also became an important variable of interest, particularly in light of the early Wolfgang (1958) findings of the disproportionate involvement of African Americans in homicide arrests and his "subculture of violence" thesis. Furthermore, in the mid-1980s it was determined that homicide was a leading cause of deaths among African Americans and constituted a public health crisis for African American males (U.S. Department of Health and Human Services, 1986).

Studies from 1988 to the Present

Continued interest is demonstrated in the contemporary problem of female drug abuse, a phenomenon that has rapidly accelerated in the past five years, even more than among males (De Witt, 1990). The connection between drug use and homicide among women in New York City is an ongoing focus of Goldstein and his colleagues, who find a "shift away from the domestic arena and towards the drug business for female homicide victims" because of women's increasing participation in the drug business (Arnold, Goldstein, Brownstein, and Ryan, 1988: 19). Barry Spunt (1992), a former research assistant of Goldstein, is currently testing several hypotheses concerning the drugs-homicide nexus with women inmates in the New York State system. This exciting research is in progress and the findings are eagerly awaited.

ORGANIZATION OF THE BOOK

Selected demographics on the study cities—Atlanta, Baltimore, Chicago, Houston, Los Angeles, and New York—are presented in chapter 2. Other homicide studies undertaken in those cities are reported with particular attention devoted to the findings on women killers. The second chapter also describes the sampling procedure, the final data base, and the methods of analysis used. A discussion of methodological quandaries that had to be overcome—for example, securing permission to make a field visit and obtaining access to police files, homicide records, FBI reports, and criminal court information—is included for the benefit of future field researchers. These experiences yielded procedural guidelines for possible replications of the original study. The chapter concludes with a brief description of the social and demographic characteristics of the study group.

While the remaining chapters describe the specific major findings of the study, in order to provide a comprehensive depiction of the phenomenon, reference is made throughout each chapter to relevant findings from the available pool of previous research shown in Table 1.1 as each topic is discussed.

Descriptions of the crime scene presented in chapter 3 include the location of the homicide (whether inside or outside the home), the specific site within a residence (for example, living room, kitchen), and whether the murder took place in the residence of the victim, in that of the offender, or elsewhere. Other ecological variables include the time, day of the week, and month each homicide occurred. The choice of weapon and the number of wounds inflicted on the victim are additional circumstances of the murder that are amplified by case examples. Chapter 3 also includes the role of the female murderer in the homicide (whether she committed it alone or with accomplices) and the contribution of narcotics and/or alcohol to her violent act. These data are disaggregated and cross-tabulated by year, city, and region according to selected relevant variables and buttressed with appropriate illustrations from individual cases.

The murder victims of the female homicide offenders are the focus of chapters 4 and 5, in which three distinct approaches are highlighted.

First, the murder is described in terms of the victim/offender relationship: child, spouse, parent, other female, friend, acquaintance, or stranger. Second, the victim's condition is examined to determine if s/he was under the influence of narcotics and/or alcohol prior to the murder, was incapacitated due to illness, a physical handicap, or age (either old or young), or was asleep when killed. The third analytic strategy focuses on whether and how key individuals—the victim, the offender, or bystanders—contributed to the homicide. A number of cases will be used to portray the victim-offender association and interaction. These data are also disaggregated and cross-tabulated by year, city, and region according to relevant variables.

More specifically, in chapter 4, the victims described are those with whom the offenders had intimate relationships, or who could be defined as "significant others." Detailed attention is devoted to *infanticide* and *filicide*, or those cases where mothers murdered their small children. The second focus of chapter 4 is on *domestic homicides* in which women killed the men and women whom they presumably loved. The majority of intimate victim cases involved domestic relationships, primarily men with whom the women homicide offenders were sexually intimate. Special attention is devoted to a seldom-reported phenomenon—the murders of lesbian lovers. Although there were only five such cases identified, the dynamics of the homosexual murders were found to parallel those involving male intimates as the victims. Throughout the chapter, relevant time and regional (south/nonsouth) analyses are included for comparisons between the years and the cities studied. A brief discussion of murders involving other family members as victims—for example, parents, siblings, cousins—closes the chapter.

Other homicide victims and murder circumstances are highlighted in chapter 5, which focuses on females who kill other females (*intragender* murder), the influence of *race/ethnicity* in female homicide offending, and the killing of *nonfamily members* (friends, acquaintances, or strangers). Particular attention is devoted to females who kill strangers, since one of the criteria used to define the alleged "new" female murderess as hardened and cold-blooded includes felony killing of strangers, killing for fun, or the thrill of killing.

Chapter 6 addresses the *criminal justice* data (prior arrests, history of victim, amount of bond, detention status) and processing of female homicide offenders from the initial charge to the final court disposition. Although none of the women received the death penalty, five were given life sentences. Women who received prison sentences are compared with those who did not, with a consideration of the possible influence of legal and extralegal factors and the length of prison sentences assigned.

Although a few researchers question whether women offenders are accorded more leniency by the criminal justice system than men, a small number of studies indicate that even when women commit the same offenses, they are not treated as punitively as their male counterparts. However, there is some evidence that gender disparity is diminishing. When the murder of a spouse is involved, the notion of preferential judicial treatment for females is questionable—women who kill their mates are found to receive harsher sanctions than men who kill their mates. In general, the question of disparate treatment due to gender has yet to be resolved, particularly when the race of female defendants is introduced. The criminal justice data in chapter 6 are disaggregated and cross-tabulated by race and other relevant variables and supplemented by case descriptions.

The final chapter of this volume summarizes the research findings and creates a synoptic profile of the contemporary female criminal homicide offender. The motives of female murderers form the nucleus of chapter 7. Case studies are especially useful for depicting the motives for homicides as well as illustrating possible fallacies in the given motives. A consistent finding of "self-defense" as the motive for murder precipitates a discussion of the "battered woman syndrome," a controversial abstraction frequently used as a rationale for self-defensive actions in female-perpetrated homicide cases. Self-defense and other motive data are compared by race, years, city, and region in chapter 7.

As in most exploratory research, several research questions were generated by the findings. In chapter 7, tentative answers are given to those questions identified earlier: economic theory as applied to women who kill, the "subculture of violence" perspective, the southern culture of violence, the "battered woman syndrome," the possible influence of drugs on homicide, whether African American lives are devalued by the courts, and if race is a factor in the criminal justice processing of female criminal homicide offenders.

Additional research questions suggested for future explorations of women who kill are centered on: the contribution to trauma-induced deaths of limited access to prompt medical care; the role of poverty in female-headed households and homicide; the relationship of the women's movement to homicide; the motive conundrum; physical size and weapon use in murder outcomes; international cross-cultural comparisons; the connection between homicides by females and other female offenses, for example, drug abuse, prostitution, and robbery; legal defense and judicial processing of female criminal homicide offenders; and differences between women who kill and receive prison terms and those sentenced to death.[12]

The book concludes with commentary related to the necessity of regarding the problem of violence as a human, not just a gender, issue.

The prevention of violence and the necessary policies and procedures to achieve that goal are also suggested.

NOTES

1. Severe assaults included acts with a higher probability of causing an injury: kicking, biting, punching, hitting with an object, beating up, threatening with a knife or gun, and using a knife or gun.

2. Chapter 4 details child murders committed by females.

3. I am indebted to the following people for their tremendous cooperation: Tricia Clark, State of California, Department of Justice, Bureau of Criminal Statistics and Special Services; Linda Booz, Florida Department of Law Enforcement, Division of Criminal Justice Information Systems; and Mark L. Cimring, State of New York, Division of Criminal Justice Services.

4. Only adult females are described in the statistics from these states.

5. Hereafter, *murder* is the term used when reference is made to UCR statistics.

6. It is reiterated that the rates of female arrests for aggravated assault in 1979 and 1983 are not much different from those today. In 1979 women accounted for 12.4 percent of all arrests for aggravated assault, and the offense ranked 11th among all female arrests at 2.1 percent. By 1983 the percentages were 13.5 percent and 2.1 percent respectively, with the ranking remaining at 11th. The 1992 figures show an increase to 14.8 percent of all arrests for aggravated assault and while the ranking is now 10th, arrests for this offense increased only modestly, to 2.4 percent of total female arrests.

7. The actual figures are: California, 325 homicide arrests out of a total of 274,068; Florida, 141 of 115,099; and New York State, 191 of 94,659.

8. Although an intergender comparison would have been optimal, the time and fiscal limitations of the study prevented the collection of data on male homicide offenders in the six-city study.

9. In recent years a flurry of books and articles have concentrated on abused or battered women who strike back, killing their abusers (for example, Browne, 1986; Johann and Osanka, 1989). This body of literature is not included because of the primarily anecdotal, clinical, or case study approach (Silverman and Kennedy, 1987). Following Wilbanks

(1982), cases such as these not only are particularistic but may also reflect the biases of the authors.

10. Some authors have published extensively from their data bases, and where relevant, information from these articles is reported. Table 1.1, however, is limited by references to a single article for each study.

11. The reader is enthusiastically referred to Volume XIV, no. 2 of the *Journal of Crime & Justice* (1991), which includes an invaluable special section on homicide research and the Wolfgang tradition.

12. Preliminary efforts are currently underway to initiate a study comparing female murderers who receive the death penalty and those who do not.

Chapter 2

The Research Design

Statistical data on murder are readily available from sources such as the Uniform Crime Reports (UCR). However the UCR do not include tabulations by race and gender so official reporting of this type cannot provide an accurate profile of female homicide offenders, much less render any particular circumstances of a murder for analysis.

A number of possible data sources and their limitations for research on lethal violence were described in chapter 1 as those from the UCR, national vital statistics, prisons, anecdotal accounts, and cities. Despite the recognized problems associated with the use of *city data*, it was determined to be the best choice for securing the deeply detailed information sought on women murderers. Since material concerning motives, circumstances of the murders, and final dispositions can be obtained from various city sources, richness of the data was presumed to be assured. Based on experience acquired in a previous Atlanta court study (Mann, 1984b), it was also reasoned that more informational resources associated with each case would be available at the city level—for example, prior police records; welfare, child and family services information; criminal court presentence investigation reports; and case court transcripts.[1] One of the major weaknesses of using a single-city data base, characterized by Wilbanks (1982: 157) as "the lack of comparative data from other jurisdictions," was partially circumvented by collecting material from six cities throughout the country. Thus, a certain "breadth" of data was secured for comparative purposes.

In addition to acquiring a city selection that, if not generalizable, was at least partially representative of the nation, an attempt was made to collect data that would permit modest comparisons over time. Since the study began in 1985, the year 1983 was chosen in hopes that prior to the time of field entry the murder cases had been either disposed of by the courts or cleared in some other legal manner (for example, *nolle prossed;* no grand jury indictment). In order to provide a time comparison, 1979 was purposely selected, also with the hope that complete records of the offenders were still available.[2] Both years were chosen as representative of years with high homicide rates.

SELECTION OF THE CITIES

The national homicide rate of 9.7 per 100,000 in 1979 (U.S. Department of Justice, 1980: 40) dropped to 8.3 per 100,000 by 1983 (U.S. Department of Justice, 1984: 43). In order to identify those jurisdictions with the highest homicide rates, the 1979 rate of 9.7 per 100,000 was used as the minimum base criterion in an examination of the homicide rates of the 50 states.[3] Table 2.1 lists the top fifteen homicide rates by state and for 1979 and 1983. Once they had been identified as meeting the homicide rate criterion, the fifteen states were scrutinized to see whether they met the ratings for both years—that is, if they had rates of at least 9.7 in 1979 and 8.3 in 1983. Thirteen of the original top fifteen states met this requirement. North Carolina and Missouri were no longer eligible based on this standard; therefore Maryland and Tennessee were substituted for these two states and included in the top fifteen.

Table 2.1

Top 15 U.S. Homicide Rates per 100,000 and Rankings, 1979 and 1983[1]

National Rate	1979		1983	
	Rate	Rank	Rate	Rank
National[2]	9.7	—	8.3	—
State Rate				
Alabama	13.2	6	9.2	11
Alaska	13.3	5	13.8	3
California	13.0	7	10.5	8
Florida	12.2	11	11.2	5
Georgia	17.1	2	8.4	15
Illinois	10.7	13	9.7	10
Louisiana	16.9	3	14.2	1
Mississippi	12.6	9	11.2	5
Maryland	9.8	14	8.5	14
Nevada	17.5	1	12.8	4
New Mexico	12.4	10	8.9	12
New York	11.9	12	11.1	7
South Carolina	12.8	8	8.8	13
Tennessee	9.8	14	9.8	9
Texas	16.7	4	14.2	1

1. Source: *Sourcebook of Criminal Justice Statistics—1981*, Table 3.57; *Sourcebook of Criminal Justice—1984*, Tabler 3.84.
2. Missouri and North Carolina were eliminated because they did not meet the criterion of a rate higher than the national rate for both years.

After the states with the highest homicide rates were identified, those cities with the highest homicide rates within each state were sought.[4] A further refinement was made by selecting those cities from states that might represent large regional areas: the Northeast (New York), Southeast (Maryland), Midwest (Illinois), South (Georgia), Southwest (Texas), and West (California). Since nine of the fifteen states found to have the highest homicide rates were in regions defined by the U.S. Census as southern (60 percent), three southern cities were among the final six cities included for study. The six cities chosen—Atlanta, Baltimore, Chicago, Houston, New York City, and Los Angeles—had homicide rates equal to or higher than the national rates for both 1979 and 1983. These cities, depicted in Table 2.2, also approximated regional representations of homicide found in the 1979 and 1983 Uniform Crime Reports.

THE STUDY CITIES[5]

Atlanta, Georgia

Incorporated in 1847, Atlanta as the capital as well as the largest city in the state of Georgia, occupied 131.8 square miles in 1990. Often called the "Gateway to the South," Atlanta is located in the northwest central part of Georgia as the seat of Fulton County. Burned almost totally to the ground during the Civil War, a rebuilt Atlanta has become the "transportation, financial, commercial, and cultural hub" of the Southeast (Carpenter and Provorse, 1992: 144).

According to the most recent (1990) statistics, the population of Atlanta comprised 52.3 percent females, 67.1 percent African Americans,

Table 2.2

Sample City Homicide Rates per 100,000, 1979 and 1983[1]

Sample City	Homicide Rate	
	1979	1983
Atlanta	54.6	31.4
Baltimore	31.1	25.5
Chicago	27.9	24.1
Houston	40.4	32.5
Los Angeles	27.5	25.9
New York City	24.4	22.8

1. Computed from UCR, and 1980 U.S. Census data, using: $R = \dfrac{\frac{C}{P}}{100,000}$

R = Population specific homicide rate; C = Homicides known to police, 1979 and 1983; P = Central city population, 1980.

and 31 percent whites. In 1979, 27.5 percent of the population was below the poverty level, and female heads of household constituted 45.1 percent of that total. The 1980 population, which is the census base used for both years studied, was 425,022. In that year, women made up 48.0 percent of the Atlanta work force.

A study of homicide trends in Atlanta between 1961–1962 and 1971–1972, reported by Munford, Kazer, Feldman, and Stivers (1976), focused on the victims of homicide. Large increases in the homicide rates for both black and white residents occurred over the ten-year study period. Although the rate for white females changed little—from 0.6 to 0.9 per 10,000 population—that for black females increased from 2.0 to 3.4 per 10,000 (Munford et al., 1976: 217). Munford et al. did not use unemployment in their analysis but described a connection between low socioeconomic status and high homicide rates, especially in the 1971–1972 time frame examined. Firearm-associated homicides increased significantly over the decade studied. While no seasonal trends were observed, black homicides were noted to occur more frequently on weekends in Atlanta.[6]

The high and elevating homicide risk levels among black Americans and the lack of attention to black victimization directed Harold Rose and Paula McClain (1990) to their multicity study of black homicide in urban environments, one of which was Atlanta.[7] Rose and McClain found "an eroding" of Wolfgang's earlier (1958) findings on black female homicide offenders:

> Although black females still are more likely to kill males with whom they have an emotional relationship, our data indicate that high percentages of them are murdering individuals with whom they had no emotional ties. Likewise, the modal place of occurrence is still the offender's home, but a higher percentage of homicides are being committed by black females outside of the house.
>
> No apparent change is observed in the role of black females in the commission of homicide. They are still sole perpetrators. Our data do indicate, however, a complete change in the type of weapon utilized. Females now primarily use firearms rather than knives, which may reflect changes that have occurred not only among females but in the overall society.
>
> . . . Additionally, on the basis of a limited number of interviews, black females apparently believe they are justified in killing a male intimate if they are the object of physical abuse. This position represents a willingness to fight back and protect oneself (Rose and McClain, 1990: 165).

Black female homicide offenders were found to have low socioeconomic status, low education levels, and to be unemployed. McClain

(1981; 1982; 1982–83) published a number of momentous articles on black female homicide offenders from the larger Rose-McClain study which are cited throughout this volume.

Baltimore, Maryland

Because of its many memorials reflecting a long history as one of the first U.S. settlements, Baltimore is known as "Monumental City." It is also called the "Birthplace of the Star-Spangled Banner," the song having been inspired by the successful defense of Baltimore during the War of 1812. The city was incorporated in 1797 and by 1990 encompassed an area of 80.8 square miles. In 1904, Baltimore's downtown area was almost totally destroyed by fire but then was rebuilt more attractively. Recent renovations and gentrification have made the city even more beautiful and a major tourist attraction today (Carpenter and Provorse, 1992: 209). Located about 40 miles northeast of Washington, D.C., Baltimore is highly respected as an educational center.

The proportion of the population below the poverty level in 1979 was 22.9 percent with 39.8 percent of households headed by women. Women also constituted 46.4 percent of the Baltimore labor force in 1980, when the 1980 central city population was 786,740. In 1990, Baltimore's population included 59.6 percent African Americans and 39.1 percent whites, with more than half of the population females (53.3 percent).

Only a few homicide studies have been undertaken in Baltimore. Cheatwood (1988), for example, found no relationship between season and homicide in an examination of the Uniform Crime Reports and other Baltimore homicide data from 1974 to 1984 (see chapter 3). As will be described more fully in later chapters, Kathleen Block (1986) researched these same years in her study of 258 female homicide offenders (see also Table 1.1).

Chicago, Illinois

Chicago is the third-largest city in the United States, with a population in 1980 of 3,005,072. Located on the southwestern shore of Lake Michigan, Chicago is the seat of Cook County in northeastern Illinois. Having recovered from the famous Chicago fire in 1871, Chicago now has "more air passengers, more railroads, and a greater dollar value of traded goods than any other U.S. city" (Carpenter and Provorse, 1992: 160). Notorious for its 1919–1933 Prohibition infamy but no longer a haven for gangland figures, Chicago nonetheless continues to have a high crime rate. Among its many nicknames, the "Windy City" and "Second City" probably best describe this major metropolis of 227.3 square miles.

Chicago's first settler (1779) was a black man, Jean Baptiste Pointe du Sable, and today (1990) 39.1 percent of Chicago's residents are

African Americans. The white population is 45.4 percent, and there are also a large number of persons of Hispanic origin (19.6 percent). Females made up 50.1 percent of the Chicago population in 1990. Women also headed 40.2 percent of the families below the poverty level in 1979 and constituted 44.9 percent of the 1980 labor force.

Chicago has been shadowed for decades by its history of violence. The days of gangsters and bootlegging killings, a number of virulent race riots, well-publicized serial murderers (for example, the recently executed John Wayne Gacy), and mass murderers such as the infamous Richard Speck have all contributed to Chicago's notorious reputation as "murder city." These factors led to several studies of homicide in Chicago. Block and Zimring (1973) studied patterns and rates of criminal homicide in Chicago from 1965 to 1970 and found that the rate had more than doubled during the six-year period. Homicide remained about 90 percent intraracial, but there were increases in firearm use and a decrease in killings of acquaintances. White (and "other") female homicide rates remained relatively stable. In 1965, this rate was 0.6 per 100,000; by 1970, the rate was 0.7. In contrast, the 1965 black female homicide rate of 11.7 per 100,000 had increased by 50 percent to 17.6 in 1970. Furthermore, while the most frequent offending age range of 25–34 years remained the same for white (and "other") females, homicide rates among black females in 1970 were substantially higher at younger ages (25–34 years) than among their 1965 counterparts, who were 35–44 years of age (Block and Zimring, 1973: Table 2, p.4).

The remarkable, highly detailed work of Carolyn Block (1985; 1987) reveals patterns of change in the commission of homicides in Chicago from 1965 through 1981 and includes an abundance of data on women offenders that are referred to throughout this look. Block's data are especially rich on the topics of race/ethnicity and the circumstances of homicides.

Houston, Texas

Named after the founder of the state of Texas, Sam Houston, the city is also known as "Space City, U.S.A.," and "Home of the Astronauts." Located in southeastern Texas, Houston is a deepwater port, the seat of Harris County, and the largest city in both the South and the Southwest. Houston was incorporated in 1836 and by 1990 boasted a total area of 539.9 square miles. As a regional cultural center and a leading educational center, the city is probably best known as the "world's major center of the petrochemical industry" (Carpenter and Provorse, 1992: 402). Despite a depression in the oil industry during the 1980s, Houston has continued to grow.

In 1980 there were 1,595,138 people in the central city; by 1990 there had been a 2.2 percent increase in the central city population and a 20.7 percent increase in the metropolitan area. Included in today's Houston population are about equal proportions of African Americans (28.1 percent) and persons of Hispanic origin (27.6 percent), with whites at 52.7 percent. Females account for 50.4 percent of Houston's citizens (1990) and in 1980 were 42.0 percent of the work force. The population below the poverty level in 1979 was 12.7 percent, with 26.5 percent of households headed by females.

One of the early studies of homicide in Houston concerned the "relationship between a specific type of crime and the places where it occurs" (Bullock, 1955: 565). Bullock was interested in developing an urban homicide theory by "tracing out the natural manner in which assailant, victim, and place become organized into a complex of ecological and interpersonal situations that result in homicide" (p. 566). An examination of the 1945 and 1949 official (police department) records of all cases of criminal homicide in Houston revealed that specific areas of the city were linked to homicide because of racial/ethnic segregation. Generally, a Houston homicide tended to occur on the weekend, was a "nocturnal phenomenon," and in 87 percent of the cases involved personal intimacy between the victim and his or her assailant (p. 572). Bullock concluded that "the process of segregation raises the probability of intra-group conflict not only by virtue of its power to generate proximity and intimacy, but also by virtue of its power to reduce respect for the areas that are segregated into deterioration" (p. 575).

Pokorny also used police department files in his Houston study reported in 1965. During the study period of March 15, 1958 through December 31, 1961, females constituted 23.8 percent of all criminal homicide offenders. In a breakdown of offenders by race, ethnic group, and gender, Pokorny found the following female offender rates per 100,000 population: Latina, 1.63; white, 2.08; and black, 16.58. Shootings accounted for 63.5 percent of the deaths; about half occurred between 8:00 P.M. and 2:00 A.M., and 58.1 percent took place away from the home, usually outdoors—on the highway, public street, alley, or field. When the murder occurred inside the home, the most common location was the bedroom. The homicide victims tended to be close friends (27.9 percent), acquaintances (4.7 percent), family members (22.9 percent), or lovers (6.6 percent) of the perpetrators. Only 1.4 percent of the victims were strangers. Excluding common-law marriages, black wives in Houston were more likely to kill their husbands (31.1 percent) than the reverse (26.3 percent). Among white couples, the proportions were identical for wife/husband (21.3 percent) and husband/wife killings (21.3 percent). Thus, wives were more likely to kill husbands (52.4 percent) than husbands were to kill wives (47.6 percent). Women also were more likely to use firearms in killing their husbands than the reverse (44.2 v. 29.6 percent). Pokorny's Houston homicide results supported Wolfgang's (1958) finding that homicide was predominantly intraracial: 91 percent were white/white homicides, 96.9 percent were black/black, and 86 percent were Latino/Latino.

In his book *Murder in Space City* (1977), anthropologist Henry Lundsgaarde reports "a cultural analysis of Houston homicide patterns." At that time, his chosen study year of 1969 had witnessed an all-time high for Houston homicides, with 23.3 known homicides per 100,000 population—a rate that was one of the highest in the nation (p. 9). Lundsgaarde apparently viewed the violence and high homicide rate as somewhat of an anomaly:

> Houston has grown from a small inland seaport and commercial town to one of the world's leading industrial centers. The city in one decade has earned a world-wide reputation as a center for technology, science, and medicine, and as a center of national and international commerce. The fact that such a concentration of human talent, technological knowledge, and capital in one city co-exists with one of the nation's highest per capita rates of serious crimes against the person is evidence that the most "civilized," "modern," or "enlightened" society may fail to apply its resources to the correction of conditions that breed violence and allow human failure (p. 5).

Lundsgaarde reviewed all 268 official homicide cases recorded by the Houston Police Department's Homicide Division in 1969. He utilized a variety of research methods, including interviews of homicide detectives, pathologists, and lawyers; examinations of official court records; and observations of homicide scenes and police interrogations. After case-by-case analyses, Lundsgaarde found that "killers and their victims tend to be more alike than different socially; that homicidal behavior occurs in a limited number of settings and social circumstances; and that similar cases generally evoke similar responses in official sanctioning" (p. 15).

Females constituted 20.7 percent of the Houston killers in Lundsgaarde's study. White females accounted for 19.6 percent, black females 74.5 percent, and Mexican Americans 5.9 of the female homicide offenders (p. 235). Wives and common-law wives were more frequently found to kill their husbands than to be killed by them (p. 54). Although not reported by gender, 40 percent of the homicide scenes were located in the home or its yard, porch, or driveway. The most frequent in-home location was the living room (24 percent), closely followed by the bedroom (23 percent). Outside of the home, a bar was the homicide scene in 46 percent of the cases. Firearms—usually .22 caliber pistols—were used in 86 percent of the homicides.[8]

Los Angeles, California

In Spanish, Los Angeles means "the angels," which is the source of its nickname "City of the Angels," but "L.A." is its most common appellation. Although the United States acquired Los Angeles in 1846 through the Mexican-American War, it was not incorporated until 1925. Located in southwestern California, the city is the seat of Los Angeles County. During the 1980s, Los Angeles surpassed Chicago in both population and area, replacing it as the second-largest U.S. city. Its astounding growth can be attributed to the "development of two industries: oil and the growth of a motion picture colony in the area (Hollywood)" (Carpenter and Provorse, 1992: 54). Los Angeles has many cultural attractions as well as a number of excellent educational institutions and despite its smog, fires, mudslides, and earthquakes, its continuing growth—including a 17.4 percent increase between 1980 and 1990—resulted in an area in 1990 of 469.3 square miles.

The proportion of the population of Hispanic origin (39.9 percent) far exceeds that of African Americans (14.0 percent). Los Angeles has a substantial number of Asian and Pacific citizens (9.8 percent) also, and whites make up 52.8 percent of the population. Of the six cities in the study, Los Angeles is the only one in which the female population (48.2 percent) is lower than the male. Also, Los Angeles had the lowest percentages of citizens below the poverty level (16.4 percent) and women as heads of households within the poverty category (29.4 percent) in 1979. The 1980 central city population was 2,968,528, and women constituted 43.4 percent of the Los Angeles work force.

Loya and Mercy's (1985) comprehensive study of homicide in Los Angeles from 1970 to 1979 used the *victim* as the unit of analysis. During the time period studied, the number of deaths from violent crime increased from 357 per year to 655, exceeding the national rate. Official records from the Los Angeles Police Department were the source from which homicide rates correlated with the age of the victims, and were derived for males, females, Anglos, Blacks, Hispanics, Asians, American Indians, and other ethnic groups. Blacks and Hispanics experienced by far the highest rates of homicide. Black males ranked highest, and the rate for black females exceeded that of Anglo males (Loya, Garcia and Sullivan, 1985). The increase in the relative incidence of homicide among Los Angeles black females was determined to coincide with an increasingly young population.

New York City, New York

New York City, known affectionately as "the Big Apple" and more sinisterly as "Gotham City," is the largest city in the United States, and its 1990 central city population of 7,322,564 ranks it fourth in the world. New York City is still growing: the 1990 population reflects a 3.5 percent increase over the 1980 population of 7,071,639. Incorporated in 1625, New York City is located in southeastern New York at the estuary of the Hudson River where it also borders the East and Harlem Rivers. The five boroughs—Manhattan, Brooklyn, Staten Island, Queens, and the Bronx—encompass 309.9 square miles, and each has unique features which when combined make New York City the "Hub of the World."

Rich in history, New York City is "a world leader in finance," home of the United Nations, and "leads the nation in retail and wholesale trading, in publishing, fashion, and art" (Carpenter and Provorse, 1992: 296). The city's endless list of accomplishments in education, music, architecture, and other points of interest make it the most popular tourist attraction in the nation. A true "melting pot," New York City contains every imaginable nationality, race, and ethnic group.

In 1990, the population of New York City included 52.3 percent whites, 28.7 percent African Americans, 24.4 percent persons of Hispanic origin, and 7.0 percent Asian and Pacific islanders. Females constituted 53.1 percent of the total population. The proportion below the poverty level in 1979 was 20.0 percent, with 41.0 percent of households within that group headed by women. Women also accounted for 45.4 percent of the New York City work force in 1980.

The Rand Institute study of criminal homicide in New York City from 1968 through 1974 concentrated on central Harlem's primarily black 28th Precinct (Swersey and Enloe, 1975). While no specific data were reported on gender, many of Rand's general findings are relevant to the study reported in this volume. Swersey and Enloe (1975: 34) suggest that changes in the number of *deliberate* killings accounted for most of the increase and decreases in criminal homicides in the 28th Precinct over the time period studied. Gun-related assaultive homicides appeared to be influential in the observed homicide increases, and indicated changes in the intent to kill; not necessarily the availability or quality of weapons. Evidence in support of this position was attributed to a reduction in weekend homicides from 56.5 percent in 1965 (*sic*) to 46.5 percent in 1974, and a similar shift in family homicides from 25 percent to 14 percent over the same time period (p. 42).

Shortly after the Rand study, the New York City Police Department (NYCPD, 1977) reported a comparison between 1976 and 1977 homicide data. During this period there was a citywide decrease in homicides, with decreases in every borough. The slight increase of 0.8 in the 28th Precinct reflected the highest increase in the Manhattan borough (Table 3, p. 12) and was the largest for the city overall (Figure 1, p. 17). Other general findings were that in 1977, homicides occurred more frequently in inside locations, specifically a residence; the largest number of homicides were recorded in December; Friday was the most common day of the week for homicides; over half of the reported homicides took place between 7:00 P.M. and 3:00 A.M.; 77.4 percent of all homicides were intraracial; firearms (56 percent) continued to be the chief weapon used in New York City homicides; and disputes constituted the most common precipitating circumstance for both male and female homicide offenders (NYCPD, 1977: 3–7).

Unlike the Rand study, the NYCPD analysis provided information on female homicide perpetrators. The 25.5 percent decrease from 106 to 79 female homicide offenders between 1976 and 1977 pertained primarily to white (− 52.9 percent) and black females (− 26.8 percent). The number of Latina perpetrators increased by 11.8 percent over the one-year period. In 1976 there were equal numbers of Hispanic and white female homicide perpetrators (both at 16.1 percent), but a year later, Latinas were 24.1 percent of the offenders, compared to white females at only 10.1 percent. Black females were those most frequently arrested for homicide in both 1976 (66.9 percent) and 1977 (65.8 percent).[9]

As noted earlier, disputes were notable as precipitating circumstances in the New York City homicides. In 1976, 70.8 percent of all homicides committed by females were triggered by a dispute (NYCPD, 1977: Table 29, pp. 62–63). Homicides resulting from disputes in 1977 occurred slightly more frequently when females were the offenders (62.5 percent) than in those cases involving male perpetrators (61.7 percent). In both years males were victims more frequently than were females. Other criminal acts not evident in the reports of 1976 female-perpetrated homicides were indicated in 1977. Robbery, for example, was associated with 6.6 percent of the homicides involving females in 1976, increasing to 9.7 percent by 1977; males were the likely victims in both years (Table 33, pp. 70–71).

Over a number of years Steven Messner and his colleagues have reported the results of their homicide studies in New York City and addressed the possible relationship between urban homicide rates, poverty, and economic inequality (Messner, 1982; Messner and Tardiff, 1986) and the application of the "routine activities" perspective to urban homicide (Messner and Tardiff, 1985). While most of their data are not gender-specific, they do suggest theoretical approaches that are addressed at the end of this chapter.

THE FEMALE HOMICIDE OFFENDER DATA BASE

In order to secure permission to access files and records and conduct the research, a lengthy series of written and verbal contacts with each of the appropriate police administrators in the six cities was required. For one city, it was necessary to travel to and personally convince the police administrator of the value of the study and thereby obtain access to the needed homicide records. Once entry was granted, most city department administrators generously assigned liaisons to coordinate the research effort.[10] These law enforcement officers, all of whom were males, ranged in status from homicide detectives to public relations officers. Initial telephone contacts were made with each liaison to obtain information on the actual numbers of women arrested for murder in 1979 and 1983 in the targeted cities. In order to complete the sampling prior to the field visits, these introductory contacts were followed up with confirmation letters and additional telephone calls.

In some of the cities the requested case numbers were received well in advance of the site visit enabling the random selection of cases. Despite the preplanning and early case sampling, additional cases for the study years were often uncovered, making it necessary for the random sampling to be repeated after arrival in the field.[11] With the exceptions of Atlanta and Baltimore, the remaining cases in the data base were randomly sampled on site through the use of a table of random numbers. Because of the small number of female arrests for murder in Atlanta and Baltimore, it was decided to include all of the cases. The city samples represented are shown in Table 2.3, which lists by city the number of female arrests for murder and the number sampled.[12]

The aggregated data for the study comprise 296 female-perpetrated homicide cases cleared by arrest in Atlanta, Baltimore, Chicago, Houston, Los Angeles, and New York City. The combined 1979 sample of 164 offenders represents 42.9 percent of the total 382 murder cases involving female offenders for the six cities. Similarly, the 1983 sample of 132

Table 2.3

Number and Percentages of Murder Arrests in Sample Cities Compared to Sample Sizes, 1979 and 1983

Year	1979			1983			TOTALS		
City	Arrests	Sample	Sample Percent	Arrests	Sample	Sample Percent	Arrests	Sample	Sample Percent
Atlanta	32	32	100.0	23	23	100.0	55	55	100.0
Baltimore	22	22	100.0	17	17	100.0	39	39	100.0
Chicago	99	33	33.3	81	27	33.3	180	60	33.3
Houston	88	30	34.1	76	24	31.6	164	54	32.9
Los Angeles	55	24	43.6	42	16	38.1	97	40	41.2
New York City	86	23	26.7	73	25	34.2	159	48	30.2
TOTALS	382	164	42.9	312	132	42.3	694	296	42.7

offenders constitutes 42.3 percent of the 312 female-perpetrated murder cases for that year. According to the Uniform Crime Reports, 2,503 females were arrested nationally for murder and nonnegligent manslaughter in 1979 (U.S. Department of Justice, 1980: 199). The comparable number in 1983 was 2,411 (U.S. Department of Justice, 1984: 186). Since the total of 694 female-perpetrated homicide cases in the six study cities represented 14.1 percent of all U.S. female arrests for murder in 1979 and 1983 (N = 4,914), the study sample of 296 constitutes about 6.0 percent of all U.S. females arrested for murder in those years. Additionally, the study provides a robust sample of 42.7 percent of females arrested for murder in the cities examined.

As noted previously, a modest attempt was made to include a regional distribution of the study cities. Since more than half of the highest homicide rates were found in southern states, it seemed logical to include southern cities as one-half of the final study sample. The sampling proportions by region are portrayed in Table 2.4.

PROCEDURES

Prior to field entry, a data collection schedule that had previously been designed and pretested in an Atlanta study of female felons was modified for use in the homicide study (see Mann, 1984b). The protocol included demographic and social characteristics of the victims and the offenders, characteristics of the murders, criminal justice histories of both the victims and offenders, and criminal justice processing data on the offenders (see Appendix A). The following condensed schematic depicts the major variables in the codebook:[13]

Table 2.4

U.S. Murder Percentages by Region Compared to Study Sample, 1979 and 1983

Region	1979[1]	1983[2]	Total Sample (1979 and 1983)	City Sample
South	42.0	43.0	50.0	Atlanta, Baltimore, Houston
Midwest	21.0	20.0	16.7	Chicago
West	20.0	20.0	16.7	Los Angeles
Northeast	17.0	17.0	16.7	New York City
TOTALS	100.0	100.0	100.0	

1. Source, Uniform Crime Reports, 1980, p. 7.
2. Source, Uniform Crime Reports, 1984, p. 7.
3. Percentages may not add to totals because of rounding.

Schematic of Research Variables

Demographics and Social Characteristics

Offender	*Victim*
Age, race, marital status, maternal status, education, employment status, number of children.	Age, race, gender.

Criminal Justice History

Offender[14]	*Victim*
Previous arrests (misdemeanor/felony), previous convictions (misdemeanor/felony), violent history, child abuse history.	Previous arrests (misdemeanor/felony), previous convictions (misdemeanor/felony), violent history.

Characteristics of the Murder

City, year, date, time, day of week, location, victim/offender relationship, premeditation, offender's role, motive, method used, number of wounds.
Alcohol/narcotics use (offender/victim), prior condition of victim, victim precipitation.

Criminal Justice Processing of Offender

Arrest date, initial charge, amount of bond, final charge, disposition, disposition date, probation time, prison time.

The Field Trips

During the summer of 1985 (Chicago, Houston, and Atlanta) and the spring and summer of 1986 (Los Angeles, New York City, and Baltimore), approximately one to two weeks were spent in each city abstracting information from police records, homicide files, FBI files, and available criminal court accounts. Each case was assigned a coded identification (ID) number to ensure confidentiality, and the data from the various sources and records were recorded for each female homicide offender on her seven-page data-collection protocol (Appendix A). The complete homicide files of the sampled cases, including all available autopsy reports, were minutely examined, and murder scene photographs and other available crime scene evidence were closely scrutinized. Other pertinent information on each female offender—for example, prior police records, fingerprint files, and FBI reports—was pursued and located.

Despite an intensive and rigorous review, missing data proved to be a serious liability. Several follow-up contacts and an unscheduled additional field trip were made to retrieve missing information, particularly those data related to final dispositions. In the final analysis, missing data introduced a serious problem and exposed another limitation to the use of city data.

Data Analysis

Coding of the data was accomplished from the field data-collection protocols, and the information for each case was transferred directly into the university computer mainframe for the analyses. A number of verification techniques to detect errors were applied to the raw data entries as part of a graduate class assignment in a course on the Statistical Package for the Social Sciences (SPSS). The instructor in the class also performed independent editing checks on the data file that resulted in an error-free or "clean" set of data for analysis.[15]

As seen in the list of major variables, most of the variables are nominal, therefore the analyses relied substantially on cross-tabulations and the Chi square statistic as the test of independence between variables. Significant differences were considered to be those with a probability of .05 or less. The intention was to determine if the selected relevant variables were dependent and had a real relationship that would seldom occur by chance, or if the variables were independent and had no relationship, thus making any association found between them due to chance (Hagan, 1982: 240). Multiple regression was used to determine which of the independent variables explained prison sentencing and the length of prison time assigned to convicted defendants.

CONCEPTUAL PERSPECTIVE AND RESEARCH QUESTIONS

In a critical analysis of theories concerning homicide and human nature, Daly and Wilson (1988: 1) disparage such perspectives as revealing "more about the prejudices of their proponents than about the causes of violence." They state further: "The manifest inadequacy of such simplistic explanations has led most scientific students of violence to shy away from general theories. Why do people kill one another? A hundred answers spring to mind, each limited in its domain tractable to investigation."

As psychologists, Daly and Wilson propose the development of an *evolutionary psychology* to "link psychological processes both to their behavioral outcomes and to the selective pressures that have shaped them" (1988: 9). Using the Darwinian theory of evolution by natural selection as the base, they attempt to explain violence on the basis of a social motive (p. 2). Darwin reasoned that organisms adapt as a result of natural selection in the struggle to survive and procreate. Favorable or advantageous variations are preserved and handed down through generations by means of the process of natural selection at the cost of less-favored variations. As applied by Daly and Wilson in what they term "selection thinking," humankind's motivational and psychological mechanisms evolved by means of natural selection to serve its interests, specifically "genetic posterity" (pp. 5–6). Thus, Daly and Wilson focus ingeniously on the kinds of psychological mechanisms that have evolved in humans and how they can explain "patterned variation in the risk of interpersonal conflict and homicide" (p. 6). Noting that "the earliest known victim of human weapons was a Neanderthal man, frontally stabbed in the chest by a right-handed antagonist more than 50,000 years ago" (p. 144), Daly and Wilson remind us also that "there can be no doubt that men have killed one another at high rates for as long as there have been men" (p. 143).

A plethora of homicide theories were classified by Thio (1978: 106–107) into three categories: *biogenic*, or those originating inside the human body; *psychogenic*, which locate the cause in the human psyche; and *sociogenic*, which find the etiology of murder in the social structure. Thio located *ethological* theory within the biogenic classification. As I have noted elsewhere:

> Ethological theory suggests that humans are far more homicidal than other animals with the instinct to kill; particularly since those dangerous animals rarely kill other animals of the same species. Ethological theorists state that other ferocious animals have an instinct to inhibit their killing instincts, but that this inhibitory instinct did not develop in humans. They attribute this to the fact that weapon development was too sudden for evolution to cope with. Since all of us have the same evolutionary past, the same killer instinct, and the same lack of instinctual inhibition against killing, according to ethological theory, we should all have the same likelihood of killing others (Mann, 1993: 75).[16]

The conceptual framework proposed in this volume is an amalgam of ethological theory and an historical application to the social-structural (sociogenic) viewpoint. In the first instance, the emphasis is on the innate violence in humans irrespective of gender. This perspective is in keeping with a notion of lethal violence as a human issue and not a gender issue. More than four decades ago, Otto Pollak (1950: 82) compared homicide statistics for a number of countries; his analysis is informative:

> The available American and British data as well as the various sex ratios referred to in the literature indicate that homicide is neither a typically male nor a typically female crime. Attacks upon human life are made by the members of either sex to such a degree that a specific deviation pattern between the male and female criminality in this respect cannot be found. The data have suggested, however, that if all types of victims and all methods of killing are included, the relative liability of women for homicide is greater than that of men.

Second, a variation on the sociogenic theme focuses on the historically inherent violence in America. As Archer and Gartner so eloquently put it, "Violence is a 'legitimate' recourse of Americans with a grievance. This legitimacy is a feature of American culture, and it is widely invoked as a partial explanation for the remarkable prevalence of violence in that affluent nation. But a reverse causal arrow is equally plausible. That which is prevalent may come to be perceived as legitimate" (1984: 290).

In sum, the conceptual perspective adopted is: *The human potential for violence and homicide that evolved over the many generations of humankind has been so exacerbated in the United States through the historically endemic execution of severe violence and murder that, over time, such behavior has become commonplace and acceptable.* Put in lay terms—if the right buttons are pushed, anyone is capable of committing murder, particularly in our historically violent nation. A refinement from Daly and Wilson (1988) is appropriate also: "The upshot is that violence may breed more violence not by "legitimizing" violence, nor by some nonadaptive process of blind "imitation," "desensitization," or "cultural conditioning" but simply by raising the perceived risks of *nonviolence*. A rational man in a violent milieu will be quicker on the trigger than the same man in a more pacific setting, although he brings the same cultural baggage to both" (p. 286).

While both of the positions reflected in the conceptualization— ethological and social-structural—can be viewed as tangentially related to Daly and Wilson's idea of evolutionary psychology, the exploratory and qualitative nature of the study precluded any attempt to devise or test theoretical models or hypotheses.

Since no extant theories specific to females who commit homicide were uncovered in the examination of the literature, there were no preconceptions of groups to be compared; however, some intergroup comparisons were generated from the data. The study was configured by a series of research questions clustered around the limited body of research literature on female homicide offenders and further guided by additional research questions that evolved from the research.

Subcultural Viewpoints

A number of references were made in chapter 1 to the pioneering homicide research reported by Marvin Wolfgang and his colleagues. It is recalled that Wolfgang and Ferracuti (1967) introduced the concept of a *subculture of violence* as one possible explanation for urban homicide: "In lower-class households and communities, the subculture of violence is passed from generation to generation and reinforced in everyday interaction" (Curran and Renzetti, 1994: 157). Even though research has shown consistently that males are more involved in crime than females, if such a phenomenon is intergenerational, it is conceivable that females would be exposed to the influences of the hypothesized subculture. There are some indications that female crimes today may be more serious, more violent, and more similar to those committed traditionally by men (Adler, 1975). Furthermore, Curran and Renzetti (1994: 159) point out that female gangs, estimated in New York City, for example, at 10 percent of the total gang membership (which numbers between 8,000 and 40,000), have diversified their criminal activities to include fighting, robbery, burglary, and auto theft, in contrast to the girls' offenses described by early theorists.

Subcultural theories primarily address the commission of homicide by urban blacks. This focus occurs despite the fact that: "Critics have maintained that the theory, by attributing violence among Black Americans to a black subculture, for example, subtly implies that the social problems of disadvantaged minorities are intrinsically generated rather than being the products of exploitation and economic opportunity, and that it is mere happenstance that the poorer classes in industrial society exhibit more face-to-face violence than the privileged, rather than the reverse" (Daly and Wilson, 1988: 287). Since African American females are reported as disproportionately represented among homicide offenders and only urban cities were sampled, an appropriate research question becomes: Is the "subculture of violence" theory applicable to African American female homicide offenders?

Similar to African American homicide rates in urban settings, persistently high homicide rates conjoined with the South's distinctive association with firearms has led to a perception of the southern region of the nation as a violent place. Concepts of a southern subculture of violence (for example, Dixon and Lizotte, 1987) or a regional culture of violence (for example, Hackney, 1969; Gastil, 1971) have been applied frequently to the southern United States. In fact, this issue has yet to be resolved.

At the June 1994 annual meeting of the Homicide Research Working Group (HRWG) in Atlanta, a panel discussed and debated the "conceptual arguments for and against a regional subculture of violence explanation for the traditionally higher rates of homicide observed in the South" (HRWG, 1994). One of the major concerns expressed by Hugh Whitt was the definition of both "South" and "southern region," or the question of where is the South? Similarly, Jay Corzine noted that there are at least fifty definitions of "culture." Corzine stressed the homogeneity of the South and its inhabitants' knowledge of and preparedness to use weapons. According to Corzine, southern culture views violence as acceptable and, in certain instances, demanded. Furthermore, women in the South are more likely to own guns than other women. In contrast, Rob Parker reported that migration variables caused the disappearance of the southern subculture of violence.

If a southern subculture of violence exists, does it extend to southern women? The fact that half of the cities included in the study are southern generated the research question: *Is there any validity to the "southern subculture of violence" as applied to women killers?*

Poverty and Economic Inequality

Many urban researchers view economic inequality as causative in homicides, largely because of racial segregation and social isolation, (for example, Blau and Blau, 1982; Liska and Chamlin, 1984; Bailey, 1984; Messner and Tardiff, 1986). As Daly and Wilson (1988: 287–88) point out, "Among the many social structural variables that criminologists have attempted to correlate with homicide rates, one of the more promising is: *income inequality:* It is not simply poverty that seems to be associated with the relatively high rates of violent crime so much as the within-society variance in material welfare."

Some female theorists introduce another perspective that pertains specifically to women: "Feminist criminologists have argued that recent downturns in the economy have impacted especially severely on women to a large extent because women are a marginalized segment of the labor force. They are concentrated in low-status, low-paying jobs and, even when educational attainment is held constant, women earn on average significantly less than men" (Curran and Renzetti, 1994: 275). Further, a study of female-headed families and homicide suggests that poverty, not race, was the possible influential factor linking homicide to the inner city (Wiltz, 1985).

The pertinent research question addressed on this subtopic is: *Is an economic theory of crime applicable to women who commit homicide?*

Substance Use

Female drug abuse in this country is not a recent phenomenon. During some time periods, female addicts have been more numerous than male addicts (Mann, 1984a). It is estimated that today women constitute about half of the drug-abusing population in the United States. Alcohol has also been consistently found to be involved in homicides (for example, Wolfgang, 1958; Abel and Zeidenberg, 1986), while the drug/murder connection is considered one of the most serious contemporary social problems. Logically, then, the question explored here is: *What is the role played by drugs (alcohol and narcotics) in female-perpetrated homicides?*

Victim Precipitation and the "Battered Woman Syndrome"

Wolfgang (1958: 255) found that women were the offenders in victim-precipitated homicides twice as often as in non-victim-precipitated homicides. Similarly, in Dade County, Florida, Wilbanks (1983a: 11) reported that 46.8 percent of the victims in female-perpetrated homicides had "participated" in the killing; that is, provoked it. The "battered woman syndrome" is a closely related concept that also implies that a female-perpetrated killing usually occurs as a form of self-defense in response to the instigation of a male victim. Since the two concepts are intertwined, a single research question is addressed: *Can victim precipitation and/or the "battered woman syndrome" predict female criminal homicide?*

Ecological Factors

A number of studies cited previously included specific ecological characteristics such as the time, month, and season when a homicide occurred; the place of occurrence; whether the murder took place inside or outside; if the homicide scene was a residence or a tavern; and, if the lethal event happened in a residence, the room that was the locale. Thus, the pertinent research question is: *Are ecological factors influential in murders committed by females?*

Racial Discrimination in Criminal Justice Processing

Research on the criminal justice experiences of males has shown consistently that men of color are treated more severely than nonminority men (see Mann, 1993). As defendants of color progress through the criminal justice system, evidence of racial discrimination accumulates— sometimes subtly, often not so subtly—both during the *pretrial stages* (bail, detention, and initial and final charging) and at the sentencing level. Prior research on the differential treatment of women of color is scarce. Little has been reported on the pretrial stages, and there are mixed findings on sentencing (for example, Wolfgang, 1958; Wilbanks, 1983a; Goetting, 1987). In light of the alleged racism in the criminal justice system, it is important to address the research question: *Are women of color who murder treated more punitively by the criminal justice system than nonminority women?*

Due to its intrinsic connection to sentencing, the *devaluation of African American lives* perspective is closely related to racial discrimination in the criminal justice system. As Darnell Hawkins (1986: 114) views the concept, American criminal law treats black life as cheap and white life as valuable. Put another way, harsher sanctions are applied when a white is murdered than when a black is murdered. This differential treatment is exacerbated when a white is killed by a nonwhite. In contrast, when a nonwhite, especially a black, is killed by a white, the sentence is more lenient. A simplified modification of Hawkins' ratings of life valuation from most to least serious is: black kills white; white kills white; black kills black; white kills black.[17] To test this proposition we ask the research question: *Does the race of the victim of a female homicide offender influence the sentencing process?*

In addition to the questions raised in the discussion of a southern subculture of violence, of further interest are comparisons of judicial treatment across the six cities studied in terms of both race and southern- ness. Possible ecological racial differences at the macrolevel lead to the final research question: *Are there city or "regional" differences in the criminal court processing of women who kill?*

These research questions are not addressed systematically as they are outlined here but instead are interspersed throughout the volume as related findings are examined in specific chapters. They are revisited in the final chapter of the book in a closing summary.

NOTES

1. As it turned out, because of the time restrictions of the field visits, the selection of some of these data sources was overly ambitious. However, at a few sites computerized data linked to other city, county, and state departments provided some of the additional information sought initially.

2. Older police records and homicide case folders are often misplaced or stored in places from which they are difficult to retrieve. Despite the attempt to avoid this hazard by advanced sampling, in some cities many of the records were extremely difficult to locate. For example, in New York City they were housed in the five individual borough homicide de- partments.

3. Puerto Rico had very high homicide rates for both years (13.8 in 1979 and 13.1 in 1983) but was excluded from consideration because distance made it unfeasible as a study site.

4. These were calculated from the UCR using the equation:

$$R = \frac{\frac{C}{P}}{100,000}$$

where R = homicide rate;
C = homicides known to police;
P = central city population, 1980

5. The city descriptions were derived from Carpenter and Provorse, 1992: 's *Facts about the Cities* (1992).

6. At this writing Atlanta has the highest homicide rate in the nation, making it the "U.S. murder capital."

7. Among the six cities studied by Rose and McClain—Atlanta, St. Louis, Detroit, Houston, Pittsburgh, and Los Angeles—three are included in the present study (Atlanta, Houston, and Los Angeles).

8. Although Houston and Los Angeles were included in their study of black homicide, Rose and McClain's (1990) aggregated city data mask any definitive information about female homicide offenders.

9. These percentages were calculated from figures listed in Table 21, p. 48 of the NYCPD study.

10. My sincere thanks and appreciation are extended to the following police administrators for their invaluable assistance: George Napper, Commissioner of Public Safety, Atlanta, Georgia; Fred Rice, Superintendent of Police, Chicago, Illinois; Bishop L. Robinson, Commissioner of Police, Baltimore, Maryland; Lee Brown, Chief of Police, Houston, Texas; Daryl Gates, Chief of Police, Los Angeles, California; and Benjamin Ward, Commissioner of Police, New York City, New York.

11. Although it may require additional field time, it is recommended that all sampling be accomplished on site.

12. The decentralization of New York City's homicide records among the individual boroughs led to the inability to find a sufficient number of 1979 cases from the various storage areas.

13. The codebook is replicated in Appendix B.

14. Statistical details of the previous arrests and convictions of offenders are located in Appendix C.

15. The contribution of Dr. Edmund True and his class was invaluable.

16. According to Daly and Wilson (1988: 144), "Where ethologists once believed that intraspecific killing was rare in the animal world in general and among our close kin a particular, we have since found that attacks by conspecifics are a major cause of mortality in many (probably most) mammals, including those most closely related to ourselves."

17. Hawkins' "scale of seriousness of homicide offenses which emerged from historical patterns of race relations in the American South" (1986: 117) is listed below:

Rating	*Offense*
Most serious	Black kills White, in authority
	Black kills White, stranger
	White kills White, in authority
	Black kills White, friend, acquaintance
	Black kills White, intimate, family
	White kills White, stranger
	White kills White, friend, acquaintance
	White kills White, intimate, family
	Black kills Black, stranger

Black kills Black, friend, acquaintance
Black kills Black, intimate, family
White kills Black, stranger
White kills Black, friend, acquaintance

Least serious   White kills Black, intimate, family (Hawkins, 1986: 118).

Chapter 3

Ecological and Other Circumstances of the Murder

In the generic sense, the ecology of crime concerns the interrelationships between humans and their physical environment. On the criminological level, social geographer Keith Harries observes, "It is no accident that the most prolific outpouring of literature on the ecology of crime has been focused at the intraurban scale" (1980: 19). The ecological examination of homicide is often conducted on the macrolevel; that is, it involves *macroenvironments* such as "large-scale socioeconomic, sociopsychological, demographic, and cultural processes that may be theoretically and/or empirically related to various aspects of criminogenesis" (Harries, 1980: 19). On that level, broad areas such as countries, regions, states, or cities and the concomitant homicide data are relevant units of analysis (Gastil, 1971; Hackney, 1971).

On the intraurban or *microenvironment* level, the relationship between homicide patterns and demographic and other social characteristics is frequently explored in terms of city blocks, or even neighborhoods. Microenvironments in homicide studies traditionally include spatial ecological factors such as the specific location of the homicides—ranging from inside or outside of residence to the particular locale within a physical structure.

Another popular ecological research approach—the study of crime and the physical environment—regards certain characteristics of the physical environment as determinants of homicidal behavior; for example, the possible impact of climate, weather, seasonality, or lunar influences and the time of the day or week that lethal violence occurs.

This study of female homicide offenders includes characterizations of both microenvironments and macroenvironments. Descriptions of the crime scene include the location (whether inside or outside the home), the actual room within a residence, and in whose residence the murder took place. Other ecological variables are the time of the murder, the day of the week and month a murder occurred, and the geographical regions of the homicides. The possible influence of seasonal variations on homicide is addressed also.

The contribution of substance use on the part of one or both participants is closely related to both the time and place of a murder. The influence of drugs (narcotics and/or alcohol) is further illustrated through individual sampled cases. Finally, choice of weapon and the number of wounds inflicted upon the victim are circumstances of the murder that are discussed in this chapter. These factors are revisited in later chapters when specific victim/offender relationships and the criminal justice processing of female homicide perpetrators are addressed.

MURDER LOCATIONS

Most studies of female homicide offenders report that murders characteristically take place in the residence of the offender, that of the victim, or the dwelling where they live together (Formby, 1986; Goetting, 1987; McClain, 1981; Totman, 1978; Weisheit, 1984; Wilbanks, 1983a; Wolfgang, 1958). The results of the present study concur with those of previous reports by finding that a majority of the murders committed by females took place in the home (70.4 percent), where the victim and offender usually lived together (42.3 percent). When the murder occurred in the residence of only one of the parties involved, it happened more often in the home of the offender than that of the victim. Occasionally the crime scene was another person's home (5.8 percent).

Previous homicide research has often reported the specific room in the house where the murder took place. Wolfgang (1958) found that the *kitchen* was a frequent site for homicides committed by females. He suggested that such murders were usually spontaneous and, in the heat of anger and passion, involved the seizure of some kitchen implement, usually a knife. Twenty years later, Totman (1978) reported that when women killed male intimates, the *bedroom* was the most frequent homicide location. More recently, Goetting (1989) also found the bedroom to be a major crime scene in mate killings.

As indicated in Figure 3.1, the *living room/family room/den*—or those locations defined here as "social areas"—were the most frequent in-residence murder sites in the present study. Social areas were followed by the bedroom, other living areas, and the kitchen as crime scenes. Since weapons are commonly found in bedrooms and kitchens, the proportion of murders taking place in the other home areas was perplexing at first. However, an examination of several individual cases revealed that weapons, usually knives, were also kept in rooms such as dens, living rooms, and family rooms. The remaining murders that occurred in or at a

Figure 3.1

Homicide Location in Residence

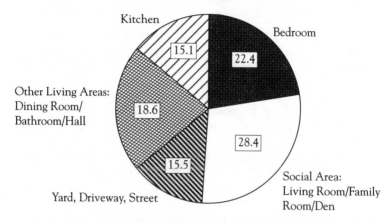

residence happened in the yard, driveway, or street, where the victim had either been killed on the way into the residence or chased from the home and murdered. The following case illustrates a typical female-perpetrated murder taking place in the street.

> *Case 4122:* At about 2:20 on a Sunday morning, Amy,[1] twenty-seven, shot her lover, a man who was ten years her senior, in the walkway to her apartment. Although both had been drinking for hours prior to the murder, they had not been drinking together. Earlier that Saturday the couple had argued, and Amy called the police to say that she was going to kill her lover. Witnesses later reported that the victim was beating Amy in the street that evening and banging her head against a wall. Amy admitted going to her mother's house and obtaining a shotgun from her mother's boyfriend. When the mother's boyfriend tried to stop her, she shot in the air, reloaded the gun, and went looking for the victim at his friends' houses. Upon returning to her home, she found him waiting for her. As the victim walked toward her, Amy claimed that somehow the shotgun went off and the homicide was an accident. Despite having a prior arrest for felonious assault with a deadly weapon and another for cruelty to a child, Amy was charged with voluntary manslaughter and sentenced to one year in jail, with three years' probation plus a fine.

In her study of African American women murderers, McClain (1981) found that 29 percent of the homicides occurred on the street. The fact that almost 20 percent of the murders in the present study took place just outside taverns, in streets, in alleys, and in yards, offers corroboration for McClain's earlier finding. The proportion of homicides that occurred in streets or alleys *away* from the residence (13.7 percent) suggests a theme of female aggressiveness such as is seen in the following representative case.

> *Case 4206:* Bea, age twenty-one, her twenty-three-year-old brother, who had a number of previous arrests for violent crimes (for example, assault with a deadly weapon, robbery), and her boyfriend, thirty-one, who had an equally violent arrest history (voluntary manslaughter, assault with intent), became involved in an argument with the thirty-five-year-old victim in the parking lot of a tavern. All of the participants had been drinking. The victim was cut in both the face and the back by Bea's male co-defendants, but it was Bea who shot the victim in the stomach with a twelve-gauge sawed-off shotgun. She was ultimately tried on a charge of voluntary manslaughter and sentenced to two years in prison.

TEMPORAL FACTORS IN THE MURDERS

Previous studies suggest that personal crimes tend to occur more frequently in the summer months and that there is a relationship between seasonality and crime (Dodge and Lentzer, 1980; Dodge, 1988). Some researchers also intimate that there is a connection between the weather and crime (Kaplan, 1960; Miller, 1968; Lab and Hirschel, 1988); they allege that homicide rates would be highest in the summer months because of the effect of heat on the human organism, as well as humidity.

In her study of female-perpetrated spousal homicide in Detroit, Goetting (1989) found that the murders were randomly distributed by month, with no obvious seasonal variations. Even if some credence were given to seasonal or climatic factors in the etiology of female homicide commission, the average temperate climates of Atlanta, Baltimore, Los Angeles, and Houston preclude any argument favoring weather as a major influence in murder, especially when compared to the weather variations in Chicago and New York City. Therefore it was not surprising to find little seasonal variation in the homicides reported here. As Figure 3.2 shows, 79 murders occurred in what are usually defined as summer months (June, July, and August), only slightly fewer than the number of murders (N = 81) in the spring months (March, April, and May), but higher than the 74 murders that took place in the winter months (December, January, and February) or the 61 murders in the fall months (September, October, and November).[2] This finding suggests that women who commit murder are no more affected by the weather, heat, or humidity than anyone else, and furthermore,

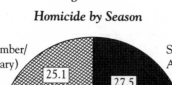

Figure 3.2

Homicide by Season

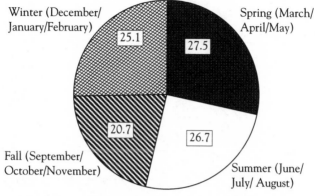

Unfortunately, seasonal studies rely on gross generalizations about weather. They ignore variations in weather conditions regardless of season, which ma promote different levels and types of activity. The use of season or months necessitates the assumption that the specific weather measures are constant across the entire period. This, however, is an untenable assumption. It is possible, even probable, that variation in weather conditions within seasons and months affects behavior differentially. That is, higher temperatures may draw people into different types of activities regardless of the time of year (Lab and Hirschel, 1988: 286).

It has generally been reported that homicides take place on weekends, particularly on Saturday nights (for example, Wolfgang, 1958). Goetting's (1987) study noted that 61 percent of the murders perpetrated by women took place on Friday, Saturday, and Sunday. Although Figure 3.3 shows that the homicides in the present study occurred most frequently on Saturday, Friday was the least likely day for the crime, and Sunday was only the third most frequent day. Tuesday was the second most popular day for murder. When the data were collapsed into weekends (Friday, Saturday, and Sunday) and averaged to account for the one-day differential (three weekend days versus four weekdays), the comparison to weekdays (Monday through Thursday) more clearly supported the notion that murder is a leisuretime, or weekend, activity.

Following social custom, it might be anticipated that the use of alcohol and drugs prior to a homicide would be more likely on weekends.

Figure 3.3

Homicides by Day of Week

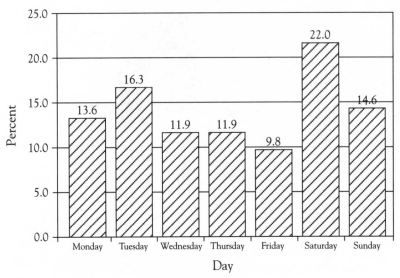

Drinking is generally considered a recreational weekend activity, but since drug use is more often associated with drug availability, logic suggests that it could occur at any time or on any day of the week. The fact that a majority of the users and nonusers were unemployed introduces the additional possibility that *both* alcohol and drug use could take place at any time. Also, such an economic status might explain the high proportion of Tuesday slayings. The findings indicated in Table 3.1 show that slightly more homicides committed by users happened on weekends, whereas the opposite was found for nonusers, who killed more frequently on weekdays. It was also found that women who had been drinking prior to the murders killed on weekends (59.4 percent). In contrast, those who had used drugs tended to commit murder on weekdays (66.7 percent).

In line with the weekend/recreational theme, it was predictable that homicides would take place in the evening hours. In the 294 (out of 296) cases for which the time of occurrence was available, the mean time of the murder was 1:39 A.M. Prior research efforts reported consistently that homicides occurred more often between 8:00 P.M. and 1:59 A.M. (Wolfgang, 1958; Pokorny, 1965; Goetting, 1987). Following the format of the previous studies, the data were collapsed into the four six-hour time

Table 3.1

Homicide Characteristics by Offender Substance Users and Nonusers[1]

| Characteristic | Offender Type | | Significance |
	Users (n = 96)	Nonusers (n = 137)	
Day of Week			
Weekday	47.9	54.7	
Weekend	52.1	45.3	
Victim-Offender Relationship			
Intimate	60.4	73.7	p = .04
Other	39.6	26.3	X² = 4.02; 1 df
Offender Role			
Alone	85.1	80.3	
With Others	14.9	19.7	
Motive			
Responsible	23.3	16.3	
Not Responsible	76.7	83.7	
Premeditation			
Yes	66.3	59.5	
No	33.7	40.5	
Victim Precipitation			
Yes	67.0	61.9	
No	33.0	38.1	
Method			
Gun	43.8	45.3	
Knife	42.7	34.3	
Other	13.5	20.4	
Number of Wounds			
One	50.5	60.6	
Multiple	49.5	39.4	

1. Does not include missing cases.

segments shown in Figure 3.4. In concurrence with earlier research, it was revealed that women who kill tend to do so at night; 62.3 percent of the homicides took place between 8:00 P.M. and 7:59 A.M.

"REGIONAL" COMPARISONS

Another ecological analysis compared the three southern cities (Atlanta, Baltimore, and Houston) to the remaining nonsouthern cities in the study, which were seen as representative of the Northeast (New York City), the Midwest (Chicago), and the West (Los Angeles). Obviously these six cities cannot be considered truly representative of regions in the United States, but the comparisons between the southern and nonsouthern cities did offer some rather intriguing findings that could serve as catalysts for future replications of this study.

Figure 3.4

Time of Homicides

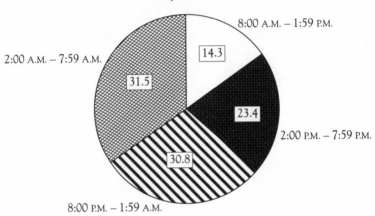

8:00 A.M. – 1:59 P.M.

2:00 A.M. – 7:59 A.M.

14.3

31.5

23.4

2:00 P.M. – 7:59 P.M.

30.8

8:00 P.M. – 1:59 A.M.

There were an identical number of aggregated homicide cases in both the southern and nonsouthern cities (N = 148), and more similarities than differences were found between the southern and nonsouthern female homicide offenders. Contrary to expectations suggested by the *southern subculture of violence* perspective, a 19.5 percent *decrease* in the number of women arrested for murder in the sampled cities between 1979 and 1983 was due primarily to a drop in the rates in the southern cities. Whereas 51.2 percent of the homicides in 1979 occurred in the southern cities, the opposite was found in 1983, when 51.5 percent of the homicides took place in nonsouthern cities.

As Figure 3.5 clearly indicates, southern women were significantly more likely than nonsouthern women to use firearms in the murders they committed (60.1 percent v. 39.9 percent).[3] African American women in the southern states were particularly prone to select firearms over other methods of killing (67.9 percent). Of the women who used long guns (rifles or shotguns) in their homicides, 68.4 percent were in southern cities. On the other hand, nonsouthern women were more inclined to use knives, and they also differed significantly from southern women in the use of homicide methods such as beating/stomping, drowning, or suffocating. This last finding may reflect the fact that nonsouthern women were more likely than southern women to kill persons under the age of twenty-five, many of whom were children.

Figure 3.5

Homicide Method by Region

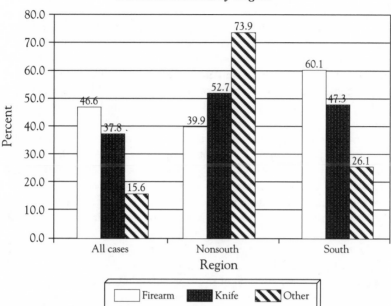

The finding that nonsouthern women more frequently inflicted multiple wounds on their victims (53.2 percent) may reflect the fact that they were also more prone to have violent arrest histories (53.5 percent). Southern female killers were also slightly more likely to have been drinking than their nonsouthern counterparts. The opposite was indicated when hard drugs were involved—nonsouthern women were implicated in 58.6 percent of the murders when drugs were used prior to the event.

Compared to southern *victims*, nonsouthern victims were not as prone to provoke their own deaths. Among those murders determined to be victim-precipitated, 58.2 percent occurred in the South. In contrast, cases defined as not victim-precipitated were more frequently found in states outside the South (67.7 percent).[4] The victims of nonsouthern women were more likely to have used hard drugs before their deaths (61.5 percent), while those killed by southern women comprised more than half of those who were drinking before the homicide (55.7 percent).[5]

SUBSTANCE USE AND MURDER

Alcohol Use

Over a third of all female homicide offenders studied had been drinking prior to the murder (35.6 percent). And, as previously indicated, more victims than offenders, especially males, were under the influence of alcohol at the time of their deaths (46.7 percent). Many of those victims were defined as legally drunk (17.0 percent). About 4 percent of the women killed their victims in or near taverns. These findings lend reinforcement to the large body of research literature suggesting a close association between homicide and the use of alcohol by both offenders and victims.

In his study of Philadelphia victims, Wolfgang (1958) reported that alcohol was present in 63.6 percent of the murders and noted, "Whether alcohol is present in the victim or offender, lowered inhibitions due to ingestion of alcohol may cause an individual to give vent more freely to pent-up frustrations, tensions, and emotional conflicts that have either built up over a prolonged period of time or that arise within an immediate emotional crisis" (ibid., p. 261). Similarly, an early sociopsychological study of incarcerated women murderers in California found that 50 percent of the cases had involved alcohol (Cole, Fisher, and Cole, 1968). Goetting (1989) reviewed all of the homicides that took place in Detroit, Michigan during 1982 and 1983, and found that 32.1 percent of offenders and 36.9 percent of victims had been drinking before the homicide. Her later analysis of homicidal wives from that study indicated that 37.5 percent of the women and 44.6 percent of their spouses had been drinking prior to the murder (Goetting, 1987).

Ward, Jackson, and Ward (1969) reported that of the 60 percent of women inmates in the Minnesota state prison who claimed alcohol was a factor in the murders they committed, 5 percent maintained that their drunkenness was influential in the homicide. In another prison study in North Carolina, Suval and Brisson (1974) found that 61.1 percent of the female homicide offenders reported frequent drinking, and over half admitted to alcoholism or a severe drinking problem. A little less than half of the women (44.6 percent) in that study were under the influence of alcohol when they committed murder. A majority of the African American women in McClain's (1982) study admitted to drinking at the time of the murder, but only 20 percent attributed the crime to alcohol.

The settings for most homicide research tend to be cities and other large urban areas, yet two studies in rural Alabama present an even more dramatic picture of an alcohol/murder relationship. Kowalski, Shields, and Wilson (1985) described imprisoned women murderers in Alabama from 1929 to 1971, 52 percent of whom were categorized as rural.

Kowalski et al. found that in 73.6 percent of the murders, at least one of the participants had used alcohol, and in 58.3 percent of the crimes both the offenders (63.2 percent) and their victims (68.6 percent) had been drinking.

Shields (1987) later expanded the study period to 1986. In the follow-up study, Shields did not report the percentage of rural cases, but assuming the same proportions held as in the earlier study, about half could be considered rural women. From 1930 to 1986, at least one of the parties had consumed alcohol in 71.5 percent of the homicide incidents, and both had been drinking in 50.3 percent. Moreover, Shields found that 11.5 percent of the murders took place at or near a tavern or in a public place.

The most recent crime report data indicate that in 1992, there were 339,269 females arrested for offenses involving alcohol (U.S. Department of Justice, 1993: 234).[6] This figure does not include the 124,690 females arrested for disorderly conduct, an offense that frequently involves drinking. These numbers suggest that the use of alcohol is clearly an influential factor in the lives of contemporary females. Furthermore, previous research leaves little doubt that high proportions of homicides have been reported as alcohol-related (Abel and Zeidenberg, 1986). As we have seen, the present study is no exception.

Drug Use[7]

While the association between alcohol use and female-perpetrated homicide is generally supported by research, the homicide/drugs nexus is not so clearly established. Despite the increasing number of female arrests for drug abuse violations—51,344, for example, in 1992 (U.S. Department of Justice, 1993: 234)—until very recently little research attention was devoted to female drug use and abuse.

Excessive use of drugs by women is much more prevalent in the United States than is realized, and it is not a recent phenomenon. Only the drugs have changed.[8] There have been periods when female addiction exceeded that of males (Mann, 1984). In the nineteenth century, for example, the drug dependence of women was described as a "significant social problem" that had existed for over one hundred years (Inciardi and Pottieger, 1986: 91). It was not unusual for women to buy "elixirs," powders, and other compounds containing opiates (Marsh and Simpson, 1986). When the Harrison Act of 1914 prohibited the legal sale of over-the-counter nonprescription narcotics, there was a decrease in the number of women addicted to those drugs. Today it is estimated that 50 percent of drug abusers are women.

In 1987, the National Institute of Justice began the Drug Use Forecasting program (DUF) in New York City. By 1993, twenty-four cities had instituted the program, which estimates drug use among arrestees. Because of their smaller numbers, *all* arrested females, regardless of charge, are included in the DUF sample. Drug use by female arrestees in 1990 ranged from 44 percent (San Antonio) to 88 percent (Cleveland). The percentage of arrested females who tested positive for any drug was higher than that for males in most of the cities (DeWitt, 1990). In 1989, 46 percent of the females arrested for homicide tested positive for drugs such as cocaine, opiates, marijuana, PCP, methadone, Valium, Quaalude, Darvon, barbiturates, and amphetamines (Maguire and Flanagan, 1991: 457).

Few of the earlier studies of female homicide offenders addressed the topic, and those that did provide an amalgam of results. Suval and Brisson (1974) reported that drugs were a factor in only 1.2 percent of the homicides in which females were the perpetrators. Similarly, Ward et al. (1969) found that 2.0 percent of the female homicide offenders studied in Minnesota were narcotics users. In their California prison study, Cole et al. (1968) associated 10 percent of the female-perpetrated homicides with narcotics. In shocking contrast, Gibbs, Silverman, and Vega (1977) found that 75 percent of Florida women killers used drugs prior to the lethal event. In a sense this Florida finding should not be too surprising, in light of the commonly reported proliferation of drugs in that state; what is surprising is that the study was reported in 1977!

The relationship between drugs, specifically cocaine, and violence, was the focus of a recent ethnographic study of 133 female drug users or distributors on the Lower East Side of New York City (Goldstein, Belluci, Spunt, and Miller, 1991). More than half of their female sample (59 percent) reported some participation in violent events (ibid.: 354). Such encounters were concentrated primarily in non-drug-related disputes such as "spouse/lover and friend/acquaintance categories" (ibid.: 357). In fact, women cocaine users were just as likely to be victims as offenders. Another New York City study that utilized Goldstein's (1985) tripartite conceptual framework,[9] classified four of twenty-one female homicide perpetrators as drug users (19 percent): three used cocaine/crack and one used alcohol (Arnold, Goldstein, Brownstein, and Ryan, 1988). Further, Arnold et al. (1988) found the drugs were associated with 29 percent of homicides when women were the killers.

Among the cases in which drug use could be determined in the present study, 12.6 percent of the female homicide offenders were under the influence of a drug at the time they committed the crimes. Many of the drug-related homicides committed by the women in the study were particularly heinous, as seen in the following two case examples.

Case 4102: The victim was a seventy-one-year-old retired barber with whom Carrie, age twenty-one, and her children lived. The victim and

Carrie were lovers. Originally, Carrie and her brother, who was allegedly dealing drugs with the victim, planned the murder. The motive involved money and drugs; Carrie was to receive $200 and the victim's car for her role in the murder. Somehow, three other co-defendants became involved, two Hispanic males and an Asian male. When they arrived at the victim's home, Carrie warned the three men that the victim was armed with an automatic gun. Using the ruse that they needed to use the telephone, the killers gained access to the house, and all of the perpetrators, including Carrie, beat the victim. After the beating, Carrie told the men, "Roll him over so he chokes on his own blood." When they refused, she eventually accomplished the act with a sheet. She then hit the victim in the neck with a cane because he was making gurgling noises. While the others left to put the victim's body in a car trunk, Carrie cleaned up the blood. After shooting the victim, who by now was in the trunk of the car, the offender's brother gave the gun to one of the co-defendants insisting that he also shoot the body to ensure his involvement in the crime. Ironically, because of an old feud over a woman, the man instead shot the brother four times. When questioned by the police, Carrie, who was white, first said that she saw three male "Negroes" beat the victim and then kidnap and rob him. Through a plea bargain, Carrie was ultimately found guilty of voluntary manslaughter and sentenced to eight and two/thirds to nine years in prison.

Case 4106: Dora, a white twenty-three-year-old, was intimately associated with African American gangs. According to police records, for four years Dora was the girlfriend of the black leader of one of the most notorious gangs involved in heavy narcotics dealing. The gang had been set up for a narcotics rip-off by a woman who, when discovered, was falsely imprisoned and stabbed nine times. She survived the attempted murder and informed the police about the attempt on her life and the gang murders. In a cafe, Dora and two of the gang members had found the men who had accomplished the drug rip-off and killed both of them for revenge and to leave a message for others who might harbor similar ideas. One victim was shot twice in the neck below the ears; the other was shot in the back and also in the neck below the ear. Dora was under the influence of drugs at the time of the murders. Among many other arrests, she had a history of felony arrests for drugs (heroin) and had been arrested also for murder. She was initially charged with murder in this case, but the charge was reduced and the case was eventually dismissed.

A Comparison of Users and Nonusers

The ninety-six women who killed while under the influence of alcohol or drugs ("users") were compared with the remaining female homicide offenders ("nonusers") in the study to determine how influential substance use was in female-perpetrated murders. Alcohol users constituted 35.6 percent of the total sample of women killers in the 233 cases for which information was available, and drug users accounted for 12.6 percent of the 230 homicides for which such data were known. In some cases the offenders were under the influence of both alcohol *and* drugs. At the time of the murder, 29.6 percent of the women had used only alcohol, 5.6 percent were influenced by drugs, and 6.0 percent had used both.

As revealed in Figure 3.6, comparison of alcohol and drug use on the part of both offenders and victims indicates that for both, alcohol use is far more prevalent than the use of drugs. Whereas victims are substantially more likely to have been drinking, their female killers are slightly more likely to have been under the influence of some hard drug.

An examination of substance use by "region" reveals that nonsouthern victims were most likely to have used drugs prior to their deaths (61.5 percent). In fact, the incidence of drug use by victims in the nonsouthern cities (17.8 percent) was twice that found among southern victims (8.1 percent).[10] In contrast, southern victims were slightly more likely to have been drinking prior to their murders. A similar pattern was found for the

Figure 3.6

Victim and Offender Substance Use by Region

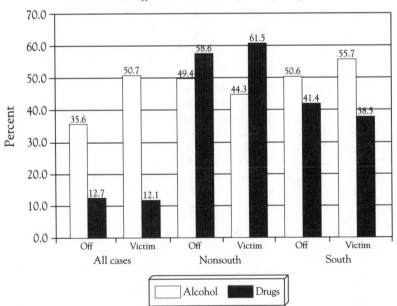

female offenders—nonsoutherners were more likely to have been using drugs than southerners, who, in turn, were more frequently found to have been drinking prior to committing homicide.

Comparisons of the social characteristics of using and nonusing offenders, depicted in Table 3.2, revealed that except for *age*, the two groups did not differ significantly on any of the features studied. The users, who ranged in age from fifteen to sixty-four years, had an average age of 32.7 years and were typically older than the nonusers (mean = 29.6 years).

It was thought that female users would be more likely to kill strangers or acquaintances and, conversely, that the victims of nonusers would be someone close to them such as their children, spouses, or relatives. Presumably, nonusers are more likely to take out their frustrations on those with whom they are sexually intimate, related by blood or marriage, or in constant, close proximity. The rationale for the first assumption was that economics are often a factor in cases involving drug users, and murder could result, for example, from a drug deal that went awry. Also,

Table 3.2

Social Characteristics of Offender by Substance Users and Nonusers (in percentages)[1]

	Offender Type		
Offender Characteristic	Users (n = 96)	Nonusers (n = 137)	Significance
Race[2]			
Black	71.9	78.8	
White	15.6	14.6	
Hispanic	12.5	6.6	
White	15.6	14.6	
Non-White	84.4	85.4	
Age (in years)			
(mean)	(32.7)	(29.6)	p = .02
Under 25	26.0	42.3	$X^2 = 5.84$; 1 df
25 and over	74.0	57.7	
Marital Status			
Ever married	58.8	59.3	
Single	41.2	40.7	
Maternal Status			
Yes	66.7	71.3	
No	33.3	28.7	
Employed			
Yes	27.2	33.9	
No	72.8	66.1	

1. Does not include missing cases.
2. There were no other racial/ethnic groups in the random sample.

the social milieu of drug use includes certain hazards such as "bad trips" or other adverse reactions to particular drugs that often lead to the initiation and/or escalation of violence. Of course, emotions also tend to run high in social drinking situations when people "begin to feel their liquor." FInally, most users' drug and drinking companions are strangers, acquaintances, or friends (see chapter 5).

As seen in Table 3.1, this prediction was supported. A significant difference was found between users and nonusers in the selection of their respective victims: nonusers killed intimates more frequently (73.7 percent v. 60.4 percent), while users killed persons other than intimates (39.6 percent v. 26.3 percent). Other features of the homicides did not distinguish the two groups.

As presented in Table 3.3, the *victims* of users and nonusers, however, were more dissimilar. Victims of users had a mean age of 35.9 years, which was significantly older than the average age of the nonusers' victims (29.7 years). Among other social and criminal justice characteristics that distinguish the victims of users and nonusers, significant differences were found in substance abuse. Just like their killers, victims of users were significantly more likely to have used both alcohol and drugs than the victims of nonusers.

Substance Use and Victim Precipitation

In line with Wolfgang's (1958) seminal findings, it was anticipated that the use of a substance, especially alcohol, would be a major precipitating factor in the female-perpetrated homicides. Wolfgang found that victims, especially men (60 percent), often instigated their own deaths by first using threats of physical force, then blows; and that drinking was highly influential in such incidents. The present study confirmed Wolfgang's earlier conclusion by finding that victim precipitation occurred more frequently among victims who used alcohol prior to their murders (55.9 percent) than it did among nondrinking victims (44.1 percent).[11] The use of some type of narcotics by a victim, however, did not seem to be as influential and reflected an opposite picture from alcohol involvement. Only 8.4 percent of victims who had used drugs instigated their deaths, while 19.4 percent of victim drug users did not.[12] These results suggest that the influence of drugs is less lethal than that of liquor, but it must be kept in mind that in the late 1970s and early 1980s, when this study was undertaken, different drugs were popular. Today the use of drugs such as crack cocaine, "ice," "cat," "speed," powerful amphetamines, and "designer" drugs of various types can lead to more erratic and volatile behavior.

Evidence was also found that the victims of female substance users who killed were significantly more likely to be users themselves. Whereas

Table 3.3

Victim Characteristics by Offender Substance Users and Nonusers
(in percentages)[1]

Victim Characteristic	Offender Type		Significance
	Users (n = 96)	Nonusers (n = 137)	
Race[2]			
Black	69.8	75.2	
White	17.7	17.5	
Hispanic	12.5	7.3	
White	17.7	17.5	
Non-White	82.3	82.5	
Age (in years)			
(mean)	(35.9)	(29.7)	
Under 25	14.6	38.7	p = .0001
25 and over	85.4	61.3	X^2 = 14.85; 1 df
Gender			
Male	86.5	78.1	
Female	13.5	21.9	
Alcohol[3]			
Yes	77.8	27.0	p = .0000
No	22.2	73.0	X^2 = 50.16; 1 df
Drugs[3]			
Yes	20.5	5.2	p = .002
No	79.5	94.8	X^2 = 9.50; 1 df
Prior Arrests			
Yes	71.9	56.2	
No	28.1	43.8	
Violent Arrest History			
Yes	52.4	40.0	
No	47.6	60.0	

1. Does not include missing cases.
2. There were no other racial/ethnic groups in the random sample.
3. Used prior to homicide.

77.8 percent of the victims of users had been drinking, only 27 percent of
the nonusers' victims had (Table 3.3). Further, victims of users were
almost four times as likely to have used drugs prior to their deaths as the
victims of nonusers (20.5 percent v. 5.2 percent). Victim precipitation
was significantly more common in the cases of women who had used
alcohol prior to the murder (79.1 percent) than among those who had
used drugs (33.3 percent).[13] Thus, a picture begins to emerge of a social
situation highly compromised by substance use on the parts of both the
women killers and their victims. In a sense, who the instigator of the
lethal violence really was becomes blurred.

In his discussion of homicide, Luckenbill (1977: 176) defines the
interaction between the victim, offender, and bystanders as a *situated*

transaction: "The transaction took a sequential form: the victim issued what the offender deemed an offensive move; the offender typically retaliated with a verbal or physical challenge; a 'working' agreement favoring the use of violence was forged with the victim's response; battle ensued leaving the victim dead or dying; the manner of the offender's exiting was shaped by his relationship to the victim and the moves of his audience."

A major component of the Luckenbill thesis is the attempt on the part of one or both of the actors in the homicide event to "establish or save face," a characteristic he found in the seventy cases he studied. Either the victim made a verbal remark that the offender considered insulting (41 percent), the victim did not honor the offender's request (34 percent), or the victim made a physical or nonverbal gesture which the offender interpreted as offensive (25 percent).

Although there are clear indications that these elements are contributory, saving face does not appear to be very influential for women who commit homicide. In the first place, most of the females were alone with their victims, whereas face-saving involves humiliation in front of others. Second, even others were present, the bystanders did not instigate, escalate, or "egg on" the female homicide offender, actions that are more common in male *intragender* victim-offender situations. Third, since most of their male victims were adults, in the majority of the *intergender* encounters there was a male "macho" element that seemed to intensify under the influence of alcohol or drugs, as demonstrated in the following case.

> *Case 6103:* Ellen, age thirty-six, and the victim, fifty-six, who had been lovers for ten years, gave a party on a Saturday night. Both had been drinking all evening. One of their guests asked Ellen if he could keep his cleaning at the house. While in the bedroom, but in earshot of the guests, Ellen repeated the request to the victim, who said "no." Ellen then retorted, "*You* tell him that!" whereupon the victim slapped her. In response, Ellen picked up a serrated steak knife with a three-inch blade and stabbed him once in the neck. The victim walked out of the house, collapsed, and died in the street. Ellen, who had a violent arrest history that included a felony cutting assault, claimed self-defense. Although she received a five-year sentence, confinement was later suspended, and Ellen was placed on five years probation.

It was anticipated that either financial reasons—for example, altercations over money in drug dealings—or the condition of being drunk or high on narcotics would be influential in the murders committed by substance users, but these assumptions were not supported by the data. There were no significant differences between user and nonusers as to the rationale for committing murder; users, however, were more likely to admit their culpability than nonusers.[14]

CHOICE OF WEAPON

The traditional means that women use to kill have generally been thought of as passive, that is, methods that put distance between the perpetrator and her victim. For this reason poisoning in one form or another has been associated with women who commit homicide, and the appellation of Lucretia Borgia is often applied. Lizzie Borden's use of an axe in the murders of which she was accused, tried, and acquitted, was considered an anomaly and undoubtedly would be viewed the same way today. A woman chain-saw killer would also stretch the most vivid imagination in any generation. But times have changed; not a single case of poisoning appeared in this study of 296 female homicide offenders. In fact, the weapons chosen by women who kill have come to more closely resemble those selected by their male counterparts.

Wolfgang's (1958) examination of female homicide offenders led him to report that wives more frequently stabbed their spouses. Whereas knives and other cutting instruments are still the preferred weapons of many women, more recent studies indicate that women who kill are turning increasingly to firearms. Guns were used by 72.6 percent of the female homicide offenders studied by McClain (1982). Firearms were used also in 55.4 percent of the cases involving homicidal wives in Detroit (Goetting, 1987). Formby (1986) examined the district attorney files on convicted homicide cases from 1970 to 1979 and reported that 57 percent of the female-perpetrated homicides in rural and semirural Alabama involved firearms. Kowalski, Shields, and Wilson (1985) also found that rural women in Alabama used firearms in murders more often than city women. And in his national calculations of firearm use, Wilbanks (1983b) reported that 57.5 percent of women chose this type of weapon, as had 59.6 percent of the women homicide offenders he studied in Miami (Wilbanks, 1983a).

The present study echoes these findings: firearms were involved in 46.6 percent of the female-perpetrated homicides, knives or other cutting implements were implicated in 37.8 percent of the cases, and the remaining murders were committed with household tools, clubbing weapons, and hands or feet.

The choice of weapon seemed to be closely related to the location of the homicide and also to the age and gender of the victim. As Decker (1993: 609) recently observed: "Clearly the intensity of relationship has an effect on the weapon used, the location, and the number of suspects involved in homicide." If a woman who killed was in the kitchen or dining room, a knife was selected; but if she was in a bedroom or living room, a gun was the most frequently chosen weapon. When the murder took place away from a residence—for example, on the street or in a tavern—the weapon carried to the scene was usually a knife. Other methods such as drowning, strangling, or the use of clubbing weapons or hands and feet typically involved child victims.

As noted earlier, geography also played a part in weapon choice. Women killers in the southern and western cities were more likely to use guns than their female counterparts in midwestern or eastern cities. Long guns (shotguns and rifles) were also more peculiar to the west (Houston and Los Angeles) than to the other cities studied. Finally, it is recalled that a significant difference in choice of homicide methods was found between the "regions": southern women killers were partial to guns, while their nonsouthern counterparts tended to select knives or other methods (Figure 3.5).

Among the 293 cases in which the victim-offender relationship was known, guns (51.7 percent) and knives (44.1 percent) were more frequently found in *domestic homicides.* Domestic killings are defined as those involving victims with whom the women offenders were sexually intimate. Such cases made up almost half of the total sample (49.5 percent).[15] Over time, however, there was a variation in the methods of killing used in domestic homicides: a firearm was a woman's weapon of choice in 1979, but by 1983, knives were more frequently used than guns. It is possible that downward changes in the economy made it more difficult for women to purchase guns, or perhaps the enactment of more rigid gun laws might explain this difference.

Based on previous studies, it was assumed that the stimulation of certain drugs, especially alcohol and psychotropic drugs such as PCP, might provoke intense emotions and result in murder. A situation could be particularly volatile if the victim and the offender were both under the influence of substances. It was further speculated that women who were using drugs or alcohol might employ the first convenient weapon reflexively. In contrast, because they were not influenced by any mind-altering substance, nonusers were expected to be less spontaneous and more calculating in their choice of homicide method even though they might be angry or emotional. As shown in Table 3.1, these presumed differences were not supported.

Number of Wounds

Initially the number of wounds inflicted in a homicide was not considered, since no previous homicide study had described such a variable. Doerner's (1983) fascinating work on the influence of the availability of medical resources on lethality was familiar, but what later became an obvious connection was not made prior to entry into the field. An examination of the homicide files and victim autopsy records in the first city visited revealed that over half of the victims had been shot or stabbed only once. A number of these victims bled to death before medical services were obtained. There were no indications that the women were experts in weapon use, much less so knowledgeable of physiological anatomy as to locate vital areas of the body to inflict single deadly wounds. Obviously the lone wound was either a stroke of luck for the female perpetrator—assuming death of the victim was a sincere goal—or perhaps the victim might have survived had emergency first aid been applied or the arrival of professional medical help been more timely. Unfortunately, ambulance and police response times, the quality of at-the-scene and emergency room medical treatment, and the caliber of postoperative care could not be determined from the accessible records. These factors in concert with the number of wounds inflicted are mentioned as provocative research ideas for future homicide studies.

Several interesting findings were generated concerning the number of wounds. First, single wounds (57 percent) were found more frequently than multiple wounds (43 percent), particularly among African American victims (58.6 percent). This finding suggests possible verification for the frequent and long-standing complaints from residents in African American, low-income, urban communities that police and medical responses to emergency calls are inadequate and also medical services are poor.

A second finding is that in 32 percent of child murders, multiple wounds were largely the result of the use of hands or feet as a weapon. Third, women who had used alcohol or drugs prior to the murder were more likely to inflict multiple wounds than those who were not under the influence of a substance. Finally, as illustrated in the following case, the homicides of substance users tended to be more brutal than those of nonusers.

> Case 1221: Flora, age fifty-four, had been drinking in her apartment with both her former beau, fifty-two, and her new beau. Soon after the new boyfriend left to get more beer, according to Flora, her former boyfriend threatened to kill her and then "jumped on her." In the ensuing fight they both fell into the bathtub where Flora hit the victim with a forty-five-inch-long iron bar. Thereafter she hit him with a broomstick and a claw hammer, and stabbed him with a pairing knife thirty-two times. The victim, who died from "cranial cerebral injury and multiple incise wounds of the head," was cut in the face, head, and throat. When the new boyfriend returned, they dragged the victim out of the tub, wrapped him in a sheet, and threw him out of the window into the apartment courtyard. Flora had an extensive arrest record for prostitution and theft, and a number of felony arrests that included

robbery and murder. She had served four years for the previous murder through a plea bargain. Flora also pled guilty to this murder in a bench trial. She was convicted on a charge of voluntary manslaughter and sentenced to ten years in prison.

SUMMARY

Ecological analyses of women murderers and their victims yielded verification for a number of previously reported findings. When women kill, most of the homicides take place in homes shared with their victims. Over three decades ago the kitchen was the most frequent murder locale. More recent studies suggest the bedroom as the usual site. In the present study, social areas such as living rooms or dens proved to be the most common homicide locations, although the bedroom was the second most frequent murder site. As others have noted, this study found female-perpetrated homicide to be a weekend, or leisuretime, even that occurs most often on Saturday night after both the offender and her victim had been drinking. Alcohol use played a significant role in the homicides committed by women. Although the victims were likely to precipitate their own deaths, especially in the southern cities, the extent of an offender's participation due to her drinking or drug use is not clear from the data. There are indications that even though her victim was provocative, the female homicide offender might have contributed to the inspiration of the lethal outcome. Victim precipitation was significantly more prevalent among women who were drinking prior to the murder than among those who had used drugs.

Only age differentiated women killers who had used alcohol or drugs prior to the homicides from those who had not. The users tended to be older than the nonusers, but on every other social characteristic examined there were no significant differences between the groups. Offender users and nonusers were also distinguished by only a single homicide characteristic: although both groups more frequently killed intimates, nonusers were significantly more likely to kill those with whom they were intimate than users, who were more prone to kill others.

In concurrence with other studies of female homicide offenders, seasonality was not found to be significant. Homicides in the warmer months of spring and summer only slightly exceeded those occurring in the fall and winter.

Comparisons between the cases of southern and nonsouthern women who killed produced some intriguing findings. Southern women more often used firearms, especially long guns, in their murders. In contrast, nonsouthern women more frequently employed other methods such as beating, drowning, and suffocating. For both groups knives were the second weapon choice. Southern victims were significantly more likely to have been drinking and to provoke their own deaths than nonsouthern victims. Whereas drinking predominated among southern victims, drug use was more prevalent among their northern counterparts. In sum, although their victims may differ slightly, except for age, women who kill are not significantly distinguished by social or homicide characteristics, southernness, or substance use.

NOTES

1. All of the offenders names are fictitious and were alphabetically assigned for easier readability.

2. This analysis was based on 295 cases since there was no indication when one child murder took place.

3. This difference is significant at the .0003 level with $X^2 = 16.52$ with 2 dfs.

4. The level of significance for this finding is .00004, with a X^2 of 16.88 at 1 df.

5. Chi square equals 4.60 at 1 df, s = .03.

6. This figure includes female arrests for driving under the influence (182,041), liquor law violations (85,316), and drunkenness (71,912).

7. Alcohol is a drug also, but it is differentiated from other "hard" drugs such as heroin, methadone, cocaine, PCP, marijuana, and the variety of pills identified as used by the female homicide offenders in this study.

8. See Inciardi, Lockwood, and Pottieger, *Women and Crack-Cocaine* (1993), for a comprehensive picture of this current female phenomenon.

9. The model categorizes drug-relatedness as psychopharmacological, economic-compulsive, or systemic.

10. S = .03 with a X^2 of 4.61 with 1 df.

11. This difference was significant at the .03 level with a chi square of 5.03 at 1 df.

12. This difference was also significant at the .03 level with a chi square of 5.03 at 1 df.

13. The X^2 of 16.88, with 2 df, was significant at the .0002 level.

14. Motives for the murders will be discussed more fully in chapter 7 when the female homicide offenders are profiled.

15. These cases will be detailed in the next chapter.

Chapter 4

Victims: The Murders of Intimates

This chapter describes the circumstances involved in female-perpetrated murders where the victim was someone to whom the offender was related by blood or marriage, or with whom she had a close relationship. *Intimate* victims have been defined to include "relatives, friends, neighbors and work associates," or, alternatively, in terms of "kinship, intimacy and shared domicile" (Saltzman and Mercy, 1993: 66). The victim/offender relationships, defined here as *significant others*, closely resemble those defined by Saltzman and Mercy in their study of fatal family and intimate assaults: "We categorized emotional intimacy between victim and offender on the basis of implied levels of closeness. We developed a list of relationships for which we presumed emotional intimacy existed. The list . . . included nuclear family members, other relatives and in-laws, married and unmarried partners, and former partners. Thus, we included spouses (legal and common law), boyfriends, girlfriends and homosexual partners, regardless of whether the partners lived together" (ibid., p. 68).

In the 293 cases for which the victim/offender relationship was known, the largest proportion (47.8 percent) involved domestic relationships: married, common-law married, lovers/living together, separated, homosexual lovers, or former lovers.[1] Children of the female homicide offenders constituted 10.6 percent of the victims, and the remaining 7.9 percent were other relatives or in-laws.

Three distinct approaches to the study of the murder of intimate victims are used. First, the victim-offender relationship is described in terms of the *choice of victim*—for example, child, domestic significant other, or other family member.[2] Second, the *victim's condition* is examined to determine if prior to the murder s/he was incapacitated due to illness, was under the influence of some substance (drugs and/or alcohol), had a physical handicap, was asleep, or if the victim's age was an influential factor. The third analytic strategy focused on the possible contribution of the victim to his/her own death. The previous chapter introduced the subject of *victim precipitation* in connection with the provocative influence of drugs or alcohol, while this chapter centers more on the deeds of victims and the interactions between the victims and their female killers.

CHILD VICTIMS

The murder of children by their parents is not new. Throughout most of world history, apathy toward children has often led to *infanticide*—the generic term for child murder—or *filicide*—the murder of one's own child. Infanticide was common in ancient periods and was routinely practiced during the eighteenth century (Empey, 1978). Straus and Gelles (1986: 466) note that the "history of Western society reveals that children have also been subject to unspeakable cruelties, including the abandonment of infants to die of exposure." Even in the early nineteenth century, the life of a child, particularly one born out of wedlock, was not highly valued, a judgment that made illegitimate children especially susceptible to homicide at the hands of their mothers (Rose, 1986). Although giving birth to a child out of wedlock is not as stigmatized as it was in earlier periods of history, the economic ramifications and the social liability of unwed motherhood often result in filicide. However, child murders are not restricted to unwed mothers. Married women may commit homicide in reaction to intense stresses in their lives: "Infanticide is sometimes resorted to by desperate mothers of illegitimate children, and parents who did not want the child to begin with are more likely to kill the baby when it is very young than when it gets older" (Shin, Jedlicka, and Lee: 1977, 403).

Homicide is one of the five leading causes of early childhood death in this country which gives the United States the shameful status of having the second-highest child homicide rate in the world (Abel, 1986). Infants under one year of age are the most vulnerable; they are four times more likely to be murder victims than children at other ages. According to Hawkins (1986: Table 1, p. 33), the homicide rate for African American infants under one year of age is 13.5 per 100,000, which makes them far more at risk than other children. In contrast, the rate for white infants in this age category is 3.6 per 100,000.

The limited research on child murder identifies women, primarily mothers, as the predominant killers (for example, Abel, 1986; Kaplun and Reich, 1976; Resnick, 1969; 1970). Like previous reports, this study focused on the murder of pre-school-age children by their mothers. Of the total sample, forty-one homicide victims were seventeen years of age or younger (13.9 percent). Within this group of minor children, the victims in twenty-five of the thirty-one cases involving offenders' offspring were pre-schoolers (8.5 percent of the study sample). Thus, children

under 6 years of age accounted for 61 percent of the minor children murdered.[3]

In a recent report on homicides of children below the age of five,
Baron (1993: 212) ranked the fifty states according to each state's
1975–1980 child homicide rate.[4] He concluded that "rates of child
homicide increase in proportion to increases in the level of gender
inequality" (ibid., p. 216). Baron defined gender inequality on the basis
of twenty-four indicators of women's status in relation to that of men,
grouped according to "the institutional sectors of politics, economics, and
legal rights" (ibid., p. 209).

When pre-school children are a source of frustration and stress to
their primary caregivers—most frequently their mothers—their helplessness and small size make them especially vulnerable. Since mothers have
more "time at risk" and provide most of the child care in a family, they
experience greater stress and, concomitantly, have higher rates of child
abuse than fathers (Straus, 1986: 449). Other factors that put mothers at
risk for abusing their children are "early marriage, unwanted children,
lack of skills in child management and isolation" (ibid., p. 459). These
reasons were also found to be determinants in the twenty-five child
murders described below.

Previous Research

Little empirical attention has been directed toward women who kill
their children, possibly because such incidents represent only a small
percentage of homicides. In the few studies located, the proportions
ranged from 2.8 percent of total homicides in an Alabama study (Kowalski, Shields, and Wilson, 1985) to 28 percent in an early California study
reported by Totman (1978). Other filicide research populations yield the
following proportions: 5 percent in both a North Carolina study (Suval
and Brisson, 1974) and one in Los Angeles, California (Loya and Mercy,
1985); 8.5 percent reported in Illinois (Weisheit, 1986) and Dade County
(Miami), Florida (Wilbanks, 1983a); 19 percent in Minnesota and California (Ward, Jackson, and Ward, 1979); and 20 percent reported by
Cole, Fisher, and Cole in 1968 in California.

Baron's (1993: 212) recent national analysis did not indicate any
clear regional patterns and concluded that "the risk of child homicide is
unevenly distributed throughout the United States." Further, according
to the 1980 Supplementary Reports of the FBI, child murders committed
by females accounted for only a small percentage of homicides nationwide.
For example, of the total 171 pre-school-age children who were murder
victims of females in 1980, 108 were under age two, and 63 were between
age two and five.[5] Whereas pre-school children constituted 7.7 percent of
U.S. victims in 1980, this study found that for the aggregated years

reported here (1979 and 1983), only 8.5 percent of the victims of female homicide offenders were pre-schoolers.

The Filicide Victims

The first six months of an infant's life are believed to be the most perilous (Resnick, 1969: 327). Kaplun and Reich (1976: 806) found that 52 percent of murdered children were less than one year old, and 26 percent were between one and five years of age. Similarly, Abel (1986) reported that most child homicide victims were from age one to four years old. In the six-city study reported here, the mean age of the child victims was a little under two years (mean = 1.99 years), 40 percent were less than one year old, and three were newborn. Two of the three neonaticides in the study suggest the shame, embarrassment, and frustration of young, unwed college coeds, while the case described below appears senseless.

> Case 5221: The twenty-four-year-old mother claimed that she did not know that she was "that pregnant" when, as she used the commode, the baby came out head first into the toilet. Neither the offender, her mother, nor her brother would remove the newborn stating that they were "afraid to pick up the baby." The female infant apparently was in the commode for fifteen to twenty minutes and was still breathing when the police arrived. She died on the way to the hospital. The police report indicated that the offender attempted to flush the baby down the toilet. The mother, who was a known prostitute with a number of misdemeanor arrests, was sentenced to a six-month jail term and five years probation for the infanticide.

Most previous studies of child homicide victims found no "racial preponderance" (Adelson, 1961: 1345), and when there was evidence of disproportionality, white children were more apt to be the victims (for example, Totman, 1978; Kowalski et al., 1985). Only 2.5 percent of the victims of African American female homicide offenders in 1975 were children (McClain, 1982–1983). Thus, in the past, African American women killed their children infrequently. More recently, a "dramatic change in the racial composition of the offender population" has been noted (Weisheit, 1986: 443). In his comparison of incarcerated women homicide offenders over time, Weisheit found that from 1940 to 1966, 72 percent of the women who killed their children were white, but by 1980 to 1983, the situation had reversed, and 71.4 percent of filicide offenders were African American. It is possible that since these women were processed and subsequently imprisoned by the criminal justice system, Weisheit's later finding may reflect more about racial discrimination in the system than about the racial composition of filicide offenders. However, more African American than white child victims (59.1 percent v. 41.9 percent) were reported by Abel in 1986. Yet Baron's study of child

homicide rates in the fifty states revealed that among the nine independent variables, including percentage black, the only three significant
contributing variables were the cirrhosis death rate, the percentage of
families headed by single females, and the level of gender equality (Baron,
1993: 215), the influence of the percentage separated or divorced having
disappeared in the analysis.

Alternatively, the present study supports Weisheit and Abel's results
by finding that African American women constituted 52 percent of those
arrested for killing their pre-school-age children, as compared to 28
percent white and 20 percent Hispanic filicide offenders. As seen in Table
4.1, African American and white children were more at risk under the
age of two years, while Hispanic children were more frequently victims
between the age of two and five.[6]

Male children are valued more highly than female children in many
cultures, including our own. This phenomenon, seen throughout time,
results primarily from the fact that family lines and inheritances were
traced through males (Empey, 1978: 63). According to a number of those
who research child killings, female children continue to be devaluated.
Totman's (1978) study of female homicide offenders yielded more female
than male child victims. Further, in her study of Chicago homicide over
a seventeen-year period (1965 to 1981), Block (1985: 46) concluded that
"for the youngest age group, race/ethnicity is not as important as gender
in homicide victimizations. The proportion of murdered females who were
killed at young ages was consistently higher than the proportion of males
who were killed at young ages." A Canadian study also found that 57

Table 4.1

Percentages of Preschool Homicide Victims by Age and Race of Victim and
Offender, 1979 and 1983

Race	Age of Victim		Total
	Under 2 years	2–5 Years	
Victim			
Black	57.1	54.5	56.0
White	28.6	27.3	28.0
Hispanic	14.3	18.2	16.0
Totals	100.0	100.0	100.0
Offender			
Black	57.1	45.5	52.0
White	21.4	36.4	28.0
Hispanic	21.4	18.2	20.0
Totals	100.0[1]	100.0[1]	100.0

1. Because of rounding the percentages may not add to total.

percent of the infanticides perpetrated by mothers involved female victims (Silverman and Kennedy, 1988: 117). In the United States, Hawkins (1986: 33) reports that the homicide rates in 1983 for both African American and white females under one year of age were higher than those for their male counterparts.

In the present study, female infants constituted 64.3 percent of the victims under one year of age, and 54.5 percent of those between the ages of two and five. The finding that, overall, females were the victims in 60 percent of the filicide cases lends credence to the devaluation of female offspring in this country.

It was noted that African American mothers predominated among the homicide offenders who killed their children. However, the higher percentage of African American victims compared to African American offenders (56 percent v. 52 percent) shown in Table 4.1 is due partially to interracial filicides such as the one in the following example.

Case 1212: The exact date of the death of a four-year-old, biracial boy was never determined. His small, decomposed body was found wrapped in plastic under the railroad tracks near a major urban university. The cause of death was "cranial injury in association with recent and old fractures" by "blunt force." Identification of the child was difficult, but ultimately his birth footprints and old medical injuries led police to the victim's thirty-five-year-old Caucasian mother, Gladys. When arrested in another state, Gladys fought extradition and claimed that she had given the boy away to another woman. Eventually, under a plea bargain, Gladys was sentenced to ten years in prison for the brutal child murder.

Offender Characteristics

Age

A Georgia study by Jason and Andereck (1983) reported a mean age of twenty-three years for females who committed fatal child abuse; 37 percent of the offenders were less than twenty years old. A similar finding was reported by Silverman and Kennedy (1988), who found that 69 percent of the mothers who killed their infants were under twenty-one years of age.

In comparison to previous research, the present six-city study found that the women who killed their young children were slightly older, with a mean age of 25.6 years. Mothers who killed their children under the age of two were slightly younger (mean = 25 years) than those whose victims were from two to five years old (mean = 26.4 years). Most of the filicide offenders ranged in age from 17 to 35; 48 percent were between 17 and 24, while another 32 percent were from 25 to 30 years of age. This age range coincides with the results of other studies. For example, Resnick

(1970) reports a range of 19 to 36 years, while the female filicide offenders in Totman's (1978) study were between 16 and 38.

Marital Status

Table 4.2 shows that married and common-law married women who were not separated from their husbands were more likely to kill their two-to-five-year-olds, whereas the child victims of single women were usually under two years of age. Divorced, separated, and single women, who were more than likely single parents or heads of household, made up 55.4 percent of the filicide offenders. While there may be some validity to Resnick's 1970 statement that "the stigma of having an illegitimate child is the primary reason for neonaticide in unmarried women today, as it has been through the centuries" (p. 1416), it is difficult to determine from the present data whether unwanted pregnancies lead to maternal filicides in contemporary America. Although single mothers were more likely to kill children under two years of age than women in other marital status categories, recent evidence indicates that single mothers who fatally abuse their children do not differ significantly from mothers in two-parent households (Jason and Andereck, 1983: 8). Further, as demonstrated in the "Murphy Brown" television series, which recently caused such a national political flap, the majority of Americans apparently no longer stigmatize single mothers as they did in the past.

Socioeconomic Status

Low socioeconomic status has been viewed as a possible contributor to both child abuse and female-perpetrated child homicide (Kaplun and Reich, 1976; Abel, 1986; Weisheit, 1986); "it is no accident that the number of parental assaults on young children has increased as the level

Table 4.2

Marital Status of Female Filicide Offenders by Age of Victim, 1979 and 1983 (in percentages)

Marital Status	Age of Victim		Total
	Under 2 years	2–5 Years	
Married	28.6	40.0	33.3
Common-Law Married	—	20.0	8.3
Divorced	7.1	20.0	12.5
Separated	21.4	10.0	16.7
Single	42.9	10.0	29.2
TOTALS	100.0[1]	100.0	100.0

1. Because of rounding the percentages may not add to total.

of unemployment has risen" (Rose, 1986: 187). All but two of the twenty-four filicide offenders studied were unemployed (91.7 percent).[7] The number of children ranged from one to eight with a mean of 2.8 children per mother. In addition to family size, other possible indicators of low income or poverty-level status found in their arrest and homicide narratives suggest the economic marginality of most of the women who killed their children. Yet, despite evidence of a possible connection between poverty and child homicide, certain cases appear that alert us to the possibility that other circumstances are also influential. The following case is illustrative.

> *Case 4216:* Harriet, a housewife, age twenty-nine, was arrested along with her husband and their family doctor for the murder of her three-year-old daughter. Harriet, who birthed eight children, had been tried previously for the murder of her eight-month-old, who choked to death from having been force-fed. There was a recorded history of abuse of all of her children, and Harriet was described as cold and indifferent toward them. According to one social worker, this was a typical case of "battered child syndrome." The victim suffered from neglect, pneumonia, emphysema, scars, cuts, bruises, burns, and fractures. Harriet claimed innocence and that the child just "stopped breathing." Although she pled "not guilty," Harriet received fifteen years in prison for involuntary manslaughter. Her husband, who stated that he was afraid of Harriet, was sentenced to five years probation for child endangerment. Their doctor, who had covered up the abuse and treated the victim both at home and in his office without reporting the incidents, was also tried for involuntary manslaughter and given two years probation.

Characteristics of the Filicides

Some researchers report that women who kill their children tend to have abused or neglected them prior to the filicide (for example, Kaplun and Reich, 1976; Totman, 1978), while others find that prior abuse is rare among child murders (Abel, 1986). The present study supports the first position, in that almost half of the filicide offenders in the study, like "Harriet," had previous recorded histories of child abuse (48 percent). This characteristic was especially true for those women whose victims were from two to five years old (90 percent). Neglect or starvation was recorded in 16 percent of the cases.

The usual method of killing a child was manual (80 percent), with hands and feet as the most common weapons (52 percent). The cases in which victims were beaten to death are differentiated from those which entailed other uses of the hands such as drowning (12 percent) or suffocation (16 percent). Clubbing weapons were used in 4 percent of the cases. Multiple wounds were found in 32 percent of the filicides, especially among victims between the ages of two and five, who made up 63.6 percent of the victims of multiple wounds. Although a mother usually committed the murder by herself (66.7 percent), another one-third had accomplices, usually a lover or spouse, particularly in cases involving neglect or starvation.

A filicide occurred typically in the residence of the offender and victim (92 percent) on a Sunday morning at about 11:00. The bathroom was the most frequent site (30.4 percent), followed by the bedroom (26.1 percent). Considering the frequency of Sunday morning filicides, it might be conjectured that the lingering effects of a Saturday night party were influential in these murders, but the data do not support such a supposition. On the contrary, the filicide offenders were usually not under the influence of a substance at the time of the offense. In those instances when alcohol or narcotics were used, however, a mother was twice as likely to have used drugs prior to the child murder as alcohol (19 v. 8.7 percent).

Comparison with Other Female Homicide Offenders

Weisheit's (1986: 447) study of women incarcerated for murder in Michigan concluded that with regard to such characteristics as race, marital status, and education, filicide offenders in the 1980s were not that different from women who had committed other homicides. A comparison of the filicide offenders with the other female homicide offenders in the present study in terms of race, employment, and marital status, controlling for age (nineteen to thirty-five years), tends to substantiate Weisheit's conclusions. Only race differentiated the two groups: African American women constituted only 52 percent of the filicide offender group but 78 percent of the other homicide offenders. In contrast, white women were twice as likely to kill their pre-school-age children (29.2 percent) as they were to murder others (13.8 percent). Latinas were also more prominent in the filicide offender group (20.8 percent) than in the overall sample of female murderers (9.0 percent).[8]

Other differences found were that filicide offenders were more likely to be or to have been married (73.9 percent) than other female homicide offenders. who tended to be single (45.3 percent). Female child killers were more frequently unemployed (91.3 percent) than women in the comparison group (73.1 percent). Finally, filicide offenders were less likely than the other homicide offenders to have previous arrest records or violent arrest histories.

City and Regional Analysis

As shown in Table 4.3, 48 percent of the child murders perpetrated in the six study cities occurred in New York City, and those most

Table 4.3

Percentages of Child Murders by Age of Victim and by City, 1979 and 1983

| | Age of Victim | | |
City	Under 2 Years (Percent)	2–5 Years (Percent)	Total (Percent)
New York	57.1	36.4	48.0
Chicago	14.3	18.2	16.0
Atlanta	7.1	18.2	12.0
Los Angeles	—	27.3	12.0
Houston	14.3	—	8.0
Baltimore	7.1	—	4.0
TOTALS	100.0[1]	100.0[1]	100.0

1. Because of rounding the percentages may not add to total.

vulnerable were children under two years of age (57.1 percent). Mothers in Houston and Baltimore were also more likely to kill their children in this younger age group. In Atlanta, Chicago, and Los Angeles, in contrast, victims were most often between two and five years of age.

The rank order of the cities according to the frequency of female-committed filicides is: (1) New York, (2) Chicago, (3) Atlanta and Los Angeles, (4) Houston and (5) Baltimore.[9] Combined, the three largest cities (New York, Chicago, and Los Angeles) accounted for 76 percent of the fatal child abuse cases. Since these three cities are located outside the South, the findings suggest that pre-school children are more at risk in urban, nonsouthern cities and that filicide is a big-city phenomenon. The stresses and other social ills prevalent in such environments undoubtedly contribute to filicide. A number of studies find that certain stressors appear to be endemic to poor, minority communities: "Marital breakdown contributes to an increase in single-parent households, which leads to unemployment and poverty insofar as adequate child care is not available, which it typically is not for members of lower socioeconomic groups. The strains of poverty, in turn, make it difficult to establish and maintain strong interpersonal relationships. Poverty and marital dissolution are thus mutually reinforcing, and they apparently combine to raise the level of violent crime" (Messner and Tardiff, 1986: 312).

In their discussion of "expressive" underlying motives that induce homicide—"anger, hostility, or other negative emotional states"—Rose and McClain (1990: 126) connect such trends with victimizations of family and acquaintances. A number of social scientists (for example, Abel, 1986; Totman, 1978) "associate the etiology of child killing with social disorganization and its concomitant ills—poverty and unemployment—and the frustrations accruing from stressful life situations" (Mann, 1993: 230).

Domestic Homicides

An old song favorite, "You Always Hurt the One You Love," certainly applies when homicide is committed—people have always been more likely to kill the ones they love. The majority of homicide studies indicate that when a woman is the offender, the one loved is most frequently a person with whom she has been sexually intimate (for example, Wolfgang, 1958; Goetting, 1987; Jurik and Winn, 1990; Kellermann and Mercy, 1992; Wilson and Daly, 1992). Such murders are commonly called domestic homicides.

Among the 20,591 murders and nonnegligent manslaughters known to the police in 1979, 4.1 percent (N = 844) were the husbands of women offenders (Flanagan, van Alstyne and Gottfredson, 1982: 315). Similarly, in the other year of this study, 1983, the 728 husbands killed were 3.9 percent of the 18,673 known murders (McGarrell and Flanagan, 1985: 419). Concomitant with the national decrease, this study revealed a decline in domestic homicides (45.5 percent) in 1983 as compared with 1979 (52.8 percent). This downward trend is continuing, "not only is marital homicide declining, but the decrease is greater than the drop in the overall rate of homicide in the United States" (Browne and Williams, 1993: 87).

Husbands constituted 30.3 percent of the domestic homicide victims in the study reported here (N = 44); the 47 common-law husbands were slightly more frequent victims than legal husbands (32.4 percent), while the 54 lovers constituted the largest subgroup of sexually intimate victims (37.2 percent). Included among the lovers were five cases involving lesbian homicides. All told, the 145 women who killed sexual intimates represent 55.1 percent of the 293 cases for which the victim-offender relationship was determined.

Victim Characteristics

A significant majority of the domestic homicide victims were non-white (91.7 percent), primarily African American (83.4 percent). Although it has been reported that black and white women are equally likely to kill men (Jurik and Winn, 1990: 235), it was found here that African American women were clearly the dominant killers of males. Hispanic and white victims were equally represented at 8.3 percent each. This finding lends support to the well-established conclusion that domestic homicides are *intraracial* (Wolfgang, 1958). In data collected from the UCR Supplementary Homicide Crime Reports, Segall and Wilson (1993:

347) found that "blacks were significantly more likely to be homicide victims than were whites in any of the regions."

The fact that female-perpetrated homicides are *intersexual* is also reinforced in this study: males accounted for 80.7 percent of the total number of victims here and 96.6 percent of the victims in domestic homicides. The male victims who were sexual intimates of the female homicide offenders ranged in age from nineteen to seventy-one and were generally over twenty-five, having a mean age of 37.9 years. As seen in Table 4.4, which compares victim and offender characteristics, domestic homicide victims were more frequently between thirty and thirty-nine years of age but were followed closely by victims in the age range of twenty to twenty-nine. A substantial proportion of the victims had prior arrest records (77.6 percent), and more than half of those previous arrests were for violent crimes (55.2 percent).[10]

A comparison of domestic and nondomestic homicide victims, depicted in Table 4.5, reveals that the two groups differ significantly. For example, the victims of women who killed in domestic encounters were 91.7 percent nonwhite, whereas among nondomestic cases the proportion

Table 4.4

Selected Victim and Offender Characteristics in Domestic Homicides, (in percentages)[1]

Characteristic	Offender	Victim
Race		
Nonwhite	91.0	91.7
White		
Age (in years)		
(Mean)	(33.6 yrs.)	(37.9 yrs.)
19 and under	3.4	2.1
20–29	42.1	28.3
30–39	24.8	29.7
40–49	19.3	24.1
50 and over	10.3	15.9
Prior arrests	49.2	77.6
Violent history	30.0	55.2
Substance use		
(before offense)		
Alcohol	36.2	58.3
Drugs	8.7	12.1
Drunk	—	22.0
Gender		
Male	—	96.6
Female	100.0	3.4
Victim precipitation	—	83.7

1. Does not include missing cases.

Table 4.5

Victim Characteristics, by Offender Type (in percentages)[1]

Victim	Offender Type		
Characteristic	Domestic	Nondomestic	Significance
Race			
Nonwhite	91.7	77.7	p = .001
White	8.3	22.3	X^2 = 10.03, 1 df
Gender			
Male	96.6	65.5	p = .000
Female	3.4	34.5	X^2 = 43.58, 1 df
Age (in years)			
(Mean)	(37.9 yrs.)	(28.7 yrs.)	p = .000
Under 25	13.1	43.2	X^2 = 31.30, 1 df
Over 25	86.9	56.8	
Arrest record			
Yes	77.6	46.2	p = .000
No	22.4	53.8	X^2 = 15.91, 1 df
Violent history			
Yes	55.2	34.5	p = .044
No	44.8	65.5	X^2 = 4.05, 1 df
Incapacitated[2]			
Yes	29.5	41.0	p = .065
No	70.5	59.0	X^2 = 3.40, 1 df
Alcohol use			
Yes	58.3	42.1	p = .021
No	41.7	57.9	X^2 = 5.36, 1 df
Drug use			
Yes	12.1	12.2	
No	87.9	87.8	

1. Does not include missing cases.
2. Victim was drunk, helpless (bound), asleep.

is significantly lower (77.7 percent). A partial explanation for this finding might be found in an observation made in a Chicago homicide study: "white males kill females with whom they are intimate twice as frequently as they are killed, whereas black males are twice as likely to be killed by their female intimates as to kill them" (Zimring, Mukherjee, and Van Winkle, 1983: 920). Block (1987: 7) also found that African Americans in Chicago were the only racial/ethnic group in which wives killed their husbands at a higher rate than husbands who killed their wives (4.94 v. 3.59 per 100,000). It is possible that the racial difference found in the present study may be attributed to felony and other types of economically motivated homicides, and the child slayings more typically representative of white homicides.

The racial/ethnic breakdown of the total victim group is 74.3 percent African American, 15.5 percent white, and 10.1 percent Hispanic. In the domestic homicides, 83.4 percent of the victims were African American, 8.3 percent were white, and 8.3 percent were Hispanic. Nondomestic homicides reveal substantially fewer African American victims (65.5 percent) and increases in the proportions of the other two racial groups (white, 22.3 percent; Hispanic, 12.2 percent).[11] These figures offer support for the frequent finding that African American males are at higher risk as both marital homicide victims and general homicide victims than any other racial/gender configuration (Segall and Wilson, 1993: 352).

The significant gender difference in victim types seen in Table 4.5 is readily explained by the fact that an overwhelming majority of the domestic relationships were heterosexual. As mentioned, there were only five cases of female intragender domestic homicide. The fact that domestic homicide victims tend to be more than nine years older than their nondomestic counterparts suggests the possibility that these victims may have had long-term relationships with their killers. On the other hand, the comparative youth of nondomestic victims appears partially related to the number of child murders as well as felony and other economically-based homicides in that more youthful group. The significant difference found in victim incapacitation further suggests that nondomestic homicide victims were less able to defend themselves because they were too old, too young, drunk, asleep, or otherwise helpless. Finally, the victims in domestic cases appear to have been more likely candidates for homicide than the nondomestic victims. As previously noted, a substantial proportion of the domestic homicide victims had previous arrest records, especially prior violent arrest records. Also they were more likely to have been drinking before their deaths. It is possible that the personal lifestyle of these victims when combined with alcohol use proved to be lethal, particularly since victim precipitation was recorded in 83.7 percent of the domestic cases. In contrast, victim precipitation was determined to have occurred in less than half of the nondomestic cases (49.3).[12] The case described below was typical of a victim-provoked, domestic homicide.

Case 2130: Ida's husband of eleven years came home about 8:30 P.M. after a "Thank God It's Friday" drinking spree to find his sisters-in-law in the house. Willie was very angry because the women were there, and a number of insults were exchanged during the ensuing domestic quarrel. Enraged, Ida, thirty-five, removed a .22 pistol from her purse and shot Willie, thirty-eight, one time in the chest. After he was shot, Willie was able to unload and break the gun down. In an effort to protect her mother, their thirteen-year-old daughter claimed that she had shot her father. An autopsy revealed that Willie had a .16 blood alcohol level. The district attorney entered a no bill in the case.

This exemplar and many more like it parallel recent findings by Rashe (1993) which emphasize the importance of verbal provocation on the part of a homicide victim. In her study of 155 homicides that took place between 1980 and 1986 in Jacksonville (Duval County), Florida, Rashe found that in 39 percent of the cases in which the victim appeared to have provoked the offender, the provocation was verbal (p. 95). Luckenbill and Doyle (1989: 422–423) introduce the intervening variable of "disputatiousness" into the equation, suggesting that being attacked by an equal in a public setting can lead to a "negative outcome" that may result in homicide:

> First, one must perceive the negative outcome resulting from another's behavior as an injury for which the other is to blame. The transformation of a negative outcome into a grievance is termed "naming." Second, the victim must express the grievance to and demand reparation from the harmdoer. The transformation of a grievance into a demand for reparation is termed "claiming." Third, the harmdoer must reject the victim's claim, in whole or in part. The rejection of a claim transforms interaction into a "dispute," a recognized conflict of interest. The victim may respond to the dispute in any of several ways, ranging from outright capitulation through mobilization of third-party assistance to perseverance and use of force. Adopting the victim's position, disputatiousness is defined as the likelihood of naming and claiming, and aggressiveness is defined as the willingness to persevere and use force to settle the dispute (pp. 422–423).

Basic to this process is a fear of showing weakness and losing face (ibid.). Clearly, in a dispute with a woman, particularly in front of others, a man may feel not only a loss of face, but also a sense of castration, particularly if the woman verbally taunts him (or his manhood) in an effective manner. This is the "stuff" of which intergender homicide is made.

Offender Characteristics

Since "women become murderers at a somewhat older age than men" (Wilbanks, 1982: 65), female homicide offenders have generally been found to be in their late twenties or early thirties (see, for example, Bunch, Foley and Urbina, 1983; Weisheit, 1984; Hewitt and Rivers, 1986; Goetting, 1988a). Hewitt and Rivers (1986) recorded an average age of 40.7 years for convicted white female homicide offenders and 39 years for nonwhites. More recently, in their national comparison of both general and marital homicide characteristics, Segall and Wilson (1993: 346) report the mean age of the offenders as 38.9 years. Most studies of women who kill in domestic situations also report the offenders as slightly older. Silverman and Kennedy (1987: 11) noted a concentration in the age range of twenty-six to forty-five among Canadian women suspects who killed their spouses (62.6 percent) or other males (45.0 percent). Zimring et al. (1983: 918) concluded from their study of intersexual homicide in Chicago, "The typical offender in all intimate homicides is older than the average offender by about ten years (a median age of thirty-one to thirty-five as opposed to twenty-one to twenty-five)." Finally, in her Detroit study, Goetting (1987) found that wives who committed homicide had a mean age of 34.1 years. Similarly, an average age of 33.6 years was found for the female domestic homicide offenders in the study reported here (see Table 4.4). This mean age was significantly higher than that of their nondomestic counterparts (28.4 years), as depicted in Table 4.6.

African American women were the most frequent domestic homicide offenders (84.1 percent), with whites (9.0 percent) and Hispanics (6.9 percent) underrepresented. A similar disproportion has been reported by numerous other studies (for example, Biggers, 1979; Formby, 1980; Goetting, 1987; Weisheit, 1984; Wolfgang, 1958). When disaggregated by year, the data reveal decreases in the African American (− 5 percent)

Table 4.6

Offender Characteristics, by Offender Type (in percentages)[1]

| Characteristic | Offender Type | | Significance |
	Domestic	Nondomestic	
Race			
Nonwhite	91.0	83.1	
White	9.0	16.9	
Age (in years)			
(Mean)	(33.6 yrs.)	(28.4 yrs.)	p = .006
Under 25	26.2	41.9	X^2 = 3.41, 1 df
25 and over	73.8	58.1	
Employed			
Yes	36.8	21.4	p = .013
No	63.2	78.6	X^2 = 6.22, 1 df
Marital status			
Single	25.2	54.4	p = .000
Once married[2]	43.5	39.2	X^2 = 34.84, 2 df
Common law	31.3	6.4	
Maternal status			
Yes	80.4	60.6	p = .003
No	19.6	39.4	X^2 = 8.51, 1 df
Alcohol use			
Yes	36.2	35.0	
No	63.8	65.0	
Drug use			
Yes	8.7	16.8	
No	91.3	83.2	

1. Does not include missing cases.
2. Includes married, divorced, separated, and widowed (not by the homicide).

and white (− 1.1 percent) percentages from 1979 to 1983, but Hispanic women, who constituted only 4.8 percent of the domestic homicide offenders in 1979, accounted for double that figure in 1983 (+ 10.0 percent).

The *socioeconomic level* of the women who killed their sexual intimates was difficult to determine because police and homicide records contain very little information on characteristics that might provide even a crude measure of socioeconomic status. This problem may be typical of female homicide offender studies since this variable is not reported often. *Education* and *employment* were examined as raw indicators of the socioeconomic level of domestic homicide offenders. The forty-five women for whom data were available had between seven and sixteen years of education, with a mean of 10.9 years, which is below the national average for females.

Employment data available on 117 of the 145 women who killed sexual intimates indicate that the majority of both domestic (63.2 percent) and nondomestic (78.6 percent) homicide offenders were unemployed. This finding coincides with other studies that report that women who kill either are unemployed or rely on prostitution or menial employment for subsistence, or on public assistance (Goetting, 1987; McClain, Weisheit, 1984). Even the domestic homicide offenders who were working at the time of the murder were employed as laborers or semiskilled workers. Although domestic killers were significantly more likely to be employed than nondomestic killers, their socioeconomic status appears to be substandard (Table 4.6).

Another possible contributor to a low income level is the number of children for whom a woman is responsible. Among the ninety-seven cases for which such information was located, women who killed sexual intimates were significantly more likely to be mothers than nondomestic homicide offenders (Table 4.6). The number of children in the domestic homicide group ranged from one to five; on average, each woman had one child.

Although domestic and nondomestic female killers were not significantly differentiated by substance abuse, Table 4.6 shows that nondomestic offenders were almost twice as likely to have used drugs prior to lethal violence.

Homicide Characteristics

As previously noted, the most frequent affiliation between victims and offenders in domestic homicides was as lovers (37.2 percent). Common-law marriage was the second most frequent relationship (32.4 percent), while husbands made up 30.4 percent of the victims.

Previous researchers who described the locations of murders perpetrated by women reported the residence of either the offender or the victim as the most common location (for example, Formby, 1986; Goetting, 1988; Kowalski, Shields, and Wilson, 1986; Weisheit, 1984; Wolfgang, 1958). Studies of domestic homicides find even higher percentages of such crimes taking place in residences (Block, 1987; Goetting, 1987). In her seventeen-year Chicago study, for example, Block (1987: 12) found that when Latina wives killed their husbands, 93.3 percent of the murders occurred in the home. She reported comparable figures for both white (77.4 percent) and African American women who killed their husbands (72.4 percent). Block also found that a street, alley, or park was the second most frequent murder site for all three racial/ethnic groups: African American (15.5 percent), whites (7.5 percent), and Latinas (6.7 percent).

In the present study, as well, the majority of the homicides took place in a residence or the yard of a residence: 57.3 percent of the murders occurred in the shared home of the offender and victim, 18.9 percent in the offender's residence, 2.8 percent in the victim's residence, and 4.2 percent in someone else's home. In the remaining cases for which the homicide location was known (143 of 145), 10.5 percent of the domestic murders happened in an alley or on the street, and 6.3 percent were scattered among business sites, taverns, and cars. As seen in Table 4.7, a significant difference between domestic and nondomestic offenders was found in terms of the homicide location—nondomestic homicides more often took place away from a residence.

The primary social room in a residence (living room, family room, or den) was the most frequent homicide location in the domestic cases. This finding is in contrast to the within-home locations found by Wolfgang (1958) and Goetting (1987), who designated kitchen and bedroom, respectively, as the common domestic homicide sites. In this study, the bedroom was the second most frequent location and the kitchen was third. It is possible that the difference between studies is related to the method of killing.

In a study reported in 1958, Wolfgang concluded that "wives usually stabbed their mates" (p. 215). Thus he felt that women were more likely to kill in the kitchen, where the familiar cutting instruments typically associated with their domestic role are found. Goetting's (1987) report that a firearm was the weapon of choice for 55.4 percent of Detroit women who killed their husbands concurs with the present study, which found that more than half of the female domestic offenders used firearms (51.7 percent). A knife was the second most frequent weapon (44.1 percent).

Other contemporary studies also indicate that firearms have become the weapons of choice for female homicide offenders. On the national level, Wilbanks (1983b) found that women used firearms in 57.5 percent

Table 4.7

Homicide Characteristics, by Offender Type (in percentages)[1]

Offense Characteristic	Offender Type		Significance
	Domestic	Nondomestic	
Location			
Home	83.2	70.1	p = .01
Other	16.8	29.9	X^2 = 10.03, 1 df
Time of week			
Weekend	49.0	44.2	
Weekday	51.0	55.8	
Weapon			
Gun	51.7	40.5	p = .000
Knife	44.1	32.4	X^2 = 29.05, 2df
Other	4.1	27.0	
Premeditated			
Yes	58.3	58.0	
No	41.7	42.0	
Offender's role			
Alone	97.2	68.5	p = .000
With others	2.8	31.5	X^2 = 39.95, 1 df
Motive			
Self-defense	58.9	19.6	p = .000
All others	41.1	80.4	X^2 = 44.39, 1 df
Victim precipitated			
Yes	83.7	49.3	p = .000
No	16.3	50.7	X^2 = 35.19, df

1. Does not include missing cases.

of their homicides. And in a study of women homicide offenders in Miami, Wilbanks (1983a) reported a slightly higher percentage, 59.6 percent. Among urban African American female killers, McClain (1982–1983) found that 72.6 percent used guns. Rural Alabama women were even more likely to select firearms (75 percent) when they committed homicide (Formby, 1986).

Among domestic homicide cases, Block's (1987) study revealed that more than half of Latina (53.4 percent) and African American (51.0 percent) women who killed their husbands in Chicago used firearms, but only 39.6 percent of white wives did. However, the white female domestic killers in Block's study were three times more likely to use long guns (7.5 percent) than African American women (2.2 percent), while no Latina women used long guns in spousal murders.

The significant difference in weapon choices between domestic and nondomestic female killers indicates that nondomestic homicide offenders, whose victims were more often children, used their hands and feet and other methods more frequently in the killings. As Table 4.7 illustrates, the use of *both* knives and guns was more evident in domestic than in nondomestic cases.

As was pointed out in the previous chapter—most homicides were reported to have taken place on weekend nights, particularly in the summer months (June, July, August), and during the Christmas season. The rationale is that tempers flare during hot months, whereas hard times prevail in the winter: "Weather was considered to be an important element in the patterning of antisocial activity by a number of classical criminologists. Peaks in violent personal crime in the summer months were attributed to the eruption of human emotions caused by the heat, whereas the relatively large amount of theft in the winter was laid at the doorstep of economic need" (Renshaw, 1980: 3).

Neither heat and humidity nor cold appeared to affect the domestic homicides studied; they were distributed fairly evenly throughout the year. During the warmer months between April and August there was a slight increase in homicides, but no observable patterns emerged.

Wolfgang (1958) reported that homicides in Philadelphia occurred more frequently on weekends. Almost thirty years later, Goetting (1987) found that nearly 61 percent of the domestic murders committed by Detroit wives also were concentrated on the weekends, with Fridays, Saturdays, and Sundays registering the highest frequencies. Block (1987) disaggregated her Chicago data by race/ethnicity over the seventeen-year study period and found that Latina and African American wives were most likely to kill their husbands on weekends (60.0 and 61.5 percent, respectively), but white wives more frequently committed domestic homicide on weekdays (56.7 percent).

Although Table 4.7 indicates that domestic homicides were slightly more likely to take place on weekdays than weekends, when averaged by the number of days, as consistently found in other studies, weekends are clearly the more frequent times for domestic homicides.[13] Also, as reported in most other studies, murders occurred most often on Saturdays (24.1 percent). It is unclear, however, why Tuesdays and Thursdays were next in frequency (both at 14.5 percent). One possible explanation is that since the majority of the women were unemployed and in the home, they could have committed homicide on any day of the week.

More than half of the domestic homicides took place between 8:00 P.M. and 3:00 A.M., a finding that reinforces other researchers who define such homicides as *nocturnal* (Goetting, 1987; Wolfgang, 1958). Interestingly, while Block (1987: 13) found the most common time of domestic homicides to be between 8:00 P.M. and 4:00 A.M., she also reports racial/ethnic differences in the time of the murders: Latina wives more frequently killed their husbands between midnight and 3:59 A.M., whereas the most frequent time of homicide occurrence for African

American and white female domestic homicide offenders was between 8:00 P.M. and 11:59 P.M.

More than a third of the domestic homicide offenders had been drinking (36.2 percent), and 8.7 percent had used some form of drug prior to committing murder (Table 4.6). Their victims were even more prone to be under the influence of either alcohol (58.3 percent) or drugs (12.1 percent) at the time they met their deaths (Table 4.5). In cases containing autopsy data, it was indicated that 22 percent of the victims were legally drunk. These findings support numerous other studies that also found that either the victims or offenders, or both, had been drinking prior to homicides (Goetting, 1987; McClain, 1982–1983; Riedel, Zahn, and Mock, 1985; Suval and Brisson, 1974; Wilbanks, 1983a; Wolfgang, 1958).

In the comparison of domestic and nondomestic homicide victims shown in Table 4.5, sexually intimate victims were significantly more likely to have been under the influence of alcohol than the victims of nondomestic killers. On the other hand, the comparison of female offenders found in Table 4.6 reveals that neither drinking nor drug use significantly differentiated domestic and nondomestic homicide offenders.

Most reports indicate that female homicide offenders do not preplan the murders and usually commit the offense alone (McClain, 1982–1983; Weisheit, 1984; Jurik and Winn, 1990). Domestic and nondomestic female killers were equally likely to commit premeditated murder (Table 4.7) but differed significantly in the role played in the lethal event.[14] Women who killed sexual intimates were the sole perpetrators far more often. In contrast, nondomestic killers more frequently had accomplices.

Year and Regional Analyses

Changes Over Time

A comparison of the domestic and nondomestic homicides for the two study years reveals interesting differences over the passage of time. Domestic homicides were more frequent than nondomestic homicides in 1979 (52.8 v. 47.2 percent), but by 1983, nondomestic murders predominated (54.5 v. 45.5 percent). In 1979, the killings of sexual intimates were also more likely to take place on weekends than were murders in nondomestic cases (60.5 v. 39.5 percent). This circumstance had reversed in 1983, when nondomestic homicides were significantly more apt to occur on weekends (61.1 v. 38.9 percent).[15]

Substance use by both victims and offenders also changed between 1979 and 1983. The proportion of victims who had used narcotics prior to their deaths increased from 7.6 percent to 18.4 percent, which was slightly more than for female offenders, whose narcotics involvement doubled over the time period (from 6.1 to 12.2 percent). The incidence of alcohol use by victims decreased from 60.9 percent in 1979 to 54 percent in 1983, but for female offenders drinking increased from 32.8 percent to 40.8 percent over that time period.

Regional Comparisons

Domestic homicides occurred more frequently in the South (53.1 percent) than elsewhere (46.9 percent). Conversely, nondomestic murders were more likely to take place outside the South (54.1 percent). "Regional" comparisons of all relevant variables yielded few significant differences between domestic and nondomestic homicides in the southern and nonsouthern cities. However, southern women were significantly more likely than nonsouthern women to use long guns when they killed sexual intimates;[16] to have not been drinking[17] or under the influence of drugs prior to the homicide;[18] and to claim that they were innocent of the crime.[19]

African American and white domestic homicide offenders were more numerous in the southern cities, whereas Hispanic women who killed sexual intimates were more frequently found in nonsouthern cities. In nondomestic homicides all three groups, but especially Latinas, were more prevalent outside the South.

Regardless of the type of homicide, southern women were more likely to be employed than the women in other regions. Also, a southern woman more frequently premeditated a domestic murder, whereas nonsouthern women more frequently planned nondomestic murders. When firearms were used, they were used more frequently by southern women in both domestic and nondomestic homicides. while nonsouthern female offenders were more likely to employ knives as murder weapons in domestic cases, southern women used knives more frequently in nondomestic homicides.

Lesbian Victims

Atlanta, Baltimore, and Los Angeles each had one lesbian homicide case, and there were two in New York City. This finding suggests that even though these homicides represented only 3.5 percent of the domestic homicide cases and less than 2 percent of the 293 cases for which the victim/offender relationship was known, the fact that such incidents occur throughout the country indicates a need for further examination of this subgroup of female killers and their female victims.

No detailed reports of female homosexual liaisons resulting in murder were identified in the literature, but Claire Renzetti's insightful book *Violent Betrayal: Partner Abuse in Lesbian Relationships* (1992) offers valuable insights into violence within such affiliations. Her research on one hundred volunteer victims of lesbian battering, 95 percent of whom were white and middle class, offers a dramatic picture of these female alliances. Renzetti reports that 64 percent of the respondents frequently were verbally demeaned in front of friends and family, and an even higher proportion (70 percent) were psychologically abused (Renzetti, 1992: 21). As in heterosexual abuse, alcohol was an important factor: "Exploring the relationship between alcohol consumption and domestic violence is particularly important when considering lesbian battering, since research indicates that substance abuse, especially alcoholism, is a serious problem in the lesbian community. Studies indicate that as many as 25% to 35% of lesbians engage in heavy drinking, have drinking problems, or are alcoholic" (ibid., p. 62). Substance abuse played a part in the intimate violence and was also used by the victim to excuse the aggression from the abusive partner in a form of rationalization (ibid., pp. 66–67). Renzetti found that violence is about as frequent in lesbian as in heterosexual relationships, but "lesbians are more likely to fight back against an abusive partner than are heterosexual women" (p. 108); and in her study 78 percent did fight back (p. 110). In her book Renzetti describes one lesbian homicide case: "On October 3, 1988, Annette Green shot and killed her lover of eleven years, Ivonne Julio, in the home the two women shared in Palm Beach County, Florida. Green was subsequently convicted of second-degree murder despite her testimony that Julio had repeatedly abused her during their relationship and that when she shot Julio, she believed she was acting in self-defense" (Renzetti, 1992: 75).

The victim and offender characteristics in the five lesbian cases in this study are quite similar to those of the other domestic homicide participants. The homicides were all *intraracial:* three of the couples were African American, one was white, and one was Hispanic. The offenders were four years younger than their victims and ranged from twenty-two to forty-one years of age, with a mean age of 32.6 years. The mean age of the lesbian victims was 36.6 years, with a range of thirty-one to forty-seven. Past criminal information was found on four of the five offenders and indicated that three had previous arrests for violent crimes. Information on the victims' criminal histories was available for only two cases: one woman had prior arrests for violence, the other did not. Three of the lesbian offenders were employed at the time of the murder: as a hotel maid, a worker in a city poverty program, and a car washer.

Weekends were the most common days for the lesbian murders, and Monday was the only other day of the week recorded. As in other domestic homicides, four out of five took place either in the residence of the offender or in a home shared by both; the remaining incident occurred in the street at the entrance to a park. When the murder happened in a residence, the most frequent site was the bedroom (three cases); one murder took place on the porch. The times of the homicides were 10:15 A.M., 6:50 P.M., 9:17 P.M., 9:30 P.M., and 9:56 P.M. Thus, for the most part, lesbian domestic homicides are also weekend and evening crimes.

Victim precipitation was determined to have occurred in three out of the four cases for which the circumstances of the murder were known. As to their rationales for the homicide, two of the offenders claimed self-defense, two stated the killing was an accident, and one maintained that the crime was justifiable homicide. Substance use clearly played a role in the lesbian homicides: four of the five offenders had been drinking, and three had used drugs prior to the homicide. Similarly, four of the five victims had used both alcohol and drugs before their deaths. A knife was the most frequently chosen murder weapon (three cases); one killing was committed with a shotgun, and the fifth case involved strangulation. Knives were involved in the two cases in which multiple wounds were inflicted.

All five women who killed their female sexual intimates were sentenced to prison. The number of years they were ordered to serve ranged from one to seven years with an average sentence of 3.4 years. As we will see in chapter 6, two of the women who killed their male sexual intimates received life sentences, and the average sentence in other such cases was ten years. Could this mean that, like that of a female child, a woman's life is also devalued? As seen in the following illustration, the question is especially pertinent when, regardless of gender, the circumstances of domestic homicides are almost identical.

> Case 5208: Jackie, age twenty-eight, and her lover, Karla, forty-seven, had lived together for thirteen years and shared the bedroom in the house they rented. Both had been drinking since noon on a Friday and were drunk when the homicide took place the following Saturday morning at 10:15. In an attempt to deal with her drinking problem Jackie had entered an alcohol treatment program. She thought that Karla should also join the program. The lovers got into an argument about this and also argued over the food they were eating. In the course of the argument, Karla spat the food she was eating at Jackie. In angry response, Jackie stabbed Karla in the stomach and the left side. Jackie, who claimed the murder was an accident, stated, "I didn't mean to do it."

Originally charged with second degree murder, Jackie, who had a previous felony arrest for assault, was convicted on a charge of attempted manslaughter and sentenced to twenty-eight months to seven years in prison. She was paroled a little over two years later.

OTHER INTRAFAMILY HOMICIDE VICTIMS

There were only eighteen homicides in which a relative (including four in-laws) other than the female offender's child or her sexual intimate was the victim. These eighteen murders represent 6.2 percent of the cases for which the victim-offender relationship was known.

Lizzie Bordon took an ax
And gave her mother forty whacks;
And when she saw what she had done
She gave her father forty-one.

This pretrial jingle is about Lizzie Andrea Borden, age thirty-two, who was acquitted of the murders of her father and stepmother by the state of Massachusetts in 1892. The female-perpetrated murder of one's parents, *parricide*, is as rare today as it was a century ago. Parents were the victims in only two incidents, and stepparents also accounted for two of the victims. Two brothers and one sister were killed; two stepchildren and five other relatives, mostly cousins, were also among the victims of the women homicide offenders. The small number of other intrafamily homicides is not unusual in female-perpetrated homicides. Straus (1986: 449) noted that among parent murders, sons are the more likely offenders rather than daughters, and males are "overwhelmingly" the killers of siblings.

When combined, murders of their children, relatives, and sexual intimates total 66.3 percent of the homicides committed by the women in the study. This finding corroborates the repeated conclusion reported by other researchers that women tend to kill those close to them. However, the *nature* of the homicides committed by women in concert with the choice of victim appears to reflect a change from the past, and is the subject of the next chapter.

SUMMARY

The predominant victims of women who kill are people close to them—their children, sexual intimates, and, to a much lesser extent, other relatives. When the victim is a child, s/he is usually under two years of age. Two decades ago African American women were not found to be killers of their pre-school-age offspring, but this study revealed them to be more than half of the filicide offenders. Whereas single mothers more frequently killed their children under two years old, the child victims of married women were usually older, between two and five years of age. These female homicide offenders were of estimated low socioeconomic status, all but two were unemployed, and they had an average of 2.8 children. They usually committed filicide by beating their young children to death in the bathroom of their home on a Sunday morning. When compared to the other females in the homicide study, only race differentiated filicide offenders from other women who committed homicide:

African American women were more likely to murder victims other than their children, while white and Latina mothers killed their children more frequently than they did others. The finding that 76 percent of the filicides occurred in the three largest cities suggests that pre-school-age children are more at risk in urban nonsouthern cities where stresses and other social structural factors may be influential.

Support was found for the frequent reports that domestic homicide is intraracial and intersexual. As noted in many other studies, African American males are those most at risk in domestic homicides. There is evidence that the victim—who had prior arrest records, especially for the commission of violent crimes, and had been drinking prior to their deaths—may have provoked their deaths. Domestic homicides usually took place in the shared home of the offender and her victim on a Saturday night between 8:00 P.M. and 3:00 A.M. Both the offender and, even more so, her victim tended to have been drinking prior to the lethal event. A comparison of domestic and nondomestic homicides revealed a number of significant differences between the offenders, their victims, and the homicide characteristics. Women who killed sexual intimates were older, were in some form of married status, were more likely to be employed, and were mothers. There were more female and more white victims in nondomestic murders, and the victims were younger than those killed by sexual intimates. The latter tended to more frequently have arrest records, including significantly more arrests for violent crimes than the victims in the nondomestic cases. Although drinking was more prevalent among sexual intimates who were killed, the victims of nondomestic female homicide offenders were more likely to be incapacitated (for example, helpless or asleep). This last finding is thought to reflect the economically motivated homicides and child killings characteristic of the nondomestic subgroup.

Women who kill sexual intimates more often commit the offenses in the home with a firearm, are the sole offenders, have been provoked into the murders by the actions of their predominantly male victims, and claim self-defense. Southern women who committed domestic homicides were also prone to claim innocence and were significantly more likely to use long guns, but they were also less likely than nonsouthern domestic killers to have used alcohol or drugs.

Lesbian domestic homicides resemble their heterosexual counterparts. Of the five cases in the study, three involved African Americans, while the remaining two included one white and one Latina homicide offender; all five cases were intraracial. The killings of female sexual intimates tended to take place on weekend nights in shared residences. Victim precipitation was indicated in the majority of the incidents, and both offenders and their victims had used alcohol and/or drugs prior to the fatal event. Knives were the weapon of choice in most lesbian domestic homicides.

Only eighteen homicides in the data set involved victims who were relatives other than the children or sexual intimates of the women who killed. The killing of one's parents (parricide) and siblings was rare; this finding supports previous research which indicates that males are the more frequent parricide offenders and killers of their siblings.

NOTES

1. There were no cases of divorced women who killed their mates.

2. Chapter 5 examines the homicides of nonrelatives, that is, friends, strangers, and acquaintances; incidents in which other females were the victims of the female homicide offenders (intrasexual murder); and interracial murder.

3. The sixteen cases of child murder omitted from this analysis include two instances of accidental killing of a child unknown to the offender, six cases in which the young victim was an acquaintance or friend, and the murders of two children of offenders' lovers, an offender's niece, and an offender's stepson. These cases are described later in the chapter under "Other Relatives as Victims." Four other cases in which the victims were children of the offenders were excluded from the analysis because their ages exceeded the parameters of theoretical interest.

4. The rank ordering of the six states in which the cities in the present study are located was: New York (6th), Georgia (8th), California (9th), Illinois (14th), Texas (18th), and Maryland (32nd).

5. This information was shared with the author by Dr. Gary Kleck, School of Criminology, Florida State University, Tallahassee, Florida.

6. No Asian American or Native American victims or offenders appeared in the study samples.

7. Employment status was the only available measure of socioeconomic level.

8. These differences were significant at the .01 level; $X^2 = 8.58$ with 2 df.

9. Recall that Baron's (1993) rank ordering of state child homicide rates was New York, Georgia, California, Illinois, Texas, and Maryland.

10. Violent arrests include assault, battery, robbery, attempted murder, accessory to murder, weapons charges, cruelty to children, and unlawful restraint.

11. The cross-tabulation by victim's race in a comparison of domestic and nondomestic homicides indicates a significant difference at the .001 level; $X^2 = 13.61$ at 2 dfs.

12. As shown in Table 4.7, this difference was statistically significant.

13. Weekdays: 51.0 percent, 4 days = 12.8 percent; weekends: 49.0 percent, 3 days = 16.3 percent.

14. Premeditation was determined from the facts in each file.

15. This finding was significant at the .02 level with a chi-square of 5.22 and one df.

16. Chi-square = 9.74 with 1 df; significance is .001.

17. Chi-square = 9.74 with 1 df; significance = .001.

18. Chi-square = 3.91 with 1 df; significance = .04.

19. Chi-square = 18.4 with 1 df; significance = .00002.

Chapter 5

Other Murder Victims

> In homicide, as in human affairs generally, otherwise equivalent conflicts
> will tend to be increasingly severe and dangerous the more distantly related
> are the principals. The other side of the coin is that people will be likelier
> to find common cause as consanguinity increases.
> —Daly and Wilson

The previous chapter described the most prevalent form of homicide—the murder of significant others. But there are other victims of
female homicide offenders whose murders not only provide additional
information about women who kill but also contribute to the understanding of violence in general. The focus of this chapter is females who kill
other females, friends, acquaintances, or strangers, and the influence of
race/ethnicity in female-perpetrated homicides.

Female intragender homicide is first examined for victims of all ages;
a second analysis deals with cases involving only adult victims. Finally,
women who kill women (intragender homicide) are compared with
women who kill men (intergender homicide). Within the nonfamily
category, acquaintances constitute the most frequent victim group,
whereas the numbers of cases involving friends and strangers are almost
identical. Descriptive statistics are provided for each of these groups.
Although a majority of the female murderers are African American,
all three racial/ethnic groups—African American, white, and Hispanic
American (Latina)—are examined. Cross-tabulations permit speculation
about female-committed interracial homicides and close the chapter.

FEMALE INTRAGENDER HOMICIDE

A 1988 article by Ann Goetting that described females who kill one
another was subtitled, "The Exceptional Case." After finding only fifteen
cases in which women were reported to have killed other females in
Detroit over a two-year period (1982 and 1983), Goetting (1988b: 181)
concluded that "female-on-female homicide is a rare form of patterned

behavior" and an "unusual type of deviance that has been totally ignored by the scholarly community." Those fifteen cases represented 11.1 percent of Goetting's sample of 136 female homicide offenders and included a total of sixteen victims—nine adults and seven pre-school female children. In the final analysis, Goetting's adult female victims represented only about 6 percent of the sample. Her finding accentuates the premise that woman-woman homicide is a very rare phenomenon.

Since most national homicide statistics are not broken down by the gender *and* age of either the victim or the offender, it is impossible to separate women who are victims of female homicide offenders from those victims who are children. According to the most recent Uniform Crime Report (UCR) statistics, we do know that 260, or 9.0 percent, of the 2,760 female murder victims known to the police in 1992 were slain by other females (U.S. Department of Justice, 1993: 17). For the years of the present study, the figures are, on average, about 1 percent higher. In 1979, for example, there were 2,927 female murder victims, 293 (10.0 percent) of whom were killed by other females (Flanagan, van Alstyne, and Gottfredson, 1982: 317). In earlier years, we were given a little more information than we are today: eighty-one of the ninety-one white female victims in 1979 were killed by white females (89 percent) and 10 were victims of African American women (11 percent). Among the African American victim group of 198, the vast majority, 192, were murdered by other African American females (97 percent), while six died at the hands of white females (3 percent). The small number of Indian females and females of "other" races (N = 4) killed by "other" females included one African American, one Indian, and two females of "other" races as perpetrators.

The other year included in this study, 1983, showed a slight decrease in the total number of female murder and nonnegligent manslaughter victims (2,822) but a modest increase in the number of female offenders involved in those murders—291, or 10.3 percent. Unfortunately, by 1983, racial breakdowns and other details were no longer provided by gender.

About 12 percent of single-offender, single-victim homicides involve female offenders/male victims; 2 to 3 percent involve female offenders/ female victims (Wilson, 1993:47). Like all statistics, these figures can be viewed another way—as the proportions of males and females murdered by females. This perspective from the point of view of the victims is rarely noted or compared.

Excluding the unknowns, nationally in 1979 there were 9,497 male murder victims, of whom 1,728 or 18.2 percent were killed by females. The adjusted figures for 1983 indicate that 1,534 of the 8,403 male murder victims in that year were killed by females, or 18.3 percent. We have already noted the proportions of females killed by other females for these years as 10.0 and 10.3 percent, respectively; thus a seldom-reported fact emerges. When the persons women kill are examined from the offenders' perspective, males clearly predominate: males are over five times more likely than females to be killed by a female (12 percent compared to 2 to 3 percent). On the other hand, examined from the viewpoint of victims, males are less than twice as likely as females to be the victims of female killers (18.3 percent versus 10.3 percent). If it can be demonstrated that the characteristics of female/female homicide are not substantially different from female/male homicide, we come closer to the underlying theme of this book—that violence is a human and not a gender issue.

Previous Research

There have been only a handful of efforts to explore the phenomenon of females killing other females, and unlike the present study, most do not differentiate the victims by age. Therefore, a majority of previous studies report only the proportions of female victims murdered by other females and do not distinguish between child and adult victims. Wolfgang (1958: 223), for example, found that 16.2 percent of murders in Philadelphia were female/female; Suval and Brisson (1974: 29), cited a figure of 11 percent in North Carolina; McClain (1982–1983) reported 14.5 percent in six U.S. cities; Wilbanks (1982) indicated 19.7 percent on a national basis; C. Block (1985; 41) found 15 percent in assault homicides and 12 percent in armed robbery homicides in Chicago; K. Block (1986) described 17.1 percent in Baltimore; Goetting (1988b) recorded 11.1 percent in Detroit; and in Canada, Silverman and Kennedy (1987: 5) cited a figure of 23 percent.

Only three recent studies delved sufficiently into intragender homicide to provide information other than proportions of the incidents. Of the twenty-one female/female homicides that took place in Washington, D.C. between 1972 and 1980, Blackbourne (1984), reports that three were associated with homosexual affairs, five were related to other love affairs, and alcohol was influential in four. In Baltimore for the period 1974 to 1984, Block (1986) found that a felony was a factor in 13.6 percent of the female/female murders, particularly those involving white females. Only 6 percent of the homicide cases were intragender in a three-state study reported by Hazlett and Tomlinson (1988). Hazlett and Tomlinson also reported that 71.8 percent of the female homicide offenders were African Americans with an average of thirty-three years. These bits and pieces of data on intragender homicide further demonstrate how little is known about the topic.

The Present Study

The fifty-seven cases of female/female homicide represent 19.3 percent of the total sample and indicate a decrease in such homicides from

1979 (thirty-two cases) to 1983 (twenty-five cases). In the fifty-six cases for which information on age was available, thirty-five involved adult female victims eighteen years of age and above, and twenty-one victims were under age eighteen. There were twenty-two women victims in 1979 and thirteen in 1983. These data on female homicide offenders and their female victims will be described in two ways: first, the typical aggregated data methods used to arrive at a profile provide a description of the female/female homicides without considering age; second, after disaggregating by age, only those females who killed adult females are examined. This subgroup is then compared with those women who killed men.

Female/Female Homicide (All Ages)

As seen in Table 5.1, which describes selected characteristics of the intragender homicides, the females who killed other females ranged in age from twelve to sixty-three years, with a mean age of 28.3. Women of color constituted 89.5 percent of the homicide offenders—73.7 percent African American and 15.8 percent Latina; 10.5 percent were white. In the twenty cases for which data on education were available, the average number of years of schooling ranged from three to fourteen, with a mean of 10.3 years of education. Over half of these offenders had completed high school (55 percent) and one listed two years of college. For the most part, the females who committed intragender homicide were single (53.8 percent) and unemployed (78.0 percent). In the forty cases for which maternal status was known, 72.5 percent of the perpetrators were mothers with an average of two children.

Undoubtedly because of the high number of children who were murdered, the mean age of the victims—who ranged in age from newborn to sixty-four years—was six years younger than that of their assailants (22.2 years). There were almost twice as many white victims (19.3 percent) as white offenders (10.5 percent), but minority females, especially African Americans (68.4 percent), were the most frequent victims. Excluding the incidents in which the victim was a daughter (30.4 percent), acquaintances (39.3 percent) constituted the most frequent relationship between the victim and her killer, followed by friends (10.7 percent) and lovers (8.9 percent). The last three categories accounted for more than half of the murders (58.9 percent) and may partially explain the finding that a little less than half of the homicides were victim-precipitated (48.1 percent). Drinking on the part of the victim appears to have been influential in female/female homicide. In one-third of the cases the victims had been drinking and, according to the homicide reports, in each instance were determined to have been drunk prior to the homicide. An offender was slightly less likely to have used alcohol (25.6 percent) than her victim (33.3 percent), but slightly more likely to have used drugs

Table 5.1

Selected Victim and Offender Characteristics in Intragender Homicides, all Ages (in percentages)[1]

Characteristic	Percentage
Offender:	(range = 12 to 63 years)
	(mean = 28.3 years)
African American	73.7
Hispanic	15.8
White	10.5
Single	53.8
Education (mean years)	10.3 (20 cases)
Unemployed	78.0
Motherhood	72.5
Prior arrests	50.9
Victim:	
Age	(range = less than 1 yr to 64)
	(mean = 22.2 years)
African American	68.4
Hispanic	12.3
White	19.3
Victim-offender	
Relationship:	
Friends	10.7
Acquaintances	39.3
Lovers	8.9
Daughter	30.4
Mother	1.8
Sister	1.8
Other relative	5.4
In-law	1.8
The Homicide:	
Victim precipitated	48.1
Committed alone	76.8
In a residence	73.7
Weekend	47.3 (aver. = 15.8%)
Weekday	52.6 (aver. = 13.2%)
Time:	
2:00 am–7:59 pm	17.9
8:00 am–1:59 pm	28.6
2:00 pm–7:59 pm	32.1
8:00 pm–1:59 am	21.4
Weapon Use:	
Gun	35.1
Knife	31.6
Other method	33.3
Single wound	51.4

1. Does not include missing cases.

(15.3 v. 13.9 percent). The influence of substance use is typified in the following case.

> *Case 1103:* Lottie, age thirty-six, was originally charged with aggravated assault against Mary Lou, age twenty-two. The two women, who were described by witnesses as acquaintances, were drinking in a tavern with a number of other patrons on a Saturday afternoon when an argument took place over a boyfriend. Although Lottie had previous misdemeanor arrests for weapon charges and aggravated battery, in her altercation with Mary Lou she did not have a weapon. A male friend gave her a ten-inch-long butcher knife, however, and Lottie stabbed Mary Lou with it. Mary Lou was taken to the hospital, but after being treated, and against medical advice, she left the hospital and subsequently died. Almost three months later, Lottie was charged with first degree murder. Once in criminal court, however, she was transferred to traffic court for outstanding warrants, and there was no further disposition related to the murder.

A majority of the females who killed other females committed the murder alone (76.8 percent). They frequently claimed self-defense (23.5 percent), that the homicide was an accident (21.8 percent), or that they were innocent of the crime (16.4 percent). Together these three explanations accounted for 61.8 percent of the rationales given by the female murderers for their homicidal actions.

Of this subgroup of female offenders, 75.5 percent killed in residences (where the murder was equally likely to take place in the living room-den area or the bedroom) or the yards of residences. The usual time of the fatal event was late afternoon or early evening, peaking between 2:00 P.M. and 7:59 P.M. (32.1 percent), with 60.7 percent of the murders occurring between 8:00 A.M. and 8:00 P.M. While there was no distinct pattern as to day of the week—for example, a homicide was equally likely to take place on a Tuesday as a Sunday (15.8 percent) or a Wednesday as a Saturday (17.5 percent)—after adjusting for the difference in the number of days in a weekend compared to weekdays, weekends were the most likely time for female intragender homicide (see Table 5.1).

Most of the intragender murders involved some form of weapon, either a gun (35.1 percent) or a knife (31.6 percent), with a single wound inflicted in over half of the incidents (51.4 percent). The majority of the remaining cases involved child victims, and the choice of method corresponds to that victim status: neglect/starvation (5.3 percent), use of hands and feet (14.0 percent), strangulation/suffocation (8.8 percent), and drowning (5.3 percent).

Adult Victim/Offender Homicides

The demographic and social characteristics of adult victims and offenders displayed in Table 5.2 show that it is of little consequence

Table 5.2

Adult Offender and Victim Characteristics, by Gender of Victims (in percentages)[1]

Characteristic	Female Victim (n = 35)	Male Victim (n = 207)	Significance
Offender:			
Age	(mean = 30.4 years) (range = 18 to 54 years)	(mean = 32.8 years) (range = 18 to 64 years)	
Under 30	48.6	49.3	
30 and over	51.4	50.7	
Race			
African American	77.1	79.7	
White	5.7	12.6	
Hispanic	17.1	7.7	
Non-white	94.3	87.4	
White	5.7	12.6	
Marital Status			
Single	53.3	33.7	p = .04
Once Married[2]	46.7	66.3	X² = 4.26, 1df
Mother			
Yes	65.0	70.7	
No	35.0	29.3	
Education	(mean = 10.6 years)	(mean = 10.9 years)	
Grammar school	5.7	2.4	
Jr. high and above	94.3	97.6	
Employed			
Yes	31.0	33.9	
No	69.0	66.1	
Arrest Record			
Yes	57.6	59.8	
No	42.4	40.2	
Violent History			
Yes	50.0	35.7	
No	50.0	64.3	
Victim:			
Age	(mean = 33.4 years)	(mean = 38.9 years) (range = 18 to 71 years)	
Under 30	42.9	29.5	
30 and over	57.1	70.5	
Race			
African American	71.4	76.8	
White	14.3	14.0	
Hispanic	14.3	9.2	
Non-white	85.7	86.0	
White	14.3	14.0	
Arrest Record			
Yes	40.0	72.0	p = .005
No	60.0	28.0	X² = 8.06, 1df
Violent History			
Yes	36.4	48.4	
No	63.6	51.6	

1. Does not include missing cases.
2. "Once Married" includes married, common law married, divorced, separated and previously widowed.

whether the victim of a woman who kills is a man or a woman. Except for marital status, the thirty-five women who killed other women did not differ significantly from the 207 women who killed men. Not surprisingly, offenders who killed women were mostly single; concomitantly, those who killed men tended to have been married at some time. The adult victims were highly similar as well, the only exception being the anticipated finding that male victims were significantly more likely to have previous arrest records than female victims.

While not statistically significant, two final observations are noteworthy: Hispanic women were twice as likely to kill a woman as a man (17.1 v. 7.7 percent), whereas white women were twice as likely to kill a man as to a woman (12.6 percent v. 5.7 percent). African American women had an almost equal number of men and women victims (79.7 percent and 77.1 percent, respectively).

Women were significantly more likely to murder a man on a weekend and a woman on a weekday. Also, as seen in Table 5.3, male victims were significantly more likely to be in intimate relationships with the women who killed them. These findings reflect the only significant victim gender differences and strongly suggest that homicide characteristics are not distinguished by a victim's gender in female-perpetrated murders.

Again, there are a few additional homicide characteristics which differentiate intra- and intergender murder that, while not statistically significant, are worth noting for future exploration. There was a tendency for men to instigate their slayings and for their killers to commit the murders alone. Also, guns—the "great equalizers"—were used more frequently against men than women victims. This finding supports Kellerman and Mercy's report that 56.4 percent of women homicide offenders used firearms as their weapon of choice, that women were five times more likely to kill a spouse, an intimate acquaintance, or a family member when they killed with guns (1990: 29). Second, men were slightly more likely to receive multiple wounds than the women who were slain. Finally, when a substance was used prior to the murder, both the women who killed and their male victims had more frequently been drinking than the parties involved in female/adult female homicides. In contrast, when narcotics or other drugs were involved, both the women who killed and the women they killed were more likely to have used such substances than in those cases involving male victims.

In sum, the process of homicides committed by women appears to be the same for both male and female adult victims. Unfortunately, since male offenders were not sampled in this study, it cannot be assumed that violence, specifically homicide, operates in the same way for men and women who kill.

Table 5.3

Homicide Characteristics by Gender of Adult Victims (in percentages)[1]

Characteristic	Female Victim (n = 35)	Male Victim (n = 207)	Significance
Year			
1979	62.9	56.5	
1983	37.1	43.5	
Day			
Weekend	31.4	48.8	p = .05
	(aver. = 10.4%)	(aver. = 16.3%)	
Weekday	68.6	51.2	X^2 = 3.63, 1df
	(aver. = 17.2%)	(aver. = 12.8%)	
Location			
Region			
Non-South	48.6	44.9	
South	51.4	55.1	
Local			
Residence	71.4	76.7	
Other	28.6	23.3	
Location in Residence			
Inside	74.1	85.3	
Outside	25.9	14.7	
Victim/Offender Relationship			
"Family"[2]	32.4	72.2	p = .00001
Non-family	67.6	27.8	X^2 = 20.79, 1 df
Offender's Role			
Alone	80.0	87.2	
With others	20.0	12.8	
Victim Precipitation			
Yes	71.9	75.2	
No	28.1	24.8	
Premeditated			
Yes	68.8	58.4	
No	31.3	41.6	
Motive Claimed			
Responsible	19.4	19.6	
Not responsible	80.6	80.4	
Victims' condition			
Helpless[3]	31.0	27.9	
Not helpless	69.0	72.1	
Alcohol Use Involved			
Offender			
Yes	36.4	42.6	
No	63.6	57.4	
Victim			
Yes	40.0	56.4	
No	60.0	43.6	
Drug Use Involved			
Offender			
Yes	18.2	12.6	
No	81.8	87.4	
Victim			
Yes	20.0	12.4	
No	80.0	87.6	

Table 5.3 *(continued)*

Characteristic	Female Victim (n = 35)	Male Victim (n = 207)	Significance
Method			
Gun	45.7	53.6	
Knife	48.6	41.1	
Other	5.7	5.3	
Number of Wounds			
Single	60.0	53.4	
Multiple	40.0	46.6	

1. Does not include missing cases.
2. "Family" includes relatives, in-laws, lovers, once married. Non-family victims are friends, acquaintances, strangers, and employer.
3. Helpless includes ill or infirm, asleep, drunk, bound or tied.

FRIENDS, ACQUAINTANCES, and STRANGERS AS VICTIMS

A number of researchers have noted classification and definitional problems associated with the victim/offender relationships under examination in this section—friends, acquaintances, and strangers (for example, Hazlett and Tomlinson, 1988; Loftin, Kindley, Norris, and Wiersema, 1987; Zahn and Sagi, 1987). Even in our personal lives many of us may have difficulty defining a friend or differentiating between a friend and an acquaintance. Although the FBI Uniform Crime Reports (UCR) provide definitions of acquaintance and stranger victims in homicides, they do not include any descriptive information on friends. On this point Riedel and Przybylski (1993: 365) comment: "While there are variations, a common aggregation is the grouping of family murders into one category, stranger murders into another and other kinds—'friends and acquaintances'—into a third category." As will be seen, this definitional strategy introduces more problems than it resolves. Therefore, keeping in mind the possible errors in such official accounts, in the following discussion friends are differentiated from strangers and acquaintances on the basis of how they were defined in the homicide reports examined in this study. Among the 296 females arrested for urban homicides in 1979 and 1983, a total of ninety-eight incidents, or 33.1 percent, involved friends (8.1 percent), acquaintances (17.2 percent), or strangers (7.8 percent).

Acquaintances are difficult to define and, as noted above, the distinction between acquaintances and friends is particularly complex (Loftin et al., 1987: 266). But "the ability to gauge accurately whether a relationship is a mere acquaintance or a friend is significant in understanding violence. . . . The distinction is particularly important: acquaintance homicides account for nearly four times as many victims as those involving friends"

(Decker, 1993: 609–610). Nomenclature such as "specific known, but nonfamily relationship" or "other known and acquainted" (Hazlett and Tomlinson, 1988) could include both friends and acquaintances. In their study of urban stranger homicides, for example, Zahn and Sagi (1987: 382) define "friends and acquaintances" as "people who have known each other in some way, ranging from neighbors and business associates to close personal friends." Acquaintances are included in the category "nonstrangers" by the U.S. Department of Justice (1986:126) "if victim and offender either are related, well known to, or casually acquainted with one another." Wolfgang's version more accurately depicts the victim/offender relationship found in the present study as one that "implies more than recognition, but less than fellowship or friendship" (1958: 205). While it appears that the definition of "acquaintance" has blurred since Wolfgang's rendition almost thirty-five years ago, Decker (1993: 587) brings us back on track.

> We distinguished acquaintances from friends on the basis of the intensity, direction, and duration of interaction in the relationship as indicated in the homicide records. Acquaintances have fewer mutually reinforcing interactions than do friends, and typically (though not always) have known each other for shorter periods. Others included in this category would be neighbors, adversaries, classmates, and coworkers. In short, although the acquaintance category contains considerable internal variation, the inclusion of "acquaintances" with "friends" clearly distorts the conventional meaning of the word.

Even the concept of "stranger" is problematic. The United States Department of Justice (1986, p. 126) categorizes a violent crime as perpetrated by a *stranger* "if the victim so stated, or did not see or recognize the offender, or knew the offender only by sight." Similarly, Loftin et al. (1987: 267) define a stranger relationship as "the lack of personal recognition of the offender by the victim." A more precise definition of a stranger is "one with whom no known previous contact existed" (Wolfgang, 1958: 205), or with whom there is "no prior relationship" (Shields, 1987). Felony homicides, or those resulting from rape, burglary, robbery, or theft, are often equated with stranger homicides (Goetting, 1988a; Zahn and Sagi, 1987). However, Riedel (1987: 249) points out that "not all stranger homicides are felony related and not all felony homicides involve strangers." Thus, using felony homicides as indicators of stranger violence risks exclusion of a substantial number of relevant cases, particularly "if variation exists across these groups, simple dichotomies mask important within-group differences" (Decker, 1993: 585). In their attribute approach to relationships between offenders and victims in homicide, Loftin et al. (1987: 259) find: "Although most studies of personal violence collect information on victim-offender relationships, the literature contains little conceptual guidance and almost no methodological research on the measurement issues. Researchers typically report results as though the distinctions between concepts such as "primary" and "secondary" or "stranger" and "non-stranger" are simple and evident."

Since the term "strangers" does not accurately define the acquaintance subgroup, and "nonstrangers" is also an inappropriate term, friends and relatives are differentiated from acquaintances in the classifications in the present study.

As mentioned, the Federal Bureau of Investigation Uniform Crime Reports (UCR) distinguish between friends, acquaintances, and strangers in murder victim/offender relationships (U.S. Department of Justice, 1980: 12; 1984: 12). For the years that are the focus of this study (1979 and 1983), and according to the most recent available UCR data, a national picture of the percentage of victims who were strangers, friends, or acquaintances of known murderers and the specific proportions by selected identified motives are presented in Table 5.4. Typically, these data are not categorized by gender and therefore are offered only for comparison in the following analysis of the data on female homicide offenders.

The national percentage of murders involving friends in 1979 was 3.3 and by 1983 had increased to 4.1 percent. Acquaintances constituted 27.4 percent of known murder victims in 1979, and by 1983 the number had increased to 29.1 percent. The comparable proportions for stranger homicides were 12.5 percent and 15 percent for the two years included in the homicide study reported here (U.S. Department of Justice, 1980: 12 and 1984: 12). According to the latest available UCR data, also given in Table 5.4, by 1992 the rate of stranger homicide increased slightly to 13.6 percent of all murders, while both friend (3.7 percent) and acquaintance homicide (27.1 percent) decreased (U.S. Department of Justice, 1993: 19).

While the overall incidence of stranger homicides may have increased since the 1948–1952 period first reported in Philadelphia by Wolfgang (1958), the *proportion* of females who kill strangers has not varied much over the years. In their California prison study, Cole et al. (1968) reported that the victims of 33 percent of the women killers were casual acquaintances or strangers. Weisheit (1984: 485) summarized results on the incarcerated women murderers he studied over a forty-three-year period by finding "fluctuation over time, but no consistent pattern of change in the percentage of victims who were strangers." Yet a twenty-five-year study of homicide convictions in Muncie, Indiana (1960–1984) reported by Hewitt and Rivers (1986) did not yield a single case of a

Table 5.4

Selected National Percentages of Non-family Victim/Offender Murder Relationships,[1] 1979[2], 1983[3], 1989[4]

Year/Motive	Victim/Offender Relationships		
	Friend	Acquaintance	Stranger
1979 (% Total)	3.3	27.4	12.5
Felony type Murder	1.4	18.1	30.6
Romantic triangle	7.5	59.1	8.6
Argument over money or property	7.5	52.0	8.6
All other arguments	4.7	36.9	8.3
1983 (% Total)	4.1	29.1	15.0
Felony type murder	1.8	23.0	38.2
Romantic triangle	7.5	51.7	9.1
Argument over money or property	14.8	52.4	8.8
All other arguments	6.4	38.7	9.6
1992 (% Total)	3.7	27.1	13.6
Felony type murder	2.5	23.8	28.1
Romantic triangle	8.4	63.3	7.5
Argument over money or property	9.7	57.0	7.9
All other arguments	6.9	36.0	11.6

1. Calculated from raw numbers in sources listed.
2. U.S. Department of Justice, *Crime in the United States, 1979* (Washington, D.C.: U.S. Government Printing Office, 1980), p. 12.
3. U.S. Department of Justice, *Crime in the United States, 1983* (Washington, D.C.: U.S. Government Printing Office, 1984), p. 12.
4. U.S. Department of Justice, *Crime in the United States, 1992* (Washington, D.C.: U.S. Government Printing Office, 1993), p. 19.

female convicted for killing a stranger. It should also be pointed out that homicide is the violent crime least likely to be committed by a stranger (Timrots and Rand, 1987: 1), especially by women. For example, in the most recent study of the phenomenon as reported by Decker (1993: 603, Table 5), only 1 percent of female/male homicides in St. Louis involved strangers, and there were no female/female stranger homicides.

A different picture emerges in the slayings of acquaintances. The reported research generally shows increases in the proportions of females who murder acquaintances both as percentages of total groups studied and within the female homicide offender groups. During the period from 1948 to 1952, Wolfgang (1958) described only 6.2 percent of acquaintance homicides as involving female offenders, but by 1978 that figure had risen to 12 percent in nine United States cities (Zahn and Sagi, 1987) and 13 percent in Canada (Langevin & Handy, 1987). Goetting (1988a) found that the victims of 18.7 percent of Detroit female killers were acquaintances in 1982 and 1983. And for three states combined (Alabama, Illinois, and Texas), Hazlett and Tomlinson (1988) reported that acquaintances accounted for 20.8 percent of the victims of females who killed in 1980 to 1984. Finally, Decker (1993: 603, Table 5) reports 23 percent female/male and 33 percent female/female acquaintance homicides. It is recalled that the present study of female homicide offenders includes 17.2 percent acquaintance victims.

It is not surprising to see in Table 5.4 that felony-type murders more frequently involved strangers and acquaintances in each of the three years listed. Friends were dramatically less likely to be killed than either strangers or acquaintances in felony murders. As regards the remaining motives of interest—romantic triangles and arguments—acquaintances were the predominant victims. Arguments over money or property were especially influential in the killing of acquaintances, accounting for more than 50 percent of such murders for all three years reported. Interestingly, strangers were generally less likely than acquaintances or friends to be killed in arguments over money or property in 1983 and 1992. On the other hand, strangers were more likely to be killed than friends when the explanation fell into the "all other arguments" group in the study years (1979 and 1983) and 1992. Since strangers were the most frequent victims of felony-type murders, this curious finding is difficult to explain.

Selected characteristics of the female offenders and their nonfamily victims are presented in Table 5.5. Only two significant differences are noted in the three-way comparison between friends, acquaintances, and strangers as murder victims. First, it appears that southern women more often kill friends than nonsouthern women. In turn, nonsouthern women tend to kill acquaintances and strangers more frequently. Second, males were the most frequent victims in every category of these nonfamily victim/offender relationships, constituting *all* of the victims in stranger homicides. With these two exceptions, neither victims nor offenders were distinguished in terms of the characteristics examined.

Although the data are not broken down by gender, in his St. Louis homicide study Decker (1993) found that friends and acquaintances were closest in age (within five years) to their killers, whereas strangers tended to be five years older than their assailants. Partial support is indicated in this study for Decker's findings: the women were within five years of age of their acquaintance victims and 8.4 years younger than strangers they murdered. On the other hand, the women killers were 7.7 years younger than the friends they killed.

As depicted in Table 5.6, there are a few significant differences with respect to the homicide characteristics involving strangers as victims. First, women are more likely to have accomplices when they kill strangers.

Table 5.5

Victim/Offender Characteristics by Non-family Relationship, in percentages[1]

Characteristic	Relationship			Significance
	Friends (N = 24)	Acquaintances (N = 51)	Strangers (N = 23)	
Year				
1979	62.5	56.9	56.5	
1983	37.5	43.1	43.5	
Region				
South	70.9	49.0	34.8	p = .04
Nonsouth	29.1	51.0	65.2	X² = 6.28, 2 df
Offender				
Age	(range = 16–64 yrs)	(range = 12–47 yrs)	(range = 16–65 yrs)	
	(mean = 32.3 yrs)	(mean = 26.6 yrs)	(mean = 26.5 yrs)	
Under 30	45.8	65.9	71.4	
30+	54.2	35.3	21.7	
Race				
African American	58.3	84.3	82.6	
White	29.2	5.9	13.0	
Hispanic	12.5	9.8	4.3	
Marital Status				
Single	68.2	65.9	71.4	
Once Married	31.8	34.1	28.6	
Motherhood				
Yes	21.4	41.2	50.0	
No	78.6	58.8	50.0	
Education	(mean = 9.7 yrs)	(mean = 10.5 yrs)	(mean = 11.7 yrs)	
Grammar school	13.3	19.0	0.0	
Jr. High and above	86.7	81.0	100.0	
Employed				
Yes	27.3	23.3	22.2	
No	72.7	76.7	77.8	
Priors				
Yes	77.3	60.0	83.3	
No	22.7	40.0	16.7	
Violent Arrests				
Yes	52.4	36.4	44.4	
No	47.6	63.6	55.6	
Victim				
Age	(range = 17–72 yrs)	(range = infant–94 yrs)	(range = infant–70 yrs)	
	(mean = 40.0 yrs)	(mean = 31.6 yrs)	(mean = 34.9 yrs)	
Under 30	3.1	51.0	39.1	
30+	60.9	49.0	60.9	
Race				
African American	58.3	78.4	60.9	
White	33.3	11.8	26.1	
Hispanic	8.3	.8	13.0	
Gender				
Male	75.0	56.9	100.0	p = .0007
Female	25.0	43.1	—	X² = 14.65, 2df

1. Does not include missing cases.

Table 5.6

Homicide Characteristics by Non-family Relationship, in percentages[1]

	Relationship			
Characteristic	Friends (N = 24)	Acquaintances (N = 51)	Strangers (N = 23)	Significance
Day of week				
Weekend (aver. = 15.9)	37.5	35.3	47.8	
Weekday (aver. = 13.1)	62.5	64.7	52.2	
Location				
Residence	66.7	2.7	36.4	
Other	33.3	37.3	62.6	
Crime Area in Residence				
Inside	76.5	75.8	77.8	
Outside	23.5	24.2	22.2	
Offender Role				
Alone	70.8	70.6	40.9	p = .03
With others	29.2	29.4	59.1	X^2 = 6.53; 2 df
Alcohol Use				
Offender				
Yes	47.4	51.4	37.5	
No	52.6	48.6	62.5	
Victim				
Yes	35.0	63.2	50.0	
No	65.0	36.8	50.0	
Drug Use				
Offender				
Yes	20.0	17.1	25.0	
No	80.0	82.9	75.0	
Victim				
Yes	10.5	13.5	21.4	
No	89.5	86.5	78.6	
Victim Precipitation				
Yes	81.8	65.3	34.8	p = .004
No	18.2	34.7	65.2	X^2 = 11.09; 2df
Premeditated				
Yes	65.2	64.6	50.0	
No	34.8	35.4	50.0	
Victim Condition				
Helpless	40.9	28.3	19.0	
Not helpless	59.1	71.7	81.0	
Motive				
Economic	4.5	4.3	22.7	p = .05
Innocent	72.7	74.5	72.7	X^2 = 9.24; 4df
Self-Defense	22.7	21.3	4.5	
Method				
Gun	45.8	39.2	73.9	p = .03
Knife	40.0	45.1	26.1	X^2 = 10.95; 4 df
Other	4.2	15.7	—	
Wound				
Single	34.8	52.0	65.2	
Multiple	65.2	48.0	34.8	

1. Does not include missing cases.

When their victims are friends and acquaintances, women usually commit the murders alone. This finding supports the suggestion that there is "an inverse relationship between the intensity of the relationship and the number of suspects" (Decker, 1993: 605). A second statistically significant finding is that strangers are less likely to precipitate their deaths than the other two categories of nonfamily victims. Third, an economic motive is five times more likely to be expressed in stranger than in friend or acquaintance homicides. Alternatively, self-defense is claimed five times more frequently by women who kill friends and acquaintances. Finally, a gun is the weapon of choice far more often in stranger killings. Knives are more frequently used by women who kill friends or acquaintances. Concurrence is found with Decker's report on weapon use as related to the victim/offender relationship: "The use of guns requires more fore-thought than does the use of objects within one's grasp, such as knives, blunt objects, or one's own hands. To use a gun most often requires a purposive effort to find, prepare, and fire the weapon. Personal contact implies what is often a more spontaneous act—grabbing whatever is at hand. Intense relationships seem more likely than more casual relation-ships to be insulated against the purposive efforts required in using a weapon" (1993: 606–607).

In order to obtain a clearer picture of any possible differences between nonfamily homicide victims, the data were further disaggregated into the comparisons shown in Table 5.7 (victim and offender characteristics) and Table 5.8 (homicide characteristics).[1] These reconfigurations—friends as compared to acquaintances, friends as compared to strangers, and acquaintances as compared to strangers—yielded few significant differences related to either victims, offenders, or characteristics of the homicide. As seen in Table 5.7, race is the only feature that significantly differentiates friend/acquaintance homicides: a white woman is almost five times more likely to kill a friend than an acquaintance. While not as dramatic a difference, nonwhites tend to murder acquaintances more frequently than they do friends. Not surprisingly, since homicide tends to be intraracial, a victim's race also distinguishes between friend and acquaintance murders: a white friend is almost three times more likely to be murdered by a white woman than is a white acquaintance. In contrast, a nonwhite acquaintance is the more likely victim of a nonwhite woman. These findings suggest that white women murder those closer to them significantly more frequently than nonwhites do.

The comparison between friends and strangers further underscores the earlier significant finding that southern women were more likely to kill friends than nonsouthern women; in contrast, nonsoutherners were more likely to kill strangers than friends.

Age and gender differences were also statistically significant in the

Table 5.7

Cross-tabulations of Victim/Offender Characteristics by Non-family Relationship, in percentages[1]

	Friends/Acquaintances	Significance	Friends/Strangers	Significance	Acquaintances/Strangers	Significance
Year						
1979	62.5		56.9		56.5	
1983	37.5		43.1		43.5	
Region						
South	70.8	p = .005 X^2 = 7.66; 1 df	51.0		34.8	p = .01 X^2 = 6.13; 1 df
Nonsouth	29.2		49.0		65.2	
Offender						
Age						
Under 30	45.8		64.7		78.3	p = .02 X^2 = 5.23; 1 df
30+	54.2		35.3		21.7	
Race						
White	29.2		5.9		13.0	
Nonwhite	70.8		94.1		87.0	
Education						
Grammar school	8.3		7.8		—	
Jr. High & above	91.7		92.2		100.0	
Employed						
Yes	27.3		23.3		22.2	
No	72.7		76.7		77.8	

Marital Status								
Single	68.2	65.9		68.2	71.4		65.9	71.4
Once Married	31.8	34.1		31.8	28.6		34.1	28.6
Priors								
Yes	77.3	60.0		77.3	83.3		60.0	83.3
No	22.7	40.0		22.7	16.7		40.0	16.7
Violent Arrests								
Yes	52.4	36.4		52.4	44.4		36.4	44.4
No	47.6	63.6		47.6	55.6		63.6	55.6
Victim								
Age Under 30	37.5	51.0		37.5	39.1		51.0	39.1
30+	62.5	49.0		62.5	60.9		49.0	60.9
Race								
White	33.3	11.8		33.3	26.1		11.8	26.1
Nonwhite	66.7	88.2		66.7	73.9		88.2	73.9
Gender								
Male	75.0	56.9		75.0	100.0		56.9	100.0
Female	25.0	43.1		25.0	—		43.1	—
	$p = .02$			$p = .01$			$p = .0002$	
	$X^2 = 5.00; 1\ df$			$X^2 = 6.59; 1\ df$			$X^2 = 14.12; 1\ df$	

1. Does not include missing cases.

Table 5.8

Cross-tabulations of Homicide Characteristics by Non-family Relationships, in percentages[1]

	Friends/Acquaintances	Significance	Victim/Offender Relationship Friends/Strangers	Significance	Acquaintances/Strangers	Significance
Day of Week						
Weekend	37.5		37.5		35.3	
Weekday	62.5		62.5		64.7	
Location						
Residence	66.7		66.7	$p = .03$	62.7	$p = .03$
Other	33.3		33.3	$X^2 = 4.22$; 1 df	37.3	$X^2 = 4.32$; 1 df
Offender Role						
Alone	70.8		70.8	$p = .04$	70.6	$p = .01$
With others	29.2		29.2	$X^2 = 4.18$; 1 df	29.4	$X^2 = 5.73$; 1 df
Alcohol Use						
Offender						
Yes	47.4		47.4		51.4	
No	52.6		52.6		48.6	
Victim						
Yes	35.0	$p = .04$	35.0		63.2	
No	65.0	$X^2 = 4.18$; 1 df	65.0		36.8	
Drug Use						
Offender						
Yes	20.0		20.0		17.1	
No	80.0		80.0		82.9	

Variable	(1)	(2)	(1) vs (2)	(1)	(3)	(1) vs (3)	(2)	(3)	(2) vs (3)
Victim									
Yes	10.5	13.5		10.5	21.4		13.5	21.4	
No	89.5	86.5		89.5	78.6		86.5	78.6	
Victim Precipitation						p = .001; X^2 = 10.19; 1 df			p = .01; X^2 = 5.91; 1 df
Yes	81.8	65.3		81.8	34.8		65.3	34.8	
No	18.2	34.7		18.2	65.2		34.7	65.2	
Premeditated									
Yes	65.2	64.6		65.2	50.0		64.6	50.0	
No	34.8	35.4		34.8	50.0		35.4	50.0	
Victim's Condition									
Helpless	40.9	28.3		40.9	19.0		28.3	19.0	
Not helpless	59.1	71.7		59.1	81.0		71.7	81.0	
Motive									p = .02; X^2 = 7.68; 2 df
Economic	4.5	4.3		4.5	22.7		4.3	22.7	
Innocent	72.7	74.5		72.7	72.7		74.5	72.7	
Self-Defense	22.7	21.3		22.7	4.5		21.3	4.5	
Method									p = .01; X^2 = 8.89; 2 df
Gun	45.8	39.2		45.8	73.9		39.2	73.9	
Knife	50.0	45.1		50.0	26.1		45.1	26.1	
Other	4.2	15.7		4.2	—		15.7	—	
Wound						p = .03; X^2 = 4.26; 1 df			
Single	34.8	52.0		34.8	65.2		52.0	65.2	
Multiple	65.2	48.0		65.2	34.8		48.0	34.8	

1. Does not include missing cases.

friend/stranger dichotomy. Women under thirty more frequently killed strangers—strangers who happened to be males (100.0 percent). The finding that the victims of stranger homicides committed by females were all males was the only significant difference in the analysis comparing acquaintance/stranger murders on the traits listed in Table 5.7.

An examination of selected characteristics of the murder displayed in Table 5.8 indicates that acquaintances who were murdered were more likely to have been drinking than friends who were murdered. As far as the homicide event is concerned, however, this is the only significant difference in the friends/acquaintances dichotomy. Most of the meaningful differences are attributed to the comparisons with stranger victims: women who kill strangers differ significantly from women who kill friends or acquaintances.

A stranger is more likely to be shot to death by a female killer in concert with an accomplice, in some place other than a residence, and for economic reasons. In contrast, a residence is the most frequent site for the murders of both friends and acquaintances, who tend to precipitate their killings. Friend/acquaintance homicides were most often committed with knives by lone women who claimed they were innocent or that they killed in self-defense.

As indicated earlier, male victims predominated in both friend (75.0 percent) and acquaintance homicides (56.9 percent). Nonetheless, female acquaintances accounted for 43.1 percent of the victims, which is a much higher proportion than the 33 percent female/female homicides reported by Decker in St. Louis from 1985 through 1989 (1993: 603, Table 5). In the cases of stranger homicide, *all* of the females killed males (100.0 percent). Analyses of the circumstances surrounding the murders of strangers offer insight into this finding. The most frequent motive, robbery, was evidenced in 45.5 percent of the stranger victim cases. Langevin and Handy (1987: 413) also found robbery to be the prevailing incentive for stranger homicide in Canada (44.4 percent). Further, among incarcerated women, Weisheit (1984) reported increases in female-perpetrated homicides during the commission of robberies between 1940 to 1966 and 1981 to 1983.

In the present study, there were ten robbery cases in which the victims were strangers—two occurred on the street in the victims' cars, three involved prostitution, drugs were implicated in another three, and two were tavern robberies. Nine of the robbery-murders were committed with accomplices, seven of whom were males and two females. The majority of the robbery homicides with strangers as victims were perpetrated by African American women (7 out of 10), two involved white women, and the remaining one was committed by a Latina. The finding of four felony murders of strangers in 1979 and six in 1983 lends modest support to the description of women homicide offenders defined by Silverman, Vega, and Danner (1993: 188) as "the instrumental offense-related murderer." "While the latter group is relatively small, it has grown in recent years. This growth may well be accounted for by increased drug use and related crime activity. If this is the case, then we can expect, given the recent increase in cocaine addiction in lower socioeconomic urban areas, to see further increases in the proportion of this more predatory type of female murderer" (ibid.).

The second most frequent circumstance involved in the killing of a male stranger was a senseless argument (31.8 percent): a former police officer tried to take his money back after purchasing sexual favors from a prostitute; an argument ensued in a park over the offender's allegedly stolen dog; and there were tavern and street fights. The female was the sole perpetrator in each of these cases.

In three cases women were initially charged with murder even though their male victims were attempting burglary at the women's residences. Similarly, in the remaining two stranger homicide cases, the women were rape victims who were charged with murder when they killed their attackers!

Since the public equates "strange with dangerous" (Sampson, 1987: 328), offenders who kill strangers are generally believed to be more violent than those who kill someone close to them in an emotional, spontaneous encounter; for example, a female "expressive relational/domestic murderer" (Silverman et al., 1993: 188). This is because killers of strangers are presumed to kill primarily for economic gain, as in robberies, or simply for the thrill or love of killing. Also, "stranger crime generates fear through its violent and unpredictable attacks" (Riedel, 1987: 257). This view is held partly because if there is resistance from the victim in felony homicides, the offender becomes more agitated and angered in response to the perceived challenge.

Recent publications on female criminality and violence appear to be divided as to whether females are becoming more violent and closing the gap between themselves and their violent male counterparts (for example, Adler, 1975; Steffensmeier, 1980). Weisheit (1984: 485) adds perspective to the dialogue: "The issue . . . is whether there have been changes over time in the extent to which victims were strangers. The image of a new breed of female killer suggests a trend toward violence against strangers, where the offender is motivated by greed or a love of violence itself."

In a recent symposium issue on stranger violence, Riedel (1987: 224) notes: "Because of its extraordinary fear-provoking nature and negative implications for the quality of urban life, it might be assumed that stranger violence would be well researched; however such is not the case." Homicide committed in urban areas is a logical focus since such areas contain larger proportions of people unknown to each other, and urbanization is a "surprisingly neglected ecological factor in explaining stranger crime" (Sampson, 1987: 333–334). In response, this section explored one possible indicator of increased violence by urban women through an examination of the subgroups of females whose homicide victims were strangers.

It is presumed that women have become more cold-blooded, hardened murderers when they kill for pleasure or profit and there is no interpersonal relationship between them and their victims. Although a number of the murders committed were quite heinous, the results reported in this study do not produce a profile of horrendous female murderers. Only minimal support was found for the notion that women are becoming more violent as measured by the commission of stranger homicide. The subgroup of females who killed strangers consists largely of single, unemployed African American women with prior arrest records who differed little from the other female homicide offenders in the sample. Thus, longitudinal studies of female homicide offenders that show little change in the proportions of females who kill strangers are generally supported by these findings.

RACE/ETHNICITY

As others have found, in this study African Americans are overrepresented among both homicide offenders and victims (see, for example, Jurik and Winn, 1990: 230). But a comparison in terms of race/ethnicity for the most part reveals that racial/ethnic status is not a distinguishing characteristic of women who kill or of those whom they kill. Regardless of race or ethnicity, female homicide offenders tend to be under thirty years of age, in some form of marital status, unemployed, mothers, and with better than a junior high school education. Hispanic women are the most likely to have been in a once-married status.

Among the selected victim and offender characteristics depicted in Table 5.9, there are only two significant differences based on race or ethnicity. First, three times as many murders committed by Hispanic women occurred in northern cities. In contrast, more homicides perpetrated by African American women took place in southern cities. The homicides of white female offenders were equally distributed between northern and southern cities. The second significant finding was that African American and Hispanic women were more likely to be mothers than the white women who killed.

Hispanic women generally had younger victims than the other two racial groups, a finding that may reflect the much lower average age of the general Hispanic population. Another possible cultural indicator is that

Table 5.9

Selected Offender and Victim Characteristics by Race/Ethnicity (in percentages)[1]

| Characteristic | *Race/Ethnicity* | | | |
	African American (n = 230)	*White* (n = 38)	*Hispanic* (n = 28)	*Significance*
Year				
1979	58.3	50.0	39.3	
1983	41.7	50.0	60.7	
Region				
South	53.0	50.0	25.0	p = .01
Nonsouth	47.0	50.0	75.0	X^2 = 7.85, 2 df
Offender				
Age				
Under 30	53.9	65.8	46.4	
30 and over	46.1	34.2	53.6	
Marital status				
Single	43.4	34.3	20.0	
Once married	56.6	65.7	80.0	
Motherhood				
Yes	68.6	56.7	95.0	p = .01
No	31.4	43.3	5.0	X^2 = 8.51, 2 df
Education				
Grammar School	3.0	5.3	7.1	
Jr. High and above	97.0	94.7	92.9	
Employed				
Yes	27.7	37.5	27.8	
No	72.3	62.5	72.2	
Prior Arrests				
Yes	54.9	55.9	47.6	
No	45.1	44.1	52.4	
Violent History				
Yes	36.4	23.5	33.3	
No	63.6	76.5	66.7	
Victim				
Gender				
Male	81.7	84.2	67.9	
Female	18.3	15.8	32.1	
Age				
Under 30	40.4	42.1	60.7	
30 and over	59.6	57.9	39.3	
Race				
African American	93.5	13.2	—	p = .0000
White	4.8	78.9	17.9	X^2 = 326.26, 4 df
Hispanic	1.7	7.9	82.1	

1. Does not include missing cases.

Hispanic women were less likely to kill men than either African American or white females.

A single significant difference was found as regards the race/ethnicity of the victims. Although the majority of murders commited by women tended to be intraracial, among the interracial homicides it was discovered that white women are more likely to kill African Americans (13.2 percent) than African American women are to kill whites (4.8 percent). Additionally, Hispanic women are more than twice as likely to have white victims (17.9 percent) as white women are to have Hispanic victims (7.9 percent). These findings are in contrast to the accounts reported in the victimization and homicide literature that whites are more often the victims of African Americans.

Homicide Characteristics

While there were a number of significant differences based on race/ethnicity among the homicide characteristics selected for analysis, as seen in Table 5.10, there are almost an equal number of features that are not differentiated. For example, regardless of race/ethnicity, women were more likely to kill a person close to them, a finding found repeatedly throughout the literature.

Murder occurred more frequently in residences, but less often for African American and Hispanic offenders than for white offenders. Women of color were more likely than white women to commit murder in the street, in a tavern, or in other places outside of the home. When the data are collapsed into white/nonwhite categories, this difference in homicide location is more pronounced and becomes statistically significant.[2] If the murder location was a residence, in all cases involving Hispanic women (100.0 percent) and in a conspicuous majority of white offender cases (94.1 percent), the fatal event happened inside the structure. Homicides outside of the residence (for example, porch, yard, driveway) occurred over three times as frequently for African American offenders. The following case illustrates such an episode.

> *Case 1122:* According to the homicide report, there was a history of spousal abuse in Nancy and Oscar's marriage. Oscar, the alleged abuser, was a thirty-seven-year-old security guard. Nancy, twenty-three, the mother of two children, claimed that Oscar threatened her during an argument and at 1:20 A.M., with Oscar in pursuit, she ran from their apartment to the gangway outside. Asserting that she felt that Oscar would shoot her first, Nancy retrieved a .38 revolver which she had stashed in the gangway earlier that day, turned, and fired. Her husband died of a single shot to the stomach. Charged with aggravated battery and voluntary manslaughter, Nancy received a sentence of four years probation.

Table 5.10

Selected Homicide Characteristics by Race/Ethnicity (in percentages)[1]

Characteristic	Race/Ethnicity			Significance
	African American (n = 230)	White (n = 38)	Hispanic (n = 28)	
Victim/Offender Relationship				
Family	66.1	65.8	67.9	
Non-Family	33.9	34.2	32.1	
Day of week				
Weekend	45.2	56.8	42.9	
	(Aver. = 15.1%)	(Aver. = 18.9%)	(Aver. = 14.3%)	
Weekday	54.8	43.2	57.1	
	(Aver. = 13.7%)	(Aver. = 10.8%)	(Aver. = 14.3%)	
Location				
Residence	75.2	89.5	66.7	
Other	24.8	10.5	33.3	
Crime Area (residence)				
Inside	81.2	94.1	100.0	p = .03
Outside	18.8	5.9	—	$X^2 = 7.00$, 2 df
Offender Role				
Alone	87.2	63.2	69.2	p = .0003
With others	12.8	36.8	30.8	$X^2 = 16.51$, 2 df
Premeditation				
Yes	59.1	51.4	61.5	
No	40.9	48.6	38.5	
Alcohol Use				
Offender				
Yes	34.5	33.3	47.8	
No	65.5	66.7	52.2	
Victim				
Yes	51.1	45.2	54.5	
No	48.9	54.8	45.5	
Drug Use				
Offender				
Yes	10.1	28.1	11.8	p = .02
No	89.9	71.9	88.2	$X^2 = 7.99$, 2 df
Victim				
Yes	9.9	18.5	26.7	
No	90.1	81.5	73.3	
Victim Precipitation				
Yes	70.5	54.1	42.3	p = .006
No	29.5	45.9	57.7	$X^2 = 10.77$, 2 df
Victim's Condition				
Helpless[2]	30.9	50.0	50.0	p = .02
Not helpless	69.1	50.0	50.0	$X^2 = 15.34$, 2 df
Homicide Method				
Gun	48.3	44.7	35.7	p = .004
Knife	40.4	23.7	35.7	$X^2 = 15.34$, 4 df
Other	11.3	31.6	28.6	
Wound				
Single	58.6	60.5	39.3	
Multiple	41.4	39.5	60.7	

1. Does not include missing cases.
2. Helpless includes ill or infirm, asleep, drunk, bound or tied.

The statistical significance in offender drug use relates primarily to white women offenders, who were more than twice as likely to have used drugs prior to the homicides (28.1 percent) than either Hispanic (11.8 percent) or African American women (10.1 percent). Although the figures are not statistically significant, the victims of white (18.5 percent) and Hispanic female offenders (26.7 percent) were also more likely than the victims of African American women (9.9 percent) to have used drugs prior to their deaths. The victims of Hispanic women were those most likely to have used drugs. While there was also no statistical difference in the extent of alcohol use by both offenders and victims according to race/ethnicity, it is interesting that both Hispanic women and their victims were more likely to have been drinking prior to the murders than their African American and white counterparts.

Racial or ethnic status had little influence on either the premeditation of the murders or the number of wounds inflicted on the victims. But, as indicated in Table 5.10, Latinas were slightly more likely to have planned their homicides and inflicted multiple wounds more frequently than the other racial subgroups.

African American women most often committed murder unassisted. In contrast, white and Hispanic women were more than twice as likely to have had accomplices. The significant difference in victim precipitation by race/ethnicity shown in Table 5.10 indicates that the victims of African American women more frequently played an active part in their deaths than the victims of the other two groups. This finding may be explained in part by another significant difference between African American, white, and Hispanic women when the victim's condition is categorized as "helpless" or "not helpless." A victim is defined as helpless when s/he is: a small child, ill, asleep, drunk, an invalid, tied up, or physically restrained in some fashion. More white and Hispanic than African American female homicide offenders were found to have helpless victims. This result is probably due to the fact that they disproportionately killed children and is supported by the finding that white and Hispanic women were also significantly more likely than African American women to use methods other than guns or knives in the murders (for example, hands and feet, strangulation, or drowning).

SUMMARY

The typical female perpetrator of intragender homicide is a single, unemployed, African American mother about twenty-eight years of age with less than a high school education, who usually killed an acquaintance, unassisted, in a residence on a weekend. A gun was used only slightly more often than knives and other means. Not only did the characteristics of the female victim strongly resemble those of the female perpetrator, but the traits were not very different from those of male victims. A male victim was significantly more likely only to be married (usually to his killer) and to have an arrest record. Thus, women who kill other women are no different from those who kill men. Except for the tendencies of nonsoutherners to kill strangers more frequently, for southerners to be more frequent killers of friends, and for males to be those most likely to be murdered, the victim/offender relationships examined were not significantly differentiated.

The few statistically significant differences involving victims indicate that male victims were most often African Americans who precipitated their own deaths. Males who were murdered were more likely to have prior arrest records, and were more often killed on weekends than female victims. If African American, male victims were less likely to be incapacitated or helpless than the victims of white or Latina female killers.

Most of the significant differences found in nonfamily victim killings support the results of previous studies. Women kill strangers for economic gain, usually with an accomplice, and a gun is frequently involved. In contrast, the murders of friends and acquaintances are accomplished alone, with the victims contributing to their own deaths through some form of provocation. Three-way cross-tabulations reinforce a number of differences found between strangers and the friend and acquaintance victim groups.

A few more significant findings were discovered among the race/ethnicity variables. Women of color who killed were more likely to be mothers than white homicide offenders. Latina killers were more concentrated in the nonsouthern cities than either whites or African Americans. While white females were more likely to kill African Americans than the reverse, Latinas were more likely to kill whites than whites were to kill Latinas. African American women tended to kill alone, whereas white and Latina killers more frequently had accomplices. Finally, white female offenders were significantly more likely to have been using drugs prior to the lethal event.

The groups of murder victims and their female killers described in this chapter—other females, friends, acquaintances, and strangers—and the race/ethnicity analyses are distinguished by the finding that very few significant differences were uncovered in the numerous comparisons undertaken.

⸰Notes

1. These additional analyses were suggested by Hal Pepinsky.

2. The probability is .04, with $X^2 = 4.2$ at 1 df.

Chapter 6

Are Women Getting Away with Murder?

A small number of studies suggest that even when women commit the same offenses as men, they are not treated as punitively by the criminal justice system as their male counterparts (Bernstein, Cardascia, and Ross, 1979; Daly, 1987, 1989; Fenster, 1979; Frazier, Bock, and Henretta, 1983; Moulds, 1978; Nagel and Weitzman, 1972; Steffensmeier and Kramer, 1982; Winn, Haugen, and Jurik, 1988). In cases of female/male homicide, this alleged leniency has led some men's groups to claim that it is "open season on men" or that women have been given a "license to kill men."[1] Reporting that 95 percent of men convicted of murdering their spouses were incarcerated in 1988 compared to only 50 percent of women who had committed the same crime, Thibault and Rossier (1992:12) are critical of the fact that: "Most of the studies of women murdering men in a household state that it is all right for these women to murder because all of these murders are self-defense. The defenseless female murderers have all been abused and the only way they can defend themselves is by murder." Citing national surveys on violence, Thibault and Rossier argue that women are just as violent as men and challenge studies which stress self-defense as a justification for female/male assaults: "Although some women may kill in the home in self defense, female killers in the home also plan to kill and kill because they want to. We need to take a close look at the courts that are letting these women get away with murder. Has our sexist society, by defending these female murderers made it open season for women to kill men, as long as the killing is in the home?"

A few researchers question whether women are actually afforded more leniency by the criminal justice system (for example, Kempinen, 1983; Kruttschnitt and Green, 1984), while other evidence suggests that some women are in fact treated more harshly (for example, Temin, 1973)—namely women of color, especially African American women (Daly, 1989; Foley and Rasche, 1979; Sarri, 1986; Hanke and Shields, 1992; Spohn, Welch, and Gruhl, 1985, 1987). There are also data that suggest that gender differences once existed but are now diminishing. It is obvious that the question of disparate treatment due to gender has yet to be resolved, particularly when the race/ethnicity of female defendants is introduced.

This chapter addresses the criminal justice history (prior misdemeanor and felony arrests and convictions), previous violent arrest history, and criminal justice processing of the female homicide offenders studied. The analyses range from the amount of bond and initial charge assigned to the final court disposition and the length of prison and probation time meted out after conviction. Although none of the women received the death penalty, five of the offenders, all of whom killed men, were given life sentences. Through a multiple regression analysis, legal and extra-legal factors were used to compare the possible influence of such variables on the length of prison time given to the women who killed.

CRIMINAL JUSTICE HISTORY AND PROCESSING: ALL CASES

An examination of Table 6.1, which details the criminal justice history of the 296 women arrested for murder, reveals that more than half of the women had prior arrests. Misdemeanor arrests were evidenced in 44.7 percent of the cases, with the number ranging from one to thirty arrests.[2] Seventy of the 115 female misdemeanants were convicted of their crimes (60.9 percent). Felony arrests ranged from one to eighteen and were indicated in 37.9 percent of the cases. A little over half of the women arrested for felonies were convicted (forty-nine of ninety-seven). With regard to these former arrests, 34.4 percent of the women murderers had been arrested for violent crimes such as assault, aggravated assault, battery, attempted murder, murder, robbery, armed robbery, carrying concealed weapons, and other violent weapons offenses.[3]

Bond Assignments

The average bond assigned was $29,716 (mode = $10,000). Even though 45 percent of the women killers were granted bonds in the range of $10,000 to $20,000, over a fourth of them were given the most substantial bonds of from $50,000 to over $100,000. The available records did not yield sufficient information to determine the proportions of the women who actually made bond or who remained in detention.

Initial and Final Charges

Initially, 92.9 percent of the women who killed were charged with murder, 4.1 percent with manslaughter, and the remaining 3 percent with justifiable or negligent homicide (the "other" category). However, as Table 6.1 demonstrates, the final charges differed dramatically. Only 26.5 percent of the female homicide offenders were tried on murder charges,

Table 6.1

Offender Criminal Justice History and Processing, all cases (in percentages)[1]

	All cases (N = 296)
Prior Record	54.4
Yes	
No	45.6
Violent History	
Yes	34.4
No	65.6
Bond Amount	(Mean = $29,716; Mode = $10,000)
$1,000–10,000	11.7
10,000–20,000	45.0
20,000–50,000	16.7
50,000–100,000 plus	26.6
Initial Charge	
Murder	92.9
Voluntary Manslaughter	2.7
Involuntary Manslaughter	1.4
Other	3.0
Final Charge	
Murder	26.5
Voluntary Manslaughter	44.4
Involuntary Manslaughter	6.6
Other	22.5
Disposition	
Prison	42.6
Probation	15.3
Other	42.1
Prison Time[2]	(Mean = 7.1 years; Mode = 5 years)
1–10 years	69.7
10–20 years	24.8
20–40 years	5.5
Probation Time	(Mean = 4.3 years; Mode = 5 years)
1–5 years	55.6
5–10 years	44.4

1. Does not include missing cases.
2. The five life sentences were excluded from the analysis.

44.4 percent on voluntary manslaughter, and 6.6 percent on involuntary manslaughter. The "other" category increased appreciably, from 3 percent of the initial charges to 22.5 percent of the final charges. Plea bargains led to charge reductions in some cases, but there were insufficient data to verify the extent of the practice.

Sentencing

In 57.9 percent of the cases the criminal court sanction was a prison term (42.6 percent) or probation (15.3 percent). An impressive proportion of final court dispositions (42.1 percent) fall into the "other" classification, which includes acquittals, dismissals, *nolle prossed* cases, mistrials, homicides determined to be justifiable, a lack of grand jury indictments, or referrals to juvenile court. More than two-thirds of the 114 convicted women were sentenced to from one to ten years in prison (69.7 percent); fewer than one-fourth were given ten to twenty years (24.8 percent), 5.5 percent received twenty to forty years, and five were sentenced to life in prison.[4]

Excluding the five life sentences, the convicted female killers received an average sentence of 7.1 years, while the average probation term was 4.3 years. Although the most frequent length of probation was one to five years, 44.4 percent of the offenders were given the more punitive terms of five to ten years (see Table 6.1).

Comparisons by Year, 1979 and 1983

Over the time period of the years studied, the slight increases in offenders' prior criminal activity were not statistically significant. But, as shown in Table 6.2, a higher proportion of women arrested for murder in 1983 had prior arrests and previous violent arrest histories than their counterparts in 1979. These changes reflect increases in both misdemeanor and felony arrests and convictions; for example, the number of arrests for misdemeanors reached a high of thirty in 1983 compared to a maximum of eighteen in 1979.

The only significant difference in the criminal justice processing of women homicide offenders from 1979 to 1983 is found in the initial charge. Female murderers were more likely to be charged with murder in 1983 than in 1979. On the other hand, women arrested for murder in 1983 were less likely than those in 1979 to receive the more serious final charges of murder or voluntary manslaughter. On the surface, many of the criminal justice practices examined suggest less punitiveness toward women killers by 1983. Although the average bond assigned was slightly higher in 1983, the mode amount of $10,000 remained the same. Also slightly more of the female homicide offenders were assigned bonds of under $20,000 in 1983 than in 1979 (60.0 percent v. 54.3 percent). Similarly, a smaller proportion of the women were assigned bonds in the highest bracket ($50,000 to $100,000 or more) in 1983 than in 1979 (see Table 6.2).

This possible lenient trend is further suggested by a slight decrease in incarcerations in 1983. Although the number of prison sentences was lower in 1983, the terms were harsher than in 1979—7.5 years compared to 6.9 years. Also, slightly higher proportions of the 1983 prison terms were in the ten-to-twenty-year and twenty-to-forty-year categories than in 1979. Further, in 1983 women murderers received an average of 4.6

Table 6.2

Offender Criminal Justice History and Processing, by year (in percentages)[1]

	1979 (N = 164)	1983 (N = 132)	Significance
Prior Record			
Yes	51.7	58.0	
No	48.3	42.0	
Violent History			
Yes	33.8	35.1	
No	66.2	64.9	
Bond Amount	(Mean = $29,428; Mode = $10,000)	(Mean = $30,120; Mode = $10,000)	
$1,000–10,000	14.3	8.0	
10,000–20,000	40.0	52.0	
20,000–50,000	14.3	20.0	
50,000–100,000 plus	31.4	20.0	
Initial Charge			
Murder	90.8	95.5	p = .03
Voluntary Manslaughter	3.1	2.2	$X^2 = 4.25$; 1 df
Involuntary Manslaughter	1.2	1.5	
Other	4.9	0.8	
Final Charge			
Murder	30.2	22.2	
Voluntary Manslaughter	46.2	42.2	
Involuntary Manslaughter	4.7	8.9	
Other	18.9	26.7	
Disposition			
Prison	43.2	41.8	
Probation	15.1	15.6	
Other	41.7	42.6	
Prison Time[2]	(Mean = 6.9 years, Mode = 10 years)	(Mean = 7.5 years, Mode = 5 years)	
1–10 years	72.9	66.0	
10–20 years	23.7	28.0	
20–40 years	3.4	6.0	
Probation Time	(Mean = 4.1 years, Mode = 3 years)	(Mean = 4.6 years, Mode = 5 years)	
1–5 years	66.7	41.7	
5–10 years	33.3	58.3	

1. Does not include missing cases.
2. The five life sentences were excluded from the analysis.

years probation compared to 4.1 years in 1979 (p = .06). A much higher proportion of the probationers were in the higher bracket of five to ten years (58.3 percent) in 1983 than in 1979 (33.3 percent). Finally, the most frequent probation term was three years in 1979 but had increased to five years by 1983.

These findings suggest that even though a significantly greater percentage of women were initially charged with murder in 1983 than in

1979, once they entered the criminal justice system they were treated differently than their earlier counterparts. A woman homicide offender was more likely to have the murder charge reduced in 1983, but thereafter the criminal justice system was less lenient in terms of both prison and probation sentencing than had been the case in 1979. It is conceivable that more scrutiny by the court system took place in 1983 than in 1979, and once the circumstances of the murders were substantiated, the women received what were viewed as deserved sentences. Perhaps, over time, women became more equal in the eyes of the criminal justice system.

CITY AND "REGIONAL" ANALYSES

Offender Criminal Justice Histories

Perhaps the most intriguing finding on the city level presented in Table 6.3 is the comparatively low percentages of female homicide offenders in New York City who had an established criminal justice background. Among the six cities studied, New York, for which samples from all five boroughs were included, had the lowest proportion of women murderers with prior arrest records and the second lowest percentage of those with violent arrest histories. The proportion of prior misdemeanor convictions was lower in New York than for any other city, and its percentage of previous felony convictions was also comparatively low (see Appendix C). In light of the notorious reputation for violence associated with this metropolis, the meaning of this finding is obscure. It is possible that female homicide offenders in New York City are less criminal than women in the other study cities. Or perhaps New York women are better criminals and do not get caught. Another possible explanation for the low percentages of misdemeanor and felony convictions compared to the initial arrest proportions found in New York City is that there was insufficient evidence to convict—a situation that is often an indication of biased arrests. One could also rely upon the traditional notion of paternalism to interpret these findings, or assume that women are treated more leniently by the criminal justice system. On the basis of these data, however, we can only ponder but not resolve this enigma.

Another surprising city result is the extremely high proportions of women murderers who had prior arrest records in Atlanta (70.6 percent) and Los Angeles (68.6 percent). Atlanta also had the highest percentage of violent arrest histories among the six cities in the study.

When the cities were reclassified into *southern* (Atlanta, Baltimore, and Houston) and *nonsouthern* (Chicago, Los Angeles, and New York City), the cross-tabulations for prior records and violent arrest histories did not distinguish the two "regions." Although a slightly higher proportion of southern female homicide offenders had prior arrest records than

Table 6.3

Offender Criminal Justice History and Criminal Justice Processing by City, in percentages[1]

	Atlanta	Baltimore	Chicago	Houston	Los Angeles	New York City	Significance
Prior Record							
Yes	70.6	47.4	58.9	44.1	68.6	33.3	p = .001
No	29.4	52.6	41.1	55.9	31.4	66.7	X² = 18.94, 5 df
Violent History							
Yes	46.0	35.3	41.8	14.3	32.4	28.6	p = .04
No	54.0	64.7	58.2	85.7	67.6	71.4	X² = 11.31, 5 df
Bond Amount	(Mean = $3,600 Mode = $1,000)	(Mean = $19,500 Mode = $10,000)	(Mean = $54,999 Mode = $99,998)	(Mean = $13,947 Mode = $10,000)	(Mean = $38,500 Mode = $10,000)	(Mean = $68,332 Mode = $9,998)	
$1,000–10,000	80.0	—	15.4	—	20.0	33.3	p = .001
10,000–20,000	20.0	50.0	30.8	84.2	30.0	—	X² = 19.74, 5 df
20,000–50,000	—	40.0	53.8	10.6	50.0	—	
50,000–100,000	—	10.0		5.2	—	66.7	
Initial Charge							
Murder	100.0	97.4	88.3	100.0	100.0	85.4	p = .007
Voluntary Manslaughter	—	—	10.0	—	—	4.2	X² = 15.82, 5 df
Voluntary Manslaughter	—	—	—	—	—	8.3	
Other	—	2.6	1.7	—	—	2.1	

Final Charge						
Murder	9.1	56.5	27.3	88.0	3.8	—	p = .00000
Voluntary Manslaughter	61.4	34.8	61.4	4.0	57.7	26.5	X^2 = 56.64, 5 df
Involuntary Manslaughter	20.5	—	2.3	—	3.8	5.9	
Other	9.0	8.7	9.0	8.0	34.7	67.6	
Disposition							
Prison	60.0	38.5	24.6	30.2	54.5	56.8	
Probation	10.2	15.4	28.1	7.5	15.2	18.9	p = .0004
Other	28.8	46.1	47.3	62.3	30.3	24.3	X^2 = 22.37, 5 df
Prison time[2]	(Mean = 8.6 years, Mode = 5 years0)	(Mean = 9.4 years, Mode = 10 years)	(Mean = 8.6 years, Mode = 6 years)	(Mean = 9.8 years, Mode = 10 years)	(Mean = 4.2 years, Mode = 1 year)	(Mean = 3.3 years, Mode = 2 years)	
1–10 years	59.3	57.1	71.4	33.3	88.9	100.0	
10–20 years	33.3	28.5	21.4	60.0	11.1	—	p = .0002
20–40 years	7.4	14.4	7.3	6.7	—	—	X^2 = 24.13, 5 df
Probation time	(Mean = 4.6 years, Mode = 5 years)	(Mean = 4.5 years, Mode = 5 years)	(Mean = 3.5 years, Mode = 4 years)	(Mean = 8.8 years, Mode = 10 years)	(Mean = 3.5 years, Mode = 3 years)	(Mean = 4.6 years, Mode = 5 years)	
1–5 years	20.0	25.0	100.0	—	81.8	20.0	p = .00001
5–10 years	80.0	75.0	—	100.0	18.2	80.0	X^2 = 31.58, 5 df

1. Does not include missing cases.
2. The five life sentences were excluded from the calculations.

their nonsouthern counterparts, an opposite trend was found in the comparison of violent arrest histories. Slightly more nonsouthern than southern offenders had violent records. Since neither of these differences was statistically significant, at least in terms of criminal histories, a "southern subculture of violence" among women is questionable.

Offender Criminal Justice Processing

Bond amounts ranged from an extremely low mean of $3,600 in Atlanta to an expected high in New York City, where bonds averaged $68,332. In Atlanta, 80 percent of the bonds were set below $10,000, and the most frequent amount was $1,000. As Table 6.3 indicates, Baltimore and Houston also had lower bonds than New York, Chicago, and Los Angeles. In two of the largest cities—Chicago and New York— more than half of the bonds assessed female homicide offenders were in the highest bracket of $50,000 to $100,000 and above. These city differences were statistically significant.

In all of the cities, women who killed tended to be initially charged with murder. Even though Chicago and New York were not as punitive as the other cities in the study, both initially charged over 80 percent of the women with murder. When the data were collapsed into murder/ manslaughter then compared to other homicide charges, a significant difference was noted between the cities on this variable. Charges in Los Angeles and Atlanta were drastically reduced from 100 percent of the women initially charged with murder to only 3.8 percent and 9.1 percent, respectively, so charged in the final stages of the criminal justice process. New York City originally charged 85.4 percent of the women who killed with murder, but not a single woman was eventually tried on this charge. Final charges of murder were also less stringently imposed in Baltimore and Chicago. Houston demonstrates the least change between initial (100.0 percent) and final charge (88.0 percent). Cross-tabulations of the reclassified variables indicate significant differences between cities with respect to the final charges brought against female homicide offenders (see Table 6.3).

After conviction, the criminal justice paths of the woman murderers became more serpentine and the cities more diverse as regards final dispositions and prison terms. Table 6.3 indicates significant differences in sentencing between the cities. In Chicago, Houston, and Baltimore, far less than half of the women killers received prison sentences. In contrast, more than half of the female homicide offenders were sentenced to prison in the remaining three cities (Atlanta, Los Angeles, and New York City). The length of prison time also significantly distinguished the cities. With the exception of Houston, there was a tendency toward lesser sentences of under ten years in prison.

An opposite trend was found for the convicted females who were given probation. The imposition of the more severe terms of five to ten years probation significantly differentiated Houston, Atlanta, New York City, and Baltimore from Chicago and Los Angeles, where terms in the lower bracket of under five years predominated.

Among the more perplexing findings on criminal justice processing are the constant fluctuations in the treatment of women homicide offenders in most of the cities. Atlanta offers a good example. As previously mentioned, 80 percent of the female murderers in Atlanta were granted low bonds, under $10,000. Yet all of the women (100 percent) were initially charged with murder. However, at some point in the process the charges were reduced, with only 9.1 percent of the Atlanta women receiving a final charge of murder. After their convictions, 60 percent of those women were sentenced to prison—the highest proportion of prison sentences among the six cities. Yet, once sentenced, 59.3 percent of the female defendants in Atlanta were accorded the *lowest* prison time of one to ten years. Although Los Angeles set higher bonds than Atlanta, the rest of the pattern described in Atlanta held in Los Angeles also, and the movement through the system was even more dramatic. Los Angeles had a higher percentage of women in the lower prison time category (88.9 percent), and not a single woman received the highest sentence of twenty to forty years! A woman murderer's path through the criminal justice system was very similar in Houston and Baltimore. Houston had the highest average prison sentence (9.8 years), closely followed by Baltimore (9.4 years). Baltimore had the highest percentage of women who received twenty-to-forty-year prison sentences, while two-thirds of Houston women who killed were sentenced to more than ten years in prison. The assessments in Table 6.4 offer some clarification of these aberrant findings.

As outlined in Table 6.4, only Chicago and New York City, which

Table 6.4

Paradigm of Criminal Justice Processing by City

	Atlanta	Baltimore	Chicago	Houston	Los Angeles	New York City
Bond	Low [1]	Low	High	Low	High	High
Initial Charge = Murder	High	High	High	High	High	High
Final Charge = Murder	Low	High	Low	High	Low	Low
Prison Sentence	High	Low	Low	Low	High	Low
Long Prison Sentence	Low	Low	Low	High [2]	Low	Low

1. Under $20,000.
2. Over 10 years.

had identical processing patterns, appear to evince consistency in the criminal justice processing of female homicide offenders:

1. high bonds—generally considered appropriate for homicide arrests;

2. high proportions initially charged with murder;

3. low proportions finally charged with murder;

4. low proportions receiving prison sentences; and

5. low proportions in the longer prison term category (over ten years).

In contrast, Table 6.4 reveals that Atlanta and Los Angeles exhibited the most erratic processing patterns. With the exception of the slightly more severe prison sentences meted out in Houston, the patterns of Houston and Baltimore are very similar and also irregular. In all the cities considered, women who kill tend to be sentenced to less than ten years in prison.

Southern/Nonsouthern Analyses

A number of significant differences were found in the comparisons between the southern and nonsouthern cities with regard to the criminal justice processing of female murderers. For example, Table 6.5 reveals that compared to southern cities, courts in nonsouthern cities assigned higher bonds in amounts over $20,000 almost three times more frequently. In addition to assessing lower bonds, southern cities were slightly less likely to initially charge women with the more serious offenses of murder/manslaughter (p = .08). When it came to final charges, however, southern cities imposed the most serious charge of murder/manslaughter in 91.3 percent of the cases, which is significantly more frequent than in nonsouthern cities (65.4 percent).

Sentences to prison did not differentiate the southern and nonsouthern cities, but a significant difference is noted between the two "regions" once prison sentences were handed down. Although both groups of cities tended toward prison terms of under ten years, southern cities were more than four times more likely to impose the harsher ten-to-forty-year terms (48.2 percent) than were nonsouthern cities (11.3 percent). The same trend held when women were assigned probation: five to ten years probation was more common in southern cities (82.4 percent), whereas nonsouthern cities were significantly more apt to give convicted female homicide offenders the lesser probation time of under five years (73 percent).

Table 6.5

Cross-tabulation of Offender Criminal Justice History and Processing, by Region (in percentages)[1]

	Nonsouth (N = 148)	South (N = 147)	Significance
Prior Record			
Yes	52.9	56.1	
No	47.1	43.9	
Violent History			
Yes	35.1	33.6	
No	64.9	66.4	
Bond Amount			
$1,000–20,000	30.8	76.5	p = .0004
20,000–100,000 plus	69.2	23.5	X^2 = 12.53, 1 df
Initial Charge			
Murder/Manslaughter	98.6	95.2	
Other	1.4	4.8	
Final Charge			
Murder/Manslaughter	65.4	91.3	p = .00001
Other	34.6	8.7	X^2 = 18.84, 1 df
Disposition			
Prison	41.7	43.0	
No prison	58.3	57.0	
Prison Time[2]			
1–10 years	88.7	51.8	p = .00003
10–40 years	11.3	48.2	X^2 = 17.56, 1 df
Probation Time			
1–5 years	73.0	17.6	p = .00001
5–10 years	27.0	82.4	X^2 = 14.44, 1 df

1. Does not including missing cases.
2. The five life sentences were excluded from the analysis.

One obvious interpretation of these "regional" findings is that the south was more punitive toward women convicted of murder/manslaughter. In the early stages of processing, southern cities assigned lower monetary bonds, but once in the system, southern women were treated more severely than nonsouthern women, particularly as regards the length of prison or probation time to be served. Perhaps southern tradition and the purported "idolization" of women played a part in the setting of lower bonds after arrests for murder, but once it was established that a woman had committed the crime, she appeared to receive the full brunt of the system. Is it possible that she acted contrary to the southern female role model?

GENDER ANALYSES

Table 6.6 lists the results of comparisons of the previous criminal records and criminal justice processing of female homicide offenders based

Table 6.6

Offender Criminal Justice History and Processing, by Gender of Victim
(in percentages)[1]

	Male Victim (N = 239)	Female Victim (N = 57)
Prior Record		
Yes	55.4	50.9
No	44.6	49.1
Violent History		
Yes	33.0	40.0
No	67.0	60.0
Bond Amount	(Mean = $29,042; Mode = $10,000)	(Mean = $32,154, Mode = $10,000)
$1,000–10,000	12.8	7.7
10,000–20,000	46.8	38.5
20,000–50,000	12.7	30.8
50,000–100,000 plus	27.7	23.0
Initial Charge		
Murder	91.6	98.2
Voluntary Manslaughter	2.9	1.8
Involuntary Manslaughter	1.7	—
Other	3.8	—
Final Charge		
Murder	27.5	23.3
Voluntary Manslaughter	44.4	44.2
Involuntary Manslaughter	6.5	7.0
Other	21.6	25.5
Disposition		
Prison	42.7	41.1
Probation	14.2	19.6
Other	43.1	39.3
Prison Time[2]	(Mean = 7.3 years; Mode = 5 years)	(Mean = 6.4 years; Mode = 4 years)
1–10 years	68.6	73.9
10–20 years	25.5	21.6
20–40 years	5.9	4.5
Probation Time	(Mean = 4.3 years; Mode = 5 years)	(Mean = 4.3 years; Mode = 3 years)
1–5 years	53.7	61.5
5–10 years	46.3	38.5

1. Does not include missing cases.
2. The five life sentences were excluded from the analysis.

upon the gender of their victims. There were no significant differences in this regard between women who killed men and those who killed women. The women who killed males were more likely to have prior arrest records than those whose victims were female; on the other hand, women who killed females tended more frequently to have violent arrest histories. Similarly, while offenders with male victims tended to have a higher number of misdemeanor arrests, female offenders whose victims were other females had more felony arrests (see Appendix C).

On average, women with female victims were assessed slightly higher bonds ($32,154) than those whose victims were men ($29,042), but $10,000 was the most common amount in both instances. Other steps in the criminal justice process shown in Table 6.6 indicate slight differences based on gender, but, as mentioned, none were statistically significant. The women homicide offenders were more frequently charged with murder or manslaughter when they killed a female, but thereafter the system was more inclined to favor a male victim. Final charges of murder and manslaughter were brought more frequently in the cases involving male victims. Prison sentences were also imposed a little more often when a male was killed. Once sentenced to prison, the offenders in female/male murders were more likely to receive the more punitive ten or more years incarceration than in female/female slayings. When males were victims, the mean number of years of prison time was 7.3 years, as compared to 6.4 years when the victims were females. Finally, although the average length of assigned probation was the same for both subgroups (mean = 4.3 years), a higher proportion of the killers of males were found in the five-to-ten-year probation category. It is emphasized that while these differences are not statistically significant, they do suggest that when a female murders a male, she is slightly more liable to receive harsher treatment from the criminal justice system than when her victim is another female.

It was expected that the removal of victims who were of minor ages from the analyses would differentiate the criminal justice histories and processing of women who killed adults, but when the data were reanalyzed controlling for the age of the victims (seventeen years and under; eighteen years and over), again no significant differences appeared. The slight tendency for women who killed men to receive longer prison and probation terms remained after the controls.

RACE/ETHNICITY ANALYSES

The examination of the possible influence of race and/or ethnicity on the criminal justice measures in female-perpetrated homicides first investigated the three offender subgroups in the study—white, African American, and Hispanic American. Thereafter, women of color were combined into a nonwhite category for comparison with the white offenders and victims. Table 6.7 lists only minor differences between the three racial/ethnic categories and the white/nonwhite subgroups, none of which were statistically significant. Contrary to expectations based upon the research literature, white female homicide offenders more frequently

Table 6.7

Offender Criminal Justice History and Processing by Race/Ethnicity, (in percentages)[1]

	Nonwhite (N = 258)	White (N = 38)	African American (N = 230)	Hispanic American (N = 28)	Significance
Prior Record					
Yes	54.2	55.9	54.9	47.6	
No	45.8	44.1	45.1	52.4	
Violent History					
Yes	36.1	23.5	36.4	33.3	
No	63.9	76.5	63.6	66.7	
Bond Amount	(Mean = $29,518 / Mode = $10,000)	(Mean = $32,500 / Mode = $10,000)	(Mean = $29,160 / Mode = $10,000)	(Mean = $32,500 / Mode = $10,000)	
$1,000–10,000	12.5	—	12.0	16.7	
10,000–20,000	42.9	75.0	44.0	33.3	
20,000–50,000	17.9	—	18.0	16.7	
50,000–100,000 plus	26.7	25.0	26.0	33.3	
Initial Charge					$p = .01$
Murder	93.4	89.5	93.9	89.3	$X^2 = 7.92$, 2 df
Voluntary Manslaughter	3.1	—	3.1	3.6	
Involuntary Manslaughter	1.2	2.6	.4	7.1	
Other	2.3	7.9	2.6	—	

Final Charge					p = .05
Murder	28.4	14.8	30.2	15.0	X^2 = 3.83, 1 df
Voluntary Manslaughter	45.6	37.0	47.0	35.0	
Involuntary Manslaughter	5.9	11.1	6.0	5.0	
Other	20.1	37.1	16.8	45.0	
Disposition					
Prison	43.2	42.9	41.5	50.0	
Probation	15.0	17.1	15.1	13.6	
Other	42.7	40.0	43.4	36.4	
Prison Time[2]	(Mean = 7.1 years)	(Mean = 7.5 years)	(Mean = 7.1 years)	(Mean = 6.9 years)	
	Mode = 5 years)	Mode = 5 years)	Mode = 5 years)	Mode = 3 years)	
1–10 years	69.8	69.2	69.4	72.7	
10–20 years	25.0	23.1	25.9	18.2	
20–40 years	4.2	7.7	4.7	9.1	
Probation Time	(Mean = 4.2 years)	(Mean = 5.1 years)	(Mean = 4.1 years)	(Mean = 5.8 years)	
	Mode = 3 years)	Mode = 5 years)	Mode = 3 years)	Mode = 5 years)	
1–5 years	59.6	28.6	62.8	25.0	
5–10 years	40.4	71.4	37.2	75.0	

1. Does not include missing cases.
2. The five life sentences were excluded from the analysis.

had prior arrest records than nonwhites. Most of the white female arrests were in the misdemeanor category. In contrast, nonwhites were more likely to have violent arrest histories.

Higher bonds, averaging $32,500, were set for both Hispanic and white women, but the lower bonds of African Americans were not significantly different from those given to the two other groups (mean = $29,160). Also, the most frequent bond sum of $10,000 was identical for all three racial/ethnic groups. Interestingly, one-third of the Latina homicide offenders were given bonds in the highest bracket, $50,000 to over $100,000.

Although previous criminal records and bond amounts did not distinguish female homicide offenders by race or ethnicity, racial/ethnic status appears to have impacted some stages of the criminal justice process: significant differences between nonwhite and white women who killed were found in the initial and final criminal charges. A higher proportion of nonwhite women were initially charged with the most serious criminal offenses of murder and manslaughter. As shown in Table 6.7, *all* of the Hispanic women were so charged. Almost 80 percent of the nonwhite female murderers also received final charges in the most serious murder/ manslaughter category, compared to only 63 percent of their white counterparts. Among the women of color, African American offenders were the predominant contributors to this last finding (83.2 percent), since only 55 percent of Hispanic women were accorded the more serious charges. In fact, Latinas were more than twice as likely as both white and African American women to receive the less punitive charges, or those in the "other" category.

Once the women murderers were charged, color seemed to play only a minor role in the further processing, since no significant differences were revealed. White and nonwhite homicide offenders were sentenced to prison in almost equal numbers, and most of the women were given terms of under ten years. Although a higher percentage of Hispanic women received prison sentences than either whites or African Americans, they were found predominantly in the shorter prison term category of under ten years. While Latinas tended to be given the harshest prison term of twenty to forty years, the average number of years of prison time was less for both Latinas (6.9 years) and African Americans (7.1 years) than for whites (7.5 years). Another difference which was not statistically significant but should be noted, is the finding that Latinas were more frequently given probation and also accorded the more stringent five-to-ten year probation sentence than either white or African American women killers. Moreover, probation time for Latinas averaged 5.8 years, compared to means of 4.1 years for African American and 5.1 years for white convicted women.

One implication of these findings is that racial discrimination may be evidenced in earlier stages of the criminal justice processing of women murderers but not in the later sentencing decisions. It is possible that the more serious charges brought initially against nonwhite defendants and sustained throughout the later stages of the process effectively labeled them as persons to be maintained in the system.

Devaluation Theory

As reported in chapter 5, most homicides are intraracial, primarily because people kill persons whom they know and those who are close to them. Also, in a racially segregated society such as ours, murder victims tend to be of the same race or ethnicity as their killers. One of the questions explored here is whether African Americans are *devalued* by the criminal justice system.[5] Possible evidence that the lives of African Americans are not deemed as valuable as those of whites is presumed found in the initial and final charges brought against the offender, the severity of the sentence, and the length of time a convicted defendant must actually serve in prison or on probation. According to the devaluation perspective, when a homicide victim is African American, the offender will be treated more leniently by the criminal justice system than when the victim is white. But another problem is introduced—the separation of possible indicators of racial discrimination in the system.

For example, contrary to the devaluation perspective, Table 6.8 reveals that a higher proportion of the women who murdered whites were assigned the lowest category of bonds—those under $20,000—than were the female killers of African Americans. If the lives of white victims were valued the most, the monetary bonds should then also be the highest. Higher *average* bonds were set in the murders of whites ($33,375). In contrast, the mean bond amount of $28,319 for cases involving African American victims was the lowest of the three racial/ethnic victim groups. On the other hand, if the criminal justice system *is* discriminating against women of color, they would be assigned higher bonds. Thus, at this juncture in our analysis, it is unclear whether devaluation of blacks or racial discrimination was influential in the bonding decisions. At any rate, since the bonding differences were not statistically significant, on this topic the question is moot.

According to the concept of the devaluation of African American lives, lesser charges should be brought against women who kill African Americans. This practice was not found with respect to either initial or final charges. Slightly higher proportions of women who murdered African Americans were initially as well as finally charged with murder or manslaughter than were women who killed whites. A three-way cross-tabulation by the race of the victim indicates a significant difference only in the

Table 6.8

Offender Criminal Justice Processing by Victim Race/Ethnicity, (in percentages)[1]

	Nonwhite (N = 250)	White (N = 46)	African American (N = 220)	Hispanic American (N = 30)
Prior Record				
Yes	53.5	59.5	53.8	50.0
No	46.5	40.5	46.2	50.0
Violent History				
Yes	34.1	35.7	34.4	31.8
No	65.9	64.3	65.6	68.2
Bond Amount	(Mean = $29,134 Mode = 10,000)	(Mean = $33,375 Mode = 10,000)	(Mean = $28,319 Mode = 10,000)	(Mean = $36,999 Mode = 5,000)
$1,000–10,000	11.5	12.5	10.6	20.0
10,000–20,000	44.2	50.0	46.8	20.0
20,000–50,000	17.2	12.5	17.1	20.0
50,000—100,000 plus	27.1	25.0	25.5	40.0
Initial Charge				
Murder	92.8	93.5	93.2	90.0
Voluntary Manslaughter	3.2	—	3.2	3.3
Involuntary Manslaughter	1.2	2.2	.5	6.7
Other	2.8	4.3	3.1	—

Final Charge[2]				
Murder	28.4	17.6	30.3	15.0
Voluntary Manslaughter	43.8	47.1	45.1	35.0
Involuntary Manslaughter	6.8	5.9	7.0	5.0
Other	21.0	29.4	17.6	45.0
Disposition				
Prison	40.8	51.2	40.2	45.8
Probation	15.4	16.0	15.7	12.5
Other	43.8	32.8	44.1	41.7
Prison Time[3]	(Mean = 7.0 years Mode = 5 years)	(Mean = 7.9 years Mode = 5 years)	(Mean = 7.1 years Mode = 5 years)	(Mean = 6.2 years Mode = 3 years)
1–10 years	70.0	68.4	68.4	81.8
10–20 years	24.4	26.4	26.7	9.1
20–40 years	5.6	5.2	4.9	9.1
Probation Time	(Mean = 4.2 years Mode = 5 years)	(Mean = 5.7 years Mode = 5 years)	(Mean = 4.1 years Mode = 3 years)	(Mean = 5.6 years Mode = 5 years)
1–5 years	58.3	33.3	62.8	20.0
5–10 years	41.7	66.7	37.2	80.0

1. Does not include missing cases.
2. p = .01, X^2 = 8.70 with 2 df in a three-way crosstabulation.
3. The five life sentences were excluded from the analysis.

final charges, but the analysis revealed that Hispanic victims were more representative of the devaluation thesis than African American victims (p = .01).[6] Whereas only 55 percent of the killers of Hispanics received the more serious final charges of murder or manslaughter, 70.6 percent of those who killed whites and 82.4 percent of the women who killed African Americans were so charged.

The final dispositions more clearly distinguish killers of whites from those who murder African Americans and nonwhites. The devaluation perspective presumes that killing an African American should result in less-punitive prison and probation sentences because the victim is deemed of little value. According to the figures reported in Table 6.8, the female murderers of both African and Hispanic Americans were less likely to be sentenced to prison than the women who killed whites, but these differences were not statistically significant. Again the data suggest that Hispanic American victims may be the most devalued, since 81.8 percent of the women who murdered Latinos were accorded the lesser prison sentence of one to ten years, and their average prison sentence was 6.2 years. The mean number of years to serve was higher for the killers of whites (7.9 years) and women with African American victims (7.1 years).

In the assignment of probation time, female homicide offenders with Hispanic victims were also treated more punitively than those who killed either whites or African Americans: 80 percent received the harsher five to ten year terms, compared to 37.2 percent of women who killed African Americans and 66.7 percent of those with white victims. The average number of years on probation was 5.7 in the cases of white victims, 5.6 if the victims were Hispanic, and 4.1 if the victims were African American (p = .09).

It is obvious that a great deal of research must be undertaken to establish the validity of the devaluation hypothesis as applied to women who kill.

Intimate Victims Analyses

Table 6.9 presents the criminal justice histories and processing of women who killed those close to them. It is recalled from chapter 4 that intimate victims were defined as "significant others" to whom the female homicide offenders were related by blood or marriage, or with whom they had close, intimate relationships—their offspring, sexual intimates, or other family members.

As Table 6.9 indicates, almost half of the women arrested for killing sexual intimates had prior arrest records. This proportion was the highest of the three "significant other" relationships. An impressive number of the female homicide offenders whose victims were family members other than their children also had prior arrest records. Women who killed their offspring were least likely to have been arrested previously, and only 23.3 percent had violent arrest histories. In contrast, 35.7 percent of the killers of other relatives and 30 percent of those who murdered those with whom they had been sexually intimate had prior arrests for violent crimes.

Despite having less criminal backgrounds, women tended to be assessed significantly higher bonds when they killed their children or other family members than when their victims were sexual intimates. Only one-fourth of the female homicide offenders who killed their offspring were accorded bonds under $20,000, while the remaining 75 percent were assigned bonds of $50,000 or more. In the cases of other family members, the proportion of offenders in the lowest bonding category was only 20 percent, while 40 percent were given bonds in the highest range. In contrast, when a sexual intimate was murdered, 70 percent of the bonds were under $20,000, and only 13.5 percent were in the $50,000 to $100,000 plus range.

The average bond amounts were also quite disparate. If a woman killed her child, the mean bond was $76,249; if the victim was another relative, the average bond assigned was $46,000; but when she murdered her husband or lover, a mean bond of only $20,066 was designated. One possible explanation for this difference is that when the bonding decisions were made, the decision makers may have assumed—as the research literature suggests—that the sexually intimate victims precipitated their own deaths. But we will see that this was not the case.

Regardless of having been given significantly lower bonds, when victims were sexual intimates, their female killers were only slightly less likely to be initially charged with murder or manslaughter than were the women who killed family members. Yet at final charging, over 80 percent of the slayers of both sexual intimates and other family members were more frequently assigned the most serious charges of murder/manslaughter than the women who killed their children (62.5 percent). In light of the fact that high bonds were set and initial charges of murder or manslaughter were brought in 100 percent of the child murder cases, this curious finding is difficult to interpret. It is conceivable that the women who killed their children may have been viewed by the court as out of control, or that their homicidal actions were perceived as a reaction to stressful life situations. Another possibility is that since the mother might have had other children to care for, perhaps the court opted to save the state money.[7] Or, alternatively, a paternalistic court may have thought that by the time a mother reached that stage of the criminal justice process she had been punished sufficiently or had suffered enough. And, finally, there is the possibility that the homicide may have been an accident, as female defendants frequently claim in filicides.

Table 6.9

Offender Criminal Justice History and Processing by Intimate Relationship, (in percentages)[1]

	Offspring (N = 31)	Sexual Intimate (N = 145)	Other Family (N = 18)	Significance
Prior Record				
Yes	35.5	49.2	42.9	
No	64.5	50.8	57.1	
Violent History				
Yes	23.3	30.0	35.7	
No	76.7	70.0	64.3	
Bond Amount	(Mean = $76,249	(Mean = $20,066	(Mean = $42,009	
	Mode = $99,998)	Mode = $10,000)	Mode = $10,000)	
$1,000–10,000	25.0	13.3	—	p = .03
10,000–20,000	—	56.7	20.0	$X^2 = 6.56$; 2 df
20,000–50,000	—	16.5	40.0	
50,000–100,000 plus	75.0	13.5	40.0	
Initial Charge				
Murder	87.1	89.6	100.0	
Voluntary Manslaughter	—	5.5	—	
Involuntary Manslaughter	12.9	—	—	
Other	—	4.8	—	

Final Charge			
Murder	16.7	28.1	30.8
Voluntary Manslaughter	20.8	52.8	38.5
Involuntary Manslaughter	25.0	4.5	15.4
Other	37.5	14.6	15.3
Disposition			
Prison	37.9	37.1	46.7
Probation	37.9	13.3	20.0
Other	24.2	49.6	33.3
Prison Time[2]	(Mean = 7.4 years, Mode = .000)	(Mean = 6.4 years, Mode = 10 years)	(Mean = 8.3 years, Mode = 1 year)
1–10 years	63.6	77.1	57.1
10–20 years	27.3	18.8	28.6
20–40 years	9.1	4.1	14.3
Probation Time	(Mean = 4.3 years, Mode = 5 years)	(Mean = 4.4 years, Mode = 3 years)	(Mean = 5.3 years, Mode = 3 years)
1–5 years	35.7	60.0	50.0
5–10 years	64.3	40.0	50.0

$p = .04$
$X^2 = 6.55$; 1 df

1. Does not include missing cases.
2. The five life sentences were excluded from the analysis.

Whatever reasoning accounted for the determination of less serious final charges in comparison to the other two groups, women who were convicted of killing their offspring were just as likely to receive prison sentences as women who killed those with whom they were sexually intimate; and, on average, their prison sentences were longer. Filicide offenders were twice as frequently given twenty to forty years in prison as women who killed their sexual intimates (4.1 percent). The mean number of years in prison for women who killed their children was 7.4 years, a year longer than the average of 6.4 years allocated to female killers of husbands and lovers.

The women convicted of murdering other family members were treated the harshest. Almost half of these offenders were sentenced to prison, and they received longer terms than the other two offending groups. Conviction for killing a family member other than one's child resulted in an average prison term of 8.3 years, the highest of the three groups. Also, a higher proportion of such murderers were sentenced to prison terms in the twenty-to-forty-year category, a percentage three times that for women who killed sexual intimates.

Probation sentences also reflect this apparent leniency toward female homicide offenders whose victims were husbands or lovers. A majority of the convicted female murderers (60 percent) were accorded the lower probationary times (one to five years). In contrast, women who killed their offspring were more frequently given the more severe probation sentences of five to 10 years (64.3 percent). As seen in Table 6.9, the average of slightly over four years probation was almost identical for both of these groups. On the other hand, the mean number of years of probation was higher for the female homicide offenders who killed other family members (5.3 years). This group was equally likely to be sentenced to one to five years as to five to ten years of probation.

NONFAMILY VICTIMS ANALYSES

The majority of females who killed persons who were not family members had prior arrest records. Not surprisingly, as seen in Table 6.10, women who murdered strangers (83.3 percent) were more likely to have previous records than those who killed friends (77.3 percent) or acquaintances (60 percent).[8] However, it was surprising to find that women arrested for murdering their friends had violent arrest histories more frequently than those who killed either strangers or acquaintances.

There was no differentiation among female killers of friends, strangers, and acquaintances with regards to the proportions initially charged with murder, and only small, insignificant differences were found between the groups when final charges were levied. The women who were assessed the most severe charges of murder or manslaughter were those who killed their friends. Inexplicably, female homicide offenders whose victims were strangers were less likely to receive the most stringent charges than those whose victims belonged to the other nonfamily groups. In light of the public (and criminal justice) conception of those who kill strangers as more dangerous and fearsome, this finding suggests that at least in terms of the charges brought against them for homicide, women who kill strangers may tend to escape such stigmatization.[9]

Once convicted, however, women who murdered strangers were significantly more likely to receive prison sentences (70.6 percent) than those who were convicted of killing acquaintances (51.1 percent), but they were still not treated as punitively as women who killed their friends (75 percent). In the murders of friends, prison time ranged from four to fifteen years with a mean of 8.8 years. Convicted female murderers were given less severe average prison terms when acquaintances were their victims (mean = 7.4 years), but the range was from less than one year to twenty-five years. Even more disparate is the finding that 75 percent of the women who killed strangers were sentenced to less than ten years in prison!

It has been reported that more severe sanctions are levied against persons who commit stranger homicides in public places and that sanctions tend to "vary inversely with the intimacy of the relationship" (Reidel, 1987, p. 252). Modest support was found for this position. A majority of the stranger homicides committed by women took place in public places (66.7 percent) and differed significantly from acquaintance homicides, which occurred more frequently in residences (65.4 percent).[10] More than half (54.5 percent) of the women who killed strangers in public places received prison sentences, while only 21.1 percent of the women who publicly killed acquaintances were so sentenced, but this difference was not statistically significant.

None of the women who murdered strangers received probation. Female homicide offenders who were sentenced to probation for killing their friends were equally likely to receive the more punitive sanction of five to ten years as they were to be assigned the lesser period of one to five years. Their average number of years on probation was 4.5. When acquaintances were their victims, the majority of female offenders (75 percent) were dispensed the least severe one-to-five-year probationary sentence and also averaged less time on probation (mean = 3.8 years) than the women convicted of killing their friends.

CORRELATION MATRIX AND MULTIPLE REGRESSION ANALYSIS

In the previously described cross-tabulations of the criminal justice variables by years of the study, "region," gender of victim, race of offender

Table 6.10

Criminal Justice History and Processing by Nonfamily Victim/Offender Relationship, (in percentages)[1]

	Friend (N = 24)		Acquaintance (N = 51)		Stranger (N = 23)		Significance
Prior Record							
Yes	77.3		60.0		83.3		
No	22.7		40.0		16.7		
Violent History							
Yes	52.4		36.4		44.4		
No	47.6		63.6		55.6		
Bond Amount	(Mean = $54,999		(Mean = $26,235		(Mean = $10,000		
	Mode = $10,000)		Mode = $10,000)		Mode = $10,000)		
$1,000–10,000	—		11.8		—		
10,000–20,000	50.0		41.1		100.0		
20,000–50,000	—		17.7		—		
50,000–100,000 plus	50.0		29.4		—		
Initial Charge							
Murder	100.0		96.1		100.0		
Voluntary Manslaughter	—		—		—		
Involuntary Manslaughter	—		—		—		
Other	—		3.9		—		

Final Charge			
Murder	30.0	25.0	30.8
Voluntary Manslaughter	50.0	44.4	23.1
Involuntary Manslaughter	5.0	—	—
Other	15.0	30.6	46.1
Disposition			
Prison	75.0	36.8	70.6
Probation	10.0	14.3	—
Other	15.0	48.9	29.4
Prison Time[2]	(Mean = 8.8 years, Mode = 5 years)	(Mean = 7.4 years, Mode = 5 years)	(Mean = 7 years, Mode = 2 years)
1–10 years	41.7	72.2	75.0
10–20 years	58.3	22.3	16.7
20–40 years	—	5.5	8.3
Probation Time	(Mean = 4.5 years, Mode = 4 years)	(Mean = 3.8 years, Mode = 4 years)	
1–5 years	50.0	75.0	—
5–10 years	50.0	25.0	—

p = .003
X^2 = 11.71; 2 df

1. Does not include missing cases.
2. The five life sentences were excluded from the analysis.

and victim, and victim/offender relationship (intrafamily; nonfamily), the only significant differences found in prison disposition were for nonfamily homicide victims and the higher number of years of prison time given in southern cities. A logical next step was to identify the factors influencing sentencing decisions to find out why some of the women murderers were sentenced to prison while others were not; and also to isolate the considerations involved in the assignment of longer prison terms to some convicted women as compared to others. Several groups of variables were examined in these analyses and were classified by characteristics of the:

offender—age, race, marital status, motherhood, employment status, and prior arrest record;

victim—age, gender, race;

features of the murder event—the victim/offender relationship, the motive, the offender's role in the event (alone or with others), the victim's condition (helpless), the victim's role in the event (provocation/precipitation), the murder method (gun), premeditation, and whether a single or multiple wounds were inflicted.

It was anticipated that certain legal factors, such as prior record and attributes of the murder—for example, premeditation or motive—would be most influential in sentencing decisions. The use of a gun and the infliction of multiple wounds were presumed to work against a defendant. Certain extra-legal factors such as gender and race were also expected to make a difference. If the criminal justice system is paternalistic, then women should be treated more leniently when victim provocation occurs. On the other hand, it is reasoned that if a woman had been drinking, using narcotics prior to the murder, or generally not performing the expected female role, the court would punish her more stringently. Further, since the literature indicates that males are valued more highly than females (see chapter 4), all things being equal, killing a male should result in harsher treatment by the criminal justice system than the murder of a female. Such an assumption is more probable when one considers that the justice system is predominantly male.

Race is included as a major variable on the basis of an abundance of literature suggesting racial bias in sentencing. It was assumed that, like their male counterparts, women of color might also experience discrimination in the form of harsher treatment. The research literature suggests that employment status is an important consideration in homicides and, concomitantly, motherhood is felt to be one of the major contributors to a woman's unemployment. Finally, it has been found that southern states mete out more severe punishments than nonsouthern states, so "region" was included in the analyses.

The zero-order correlations with prison disposition are displayed in the first column of Table 6.11; the second column contains contains the correlations with prison time. As is readily observed, most of the correlations are low and do not assume statistical significance. However, a few of the predicted variables were significantly associated with the assignment of a prison sentence—unemployment, prior arrest history, "region," gender of the victim, and prison time. Prison time is significantly associated with both unemployment status and the age of the victim. The results of this analysis suggest that being unemployed affects whether a woman murderer is sentenced to prison and also impacts the length of time she must serve (p = <.01). Further, if a woman who kills has a prior arrest record, the odds of her receiving a prison sentence are increased, especially in the southern cities (p = <.01). In addition, the length of time in prison is negatively correlated with the age of the victim; that is, higher prison terms were imposed when the victims were younger (p = <.01). While not attaining the significance level of the other variables described, killing a male was correlated with a prison disposition (p = <.05) but had no apparent effect on prison time.

While some of the results in the correlation matrix were anticipated, it is possible that some of the variables are masking other associations with the dependent variables. To reduce the possibility of such effects, the preliminary correlation analysis is augmented by the multiple regression analysis presented in Table 6.12, where prison time (actual years, excluding life sentences) is the dependent variable.

The number of variables was reduced to the five most representative as explanatory in the sentencing literature (region, prior arrests, motive, premeditation, victim precipitation) while maintaining the gender of the victim in order to test paternalism theory and the devaluation of female lives. When applied to the length of prison time allocated, this more parsimonious regression equation of six variables indicates that region (Beta = .405719; p = .0000), motive (Beta = −.310252; p = .0009), and victim precipitation (Beta = −.262476; p = .008) are significant predictors of the prison time given to women convicted of murder (R^2 = .30). The data presented in Table 6.12 on length of prison time are somewhat more straightforward after the original nineteen independent variables are entered into the regression equation. As anticipated, motive for the murder (p = .009) and "region"—southern/nonsouthern—(p = .0005) were found to be significant predictors of the number of prison years assigned. If the offender had been drinking prior to the murder, the probability of receiving a longer sentence was increased but did not reach an acceptable significance level (p = .08). Although considerably more

Table 6.11

Correlation Matrix (N = 296)

Variable	1	2	3	4	5	6	7	8	9	10	11	12	13	14	15	16	17	18	19	20	21
1) Prison Disposition	1.00																				
2) Prison Time	.41**	1.00																			
3) Age of Offender	.01	-.03	1.00																		
4) Race of Offender	.01	-.02	.06	1.00																	
5) Employment	.19**	-.12**	.03	.02	1.00																
6) Motherhood	.05	-.04	.16**	.10	.17**	1.00															
7) Prior Arrests	.27**	.11	.07	.02	.27**	.10	1.00														
8) Age of Victim	-.09	-.17**	.39**	.00	.01	.17**	.03	1.00													
9) Race of Victim	-.01	.04	.09	.67**	.04	.04	.06	-.15*	1.00												
10) Gender of Victim	.12*	.04	.11*	-.03	.05	.01	.13*	.28**	.05	1.00											
11) Victim/Offender Relationship	.09	.08	.02	.04	.03	-.01	.05	.07	-.04	-.03	1.00										
12) Motive	-.03	-.02	.09	.01	.01	.08	-.05	.08	.03	-.03	.26**	1.00									
13) Method	-.03	.00	.21**	.02	.01	.11	-.15*	.21**	.01	.11	.11	.09	1.00								
14) Wound	-.04	.01	.00	.05	-.00	.08	-.03	.09	.04	.07	-.06	.21**	.07	1.00							
15) Offender's Role	.11	.04	.21**	.11	.06	.05	.09	.04	.04	.02	.46**	.28**	.03	-.02	1.00						
16) Premeditation	.06	-.02	.11	.06	.06	.05	-.03	.04	.02	-.11	.26**	.38**	-.01	.09	.36**	1.00					
17) Victim Precipitation	.04	.09	.14*	.07	-.01	.09	-.03	.14*	.06	.05	.26**	.55**	.13*	.35**	.35**	.40**	1.00				
18) Victim's Condition	.01	.08	-.00	.07	-.00	.25**	-.03	.08	.05	-.00	.32**	.29**	.19**	.14*	.13*	.21**	.36**	1.00			
19) "Region"	-.18**	-.00	.09	.00	-.01	-.08	.13*	.15*	-.02	.06	.10	.05	.11	-.06	.09	-.01	.12*	-.07	1.00		
20) Offender Alcohol	-.04	.04	.04	.15**	-.01	.28**	.01	.11*	.14*	-.03	.19**	.22**	.19**	.15*	.14*	.11	.21**	.44**	-.09	1.00	
21) Offender Drugs	-.04	.07	-.04	.05	.05	.21**	-.01	.04	.09	-.02	.18**	.22**	.10	.07	.05	.02	.16**	.47**	-.17**	.80**	1.00

*Significant at p < .05
**Significant at p < .01

Table 6.12

Multiple Regression Analysis of Prison Time (N = 296)

Independent Variable	b	B	SE Beta	Significance of t
Region	5.553	.436	.118	.0005
Race	.947	.049	.157	.7520
Victim/Offender Relationship	.020	.002	.140	.9917
Number of Wounds	.284	.022	.115	.8472
Offender Alcohol	−2.922	−.221	.122	.0765
Motive	−4.842	−.315	.117	**.0093**
Premeditation	−1.018	−.079	.118	.5062
Victim's Condition	2.229	.168	.121	.1699
Offender's Age	−.051	−.089	.137	.5188
Victim's Gender	.860	.054	.120	.6575
Prior Arrests	−.591	−.046	.119	.6979
Employment Status	.052	.004	.118	.9747
Offender Narcotics	2.553	.134	.122	.2776
Method	−.382	−.030	.122	.8059
Offender's Role	−2.907	−.174	.134	.1993
Victim Precipitation	−2.625	−.196	.142	.1721
Motherhood	1.823	.132	.140	.3496
Victim's Age	.054	.144	.146	.3294
Victim's Race	.071	.004	.156	.9793

$R^2 = .41$

variance is explained by prison time than by disposition, the question persists whether other events or nuances of the courtroom setting sway such decisions when women are defendants.

Since a great deal of the variance is left unexplained, it is suggested that more subtle extralegal influences on women's murder case dispositions may occur in the criminal courts that are not picked up from the facts found in police and homicide records. It is only in those cases where the women are possibly viewed by the court as particularly "evil" because they preplanned the murders that statistical significance is attained.

THE LIFE SENTENCE CASES

The five women murderers in the study who received life sentences committed their homicides in jurisdictions with capital punishment statutes (Georgia, Maryland, and Texas). An examination of the particulars in these cases demonstrates calloused behavior as well as heinous crimes. For example, in case #2221, when the offender's husband of eleven years, who was age fifty-six, told her that she was getting too old for him and that he wanted a divorce *and* a younger woman, the forty-seven-year-old offender shot him in the back. The victim ran from her into the bedroom, where he fell. The offender then shot him four more times as he lay on the floor. According to a witness, the offender was "highly intoxicated."

In a second case, the offender, age twenty-two, told a witness to the murder that she was going to kill her live-in lover of two years because she did not like the way he treated her. With a knife in one hand and scissors in the other, the offender repeatedly stabbed her twenty-six-year-old lover, who was asleep at the time, in front of the witness. Later the offender was in front of the building, claiming to the police that she had "killed the motherfucker." When the medics were taking the victim to the ambulance, the offender had to be restrained by the police for trying to kick him as she screamed, "I thought I had killed the motherfucker!"

Three lesbian lovers were co-defendants in the murder of a fifty-seven-year-old male; two were given life sentences and the third was sentenced to fifteen years in prison. The victim and one of the offenders, age nineteen, had lived together as lovers. Prior to the murder, the three women had tied up the victim with extension cords and tortured him. A neighbor later reported that the victim was crying and making choking sounds—undoubtedly because the three women had poured hot water down his throat and tried to strangle him. They also stabbed him repeatedly with an eight-to-nine-inch knife, causing several wounds which were five inches deep, and then slashed his wrists. The three were together at the time of their arrests and admitted reluctantly that they knew the victim, but they denied any knowledge of the homicide. In contrast to the first two cases in which neither woman had a prior arrest record, all three women in this case had previous records, primarily for vice crimes.

The final case of a life sentence involved a nineteen-year-old offender who had numerous previous arrests ranging from misdemeanor drug possession to several arrests for aggravated assault, auto theft, firebombing, and carrying concealed weapons. At the time of the murder she was allegedly dealing hard drugs. A shoe box full of money was found at her mother's house, where the homicide took place. Apparently the money was a primary factor in the murder of a twenty-eight-year-old male friend who was shot to death by the offender.

Three of the five women (60 percent) who received life sentences were African American and two were white. Jose-Kampfner (1990) interviewed seventy women who were serving life terms or sentences of ten years or longer, a disproportionate number of whom were women of color. Of the women interviewed, 45 percent were imprisoned for killing their lover, 15 percent for conspiracy to kill their lover, 20 percent for being accomplices to a crime, and the remaining 20 percent were serving long sentences as habitual offenders (ibid.: 112).

ARE WOMEN GETTING AWAY WITH MURDER?

Previous research that suggests more lenient sentencing of women who committed the same crimes as men—for example, the excellent and provocative reports by Kruttschnitt (1984), Kruttschnitt and Green (1984), and Daly (1987; 1989)—addressed less serious offenses or nonviolent crimes, and did not focus on the crime of murder.

Although prison commitments for murder are not available for the years of the study by gender, new court commitments to state prisons for murder in 1989 show few within-group gender differences. In their work on women in prison, Greenfeld and Minor-Harper (1991: 3) report that "violent female offenders were more likely to have victimized a male (61.4%) than violent male offenders were to have victimized a female (52.7%)." Of all females committed to state prison in 1989, 1.8 percent were incarcerated for murder; the proportion for men was 2.2 percent (Perkins, 1992:12).

Sentence lengths vary by gender. According to the latest available figures, the average maximum sentence length in state prisons that men received for murder in 1991 was 32.2 years (386 months). In contrast, women had a mean of 25.8 years (310 months), or almost six and a half years less for the same crime (Snell and Morton, 1994: 4, Table 6). These differences suggest that compared to men, women do receive more lenient sentences for murder. There are indications that this disparity is changing.

In 1986, the mean maximum sentence length for new female court commitments for murder was 16.7 years (Greenfeld and Minor-Harper, 1991: 4). Thus, from 1986 to 1991 there was an average increase of nine years in the sentence length of women incarcerated for murder. Further, in 1986 the women who served time in prison for murder and were released had served an average of 3.5 years (Greenfeld and Minor-Harper, 1991: 4), but by 1989 the mean number of years women had served by the time of release was 4.9 years, an increase of 1.4 years from the earlier period (Perkins, 1992: 26). As Champion (1990: 325) observes, it is conceivable that as determinate and mandatory sentencing policies become consistent practices, in the future there will be a gradual elimination of differences in sentencing based on gender.

The lack of male comparison groups in this study makes it difficult to establish whether women are "getting away with murder" or have an "open license to kill," as some have charged. Considering the seriousness of the crime, there is some evidence that as indicated by the official reports cited earlier, women murderers are not treated as harshly by the criminal justice system as one would expect. Killing a stranger, particularly when the motive is economic, is generally viewed as the victim-offender relationship most severely punished. Possible support for the position of more lenient treatment of female offenders by the courts is suggested by the finding that more than half of the women sentenced to prison for murdering strangers and acquaintances—that is, people they didn't know or hardly knew—received prison time of under ten years. In fact, the average sentence for killing *anyone* was only 7.1 years (Table 6.1). As mentioned earlier, the mean length of sentence women received for murder in 1986 was 16.7 years, which by 1989 had increased to 19.7 years; both of these averages are more than twice the prison time allocated in this study. Even though the average length of sentence for murder dispensed to females is less than that of males, it is apparent that over the years the criminal justice system has become increasingly more stringent toward women murderers.

If women are "getting away with murder," or are treated less punitively when they murder men, more lenient treatment would be expected when they killed males than when their victims were other females. Yet there were no significant differences in the criminal justice processing of women based on the gender of their victims. On the contrary, while the differences were not statistically significant, prison sentences were slightly more frequent among women who killed males and longer prison times were meted out in such cases than to those women who murdered females. The question of whether women are getting away with murder remains unanswered.

SUMMARY

Women arrested for killing other human beings in 1979 and 1983 began their journey through the criminal justice system in the usual way—with reasonable bonds and, for most, an initial charge of murder. But as they moved further into the system, almost two-thirds of the charges were reduced from murder to some form of manslaughter or a lesser charge, fewer than half received prison sentences, and those who did were assessed an average prison time of 7.1 years. Since more than half of the female homicide offenders studied had prior arrest records, including over one-third who had previously been arrested for violent crimes, it might be concluded that indeed women were "getting away with murder." Further analyses challenge such a notion but do not erase it.

There is a great deal of variation in the female murderers' criminal justice histories and processing across the six cities studied, and significant differences between the cities on these indices, suggesting that perhaps women are getting away with murder in some U.S. cities. But this does not appear to be true in southern cities that were significantly more likely than nonsouthern cities to assess a final charge of murder or manslaughter to female killers, and to impose longer prison and probation terms.

An essential part of the argument that women are getting away with murder is gender-based. Those making such a claim are really insisting that women are getting away with the murder of men. The data do not support such a notion. Comparisons between the defendants' criminal justice processing based on whether the victim is male or female reveal no significant differences between any of the variables examined. However, the differences found do indicate that women who kill men receive more serious final charges, and are sentenced to prison more frequently and for longer periods of time than women with female victims.

Another well-established view is that men of color, especially African American men, are treated more harshly by the criminal justice system because of racial discrimination endemic in the system. Although nonwhite women who killed were slightly less likely to have prior arrest records than white homicide offenders, they were significantly more likely to be initially and finally charged with the most serious crimes of murder or manslaughter. This was particularly true for African American female homicide offenders. Despite the more critical charges, nonwhites did not differ significantly from whites in prison sentences or prison time to serve.

This study of women murderers also tested the "devaluation of black lives" theory. According to this thesis—which is more frequently applied in death penalty analyses—stricter sentences would be dispensed to the killers of whites than to those who killed blacks. An expanded application of devaluation theory examined here suggests that every step of the criminal justice process could also indicate devaluation of black lives: lower bonds set, less serious initial and final charges, fewer prison dispositions, and less prison time imposed in cases with black victims. Little statistical support was found for the devaluation perspective as applied to the homicide victims of women. The single difference supporting *a* devaluation theory was that the average prison sentence of women who killed whites was significantly higher than that for women who killed nonwhites. But the devaluation theory was found to be more applicable to Hispanic Americans: killers of Latino victims were more leniently treated than those who murdered African Americans.

Analyses based on the victim/offender relationship revealed few significant differences in criminal justice processing. Women who killed their children were assigned the highest bonds significantly more often than those who killed other family members or sexual intimates, but were least likely to receive the more serious final charges of murder or manslaughter. A comparison of nonfamily victim/offender relationships disclosed a single significant result—the killers of friends and strangers received prison sentences more frequently than women who killed acquaintances.

Two independent variables were significant in the multiple regression analysis of prison time. Region, the first variable, and a major contributor to longer prison sentences, corresponds with the previously identified punitiveness in the criminal justice systems of the southern cities. The second variable, motive for the murder, while reflecting logical and legal reasoning as a determinant of the length of a prison sentence, also presents a number of definitional problems. These are addressed in the next chapter.

NOTES

1. Over the past six years, such comments have been received by the author in the form of telephone calls and correspondence from a number of men representing groups who challenge the notion of the "battered woman syndrome" as a defense for spousal murder and the leniency in the sentencing of women who kill men.

2. Tables containing detailed information on misdemeanor and felony arrests and convictions are located in Appendix C.

3. Child abuse is a separate category.

4. These five women are not included in the statistical calculations.

5. For an in-depth explanation of this concept, see Hawkins (1986). As applied to women homicide offenders, see Mann (1990).

6. $X^2 = 8.70$ with 2 df.

7. In criminal court observations, Mann (1984b) reports that some of the judges in the study felt that sending a woman felon who had children to prison would result in a double financial burden on the state: the costs of maintaining the woman in prison and the costs of providing for her children while she serves her sentence.

8. As indicated earlier, the female homicide offenders who were intimately related to their victims also tended to have had previous dealings with the criminal justice system. These women differed significantly in such experience from those whose victims were acquaintances or strangers. A comparison of stranger/acquaintance homicides with cases in which the victims were well known (intimate plus friends) revealed a significant difference in prior arrest records between these groups (p = .03; $X^2 = 4.67$ at 2 df). However, the groups were not distinguished in terms of violent arrest histories.

9. Further support for this position is seen in the finding that offenders whose victims were well known to them did not differ significantly with regard to prison sentences from the subgroup with stranger or acquaintance victims. While 42 percent of the female homicide offenders who killed someone close to them received prison sentences, so did 44.8 percent of those who killed strangers or acquaintances.

10. The significance of this difference was .02, $X^2 = 5.01$ at 1df.

Chapter 7

A Profile of Today's Female Killer

More than three-fourths of the females who were arrested for murder in the six cities included in this study were African American; 12.8 percent were white and 9.5 percent were Latina. No other racial/ethnic groups surfaced in the city samples. The offenders ranged from twelve to sixty-five years of age, with a mean age of thirty-one. Most of the arrestees were in a status defined as *once married*, that is, either married, common-law married, separated, divorced, or widowed (which does not include widowhood resulting from the homicide). Only 40 percent were single. A majority of the women who killed were mothers (69.5 percent). They had on average almost eleven years of education and tended to be unemployed (71.0 percent). More than half had records of previous arrests, and 35 percent had prior arrest histories for the commission of violent crimes.

Thus, a summary profile of today's typical female homicide offender reveals her to be a single, thirty-one-year-old, unemployed African American mother with less than a high school education who has been arrested in the past. This description fits the profile of female homicide offenders that Hanke and Shields (1992) recently referred to as "ordinary." In their study of the records of 746 women incarcerated for murder in Alabama over five and a half decades (1929 to 1985), Hanke and Shields report:

> Contrary to the negative and exotic images of the female homicide offender given to us through the media's eyes, these women did not appear to be anything except ordinary women. Even the circumstances appeared ordinary; that is, these homicides occurred in homes, were committed against known persons (family or friends), usually happened as the result of some type of quarrel, and were most frequently carried out by means of knives or firearms, readily available to most people. Images of warped and strange methods of operation or lady-like poisonings were not borne out across 5-1/2 decades of Alabama women homicide offenders (Hanke and Shields, 1992:21).

The Victims and Their Homicides

The demographics of the victims closely resembled those of their killers: 74.3 percent were African American, 15.5 percent white, and 10.1 percent Hispanic. There were slightly fewer African Americans and more whites and Hispanics within the victim group than in the offender group. The homicide victims were also a little older than their killers, having a mean age of thirty-three years, and ranging in age from one to ninety-four. Males predominated among the victims (80.7 percent), and 62.6 percent of them had prior arrest records; 45.1 percent had previous arrests for the commission of violent crimes. Of the victims, 44.3 percent were in intimate interpersonal relationships with their killers, 25.6 percent were friends and acquaintances, 10.9 percent were the offenders' own children, and 7.5 percent were strangers; other relatives made up the remaining homicide victims.

The typical murder took place on a weekend, usually after midnight on a Friday or Saturday, and occurred in the living room of a residence that was shared by the offender and her victim. In only a few instances were accomplices involved; the woman was usually the lone perpetrator (82.2 percent). More than one-third of the women offenders and almost half of the victims had been drinking at the time the homicide took place. The female offenders were slightly more likely than their victims to have used drugs prior to the homicide. A firearm was the weapon of choice in 46.6 percent of the murders, followed by a knife (37.8 percent).

It appeared that victims contributed to their own deaths in a significant number of the cases (65.7 percent). Although self-defense was the most frequent motive given by the female homicide offenders, in 92.2 percent of the cases they were initially charged with murder. From the records it was determined that more than half of the killings were premeditated, and 79.3 percent of those perpetrators were charged originally with first degree murder. But in the final court determinations, only 26.5 percent of the women were accorded a first degree murder charge. Less than half of the defendants received prison sentences (42.6 percent), ranging from one year to life, with an average term of 7.1 years. Overall, more than two-thirds of the convicted female murderers were sentenced to less than ten years in prison.

ADDRESSING THE RESEARCH QUESTIONS

1. *Is the "subculture of violence" theory applicable to African American female homicide offenders?*

Subculture theory asserts that violent behavior and homicide are especially endemic in African American urban communities, and since the related crime-causing values are transmitted through generations, presumably females would not be exempt from their effects. No statistical evidence was found among either the demographic or the criminal justice history variables to suggest that the subculture of violence theory is applicable to African American women who kill.

The comparisons of the female homicide offenders on a number of demographic characteristics by race and ethnicity presented in Table 7.1, and previously detailed in chapter 5 (see Tables 5.9 and 5.10), indicate that most social characteristics of women who kill are not differentiated by race/ethnicity. In fact, the demographic profile reveals only two statistically significant differences between white, African American, and Latina homicide offenders. First, the significant difference in education found between the three racial/ethnic subgroups is primarily related to the low average number of years of schooling attained by Latinas. In mean number of years of education, Latinas lagged more than three years behind African Americans and more than two years behind whites. Although African American offenders had the highest average number of school years completed, a higher proportion of whites had some college education. None of the Latinas had progressed beyond high school.

The second significant racial/ethnic difference is that women of color, particularly Latinas, were more likely to be mothers. Also, while not a significant difference, it should be noted that compared to their white and African American counterparts, Latinas who killed were most likely to be married or once married (p = .06). Whereas 80 percent of Latinas and 65.7 percent of whites were described as having some form of marital status, only 56.6 percent of the African American women fell into this category.

2. *Is there any validity to the "southern subculture of violence" theory as applied to women killers?*

One of the major tenets of those suggesting that southerners are more violent than citizens in other regions is the alleged southern affinity for guns. Southern women murderers in the study were significantly more likely to use firearms, especially long guns, in their murders. In turn, their victims were also significantly more likely to have been drinking prior to their deaths and to have precipitated the murders. Overall, however, the southern and nonsouthern female homicide offenders in the study were more similar than dissimilar; thus, only very modest support was found for the application of the southern violence theory to women who kill.

3. *Is an economic theory of crime applicable to women who commit homicide?*

There are at least two ways to approach an examination of economics as the basis for homicide. The standard explanation involves poverty or

Table 7.1

Demographic Profile of Offenders by Race/Ethnicity, in percentages[1]

Characteristic	All Cases (N = 296)	White (N = 38)	African American (N = 230)	Hispanic American (N = 28)	Significance
Age	(Mean = 31.0 years)	(Mean = 29.2 years)	(Mean = 31 years)	(Mean = 33.3 years)	
19 and under	10.8	5.3	12.6	3.6	
20–29	43.9	60.5	41.3	42.9	
30–39	24.3	18.4	24.3	32.1	
40–49	13.9	5.3	15.2	14.3	
50 and over	7.1	10.5	6.5	7.1	
Education	(Mean = 10.7 years)	(Mean = 9.7 years)	(Mean = 10.9 years)	(Mean = 7.5 years)	
0 thru 8 years	3.7	5.3	3.0	7.1	p = .006
9 thru 12 years	28.7	23.7	33.0	92.9	X^2 = 14.46, 4 df
13 years and above	67.6	71.1	63.9	—	
Employed					
Yes	29.0	37.5	27.7	27.8	
No	71.0	62.5	72.3	72.2	
Marital Status					
Single	39.9	34.3	43.4	20.0	
Once Married	60.1	65.7	56.6	80.0	
Motherhood					
Yes	69.5	56.7	68.6	95.0	p = .01
No	30.5	43.3	31.4	5.0	X^2 = 8.51, 2 df

1. Does not include missing cases.

similar indices of the lack of material wealth. From this viewpoint, the argument is that the stresses and strains of unemployment, underemployment, or low income, especially in urban areas, can lead to insurmountable frustrations that result in murder. In such instances the victims tend to be those close to their killers, and domestic homicide results. Unfortunately, employment was the only available measure of economic status. While a number of offender and homicide characteristics significantly differentiated domestic from nondomestic murders, the data are insufficient to support this aspect of the economic theory of homicide, particularly since it was found that the domestic killers were more frequently employed (Table 4.6). The findings that female domestic killers were also significantly more likely to be mothers, to claim self-defense, and to face victims who precipitated their murders, might suggest situations indicative of frustration, but the link to economics is missing.

A second possible indication of economic motivation in female-perpetrated homicide is found in the commission of felony murder for economic gain, the most common example of which is the killings of strangers. Although the evidence is not compelling, there seems to be reserved support for this aspect of economic theory. Women were significantly more likely to kill strangers for economic benefit in the classic fashion—with little victim provocation, outside of residences, with accomplices, and with guns.

4. *How significant is the role played by drugs (alcohol and narcotics) in female-perpetrated homicides?*

The use of alcohol by both female offenders and their victims was far more prevalent than drug (narcotics) use prior to the murders. More than a third of the women killers had been drinking, as had 46.7 percent of their victims. In 17 percent of the cases, autopsies revealed that the victims were legally drunk. Comparisons of the social characteristics of offenders who had used substances with those who had not revealed only a single significant difference—female users tended to be older. However, an examination of the prior arrest records of the women killers, shown in Table 7.2, indicates that, as a group, women users had significantly more previous arrests and violent arrests than the nonusers. While this finding implies a more marginal or criminal user group, it is the differences between victims that suggest that alcohol, but not drugs, does play a major role in female-perpetrated homicide.

As reported in chapter 3, victims who had been drinking were also much more likely to have precipitated their own deaths. This significant difference supports earlier research indicating that alcohol further loosens inhibitions in already volatile situations, and can result in lethal violence. Also, the finding that the victims of substance users were significantly more likely to be drinking than the victims of nonusing offenders rein-

Table 7.2

Criminal Justice Characteristics by Substance Users and Nonusers[1]

	Offender Type		
Characteristic	Users (N = 96)	Nonusers (N = 137)	Significance
Prior arrests			
Yes	70.9	39.8	p = .0000
No	29.1	60.2	X² = 18.08; 1 df
Violent arrest history			
Yes	50.0	22.5	p = .0001
No	50.0	77.5	X² = 14.81; 1 df
Initial charge			
Murder/manslaughter	96.8	98.5	
Other	3.2	1.5	
Final charge			
Murder/manslaughter	76.9	73.3	
Other	23.1	26.7	
Final Disposition			
Prison	44.9	41.0	
No prison	55.1	59.0	
(mean years)	(5.7)	(6.9)	
Prison time			
Under 10 yrs.	78.9	71.1	
10 yrs. and over	21.1	28.9	

1. Does not include missing data.

forces the negative influence of alcohol on homicide. In other words, women who had used alcohol themselves encountered victim precipitation from alcohol-using victims significantly more frequently than women who had not been drinking.

Considering the types of drugs most commonly used in the time period of the study, the use of drugs such as "crack" cocaine was not the influential factor in homicide it is believed to be today. Although many of the murders committed by the 12.6 percent of women who had used drugs prior to the lethal event were heinous, the possible influence of drug use in female-perpetrated murder could not be determined.

5. *Can victim precipitation and/or the "battered woman syndrome" predict female criminal homicide?*

The finding that 65.7 percent of the homicides in this study were victim-precipitated seems somewhat high and more closely resembles the confrontational outcomes in male-perpetrated homicides. For example, Wolfgang (1958: 255) reported that 94 percent of the men killed in his Philadelphia study had instigated their murders, but only 29 percent of the victim-precipitated homicides in that study were committed by females against males (ibid., p. 259). A slightly higher proportion of 50 percent was reported some twenty years later by Gibbs, Silverman, and Vega (1977). And more recently, Winn, Haugen, and Jurik (1988) found that male offenders were more likely than their victims to escalate a confrontation into a physical attack. They report an opposite finding when women were the homicide offenders—in only 25 percent of the cases involving male perpetrators did the victims provoke the crime, but when women killed, their victims started the altercation that culminated in their deaths 50 percent of the time.

Even though the proportion of women who were provoked into killing is higher in this study than in others, it seems clear that victim precipitation is a major contributing factor in female-perpetrated murders. As we will later demonstrate, the higher frequency found is probably related to the problem of defining victim precipitation in this study.

The "Battered Woman Syndrome"

Since the battered woman syndrome could not be specifically tested in this study, it is difficult to reject its applicability to these findings. The importance of this significant social problem and the plight of the desperate women who face abuse on a daily basis cannot be ignored. Nonetheless, evidence of the battered woman syndrome *as legally defined* and reported in the literature cannot be established conclusively by these findings.

Among many findings listed by Lenore Walker, who is one of the most respected experts on the battered woman syndrome, three-fourths of her sample of battered women were employed, "the violence always escalated in frequency and severity over time," and the women were more likely to be married to their batterers (1984: 148–49). Also, 80 percent of the battered women in her sample were white, 8 percent were Hispanic, and 6 percent were African American (ibid., p. 156). None of these characteristics coincide with the profile of the female homicide offenders in this study—the majority of whom were single, African American, and unemployed. Nor was there evidence of frequent violence against the majority of the offenders. On the contrary, it appeared that if there was a domestic fight, these women won.

"Learned helplessness" is a psychological state frequently attributed to battered women. In this condition "the woman is psychologically locked into her situation due to economic dependence on the man, an abiding attachment to him, and the failure of the legal system to adequately respond to the problem" (Schneider, 1989:57). There were no indications that the women in this study were experiencing "learned helplessness." Since 40 percent of the offenders were single and 31.3 percent were in not a legal but a common-law marriage with their victims, if they were being maltreated, presumably they could have left the abuser.

In any event, intensive examination of the cases did not produce a profile of these women that suggested helplessness.

The battered woman syndrome is frequently employed in homicide cases as a rationale for self-defense and implies that the murder was "reasonable and necessary" because the offender "reasonably believed she was in imminent danger of serious bodily harm or death and that the force she used was necessary to avoid that danger" (Thar, 1982: 353). Several of the findings in this study are contrary to such a defense. The finding of premeditation in more than half of the cases challenges both the idea of "reasonableness" and the "objective immediacy standard," that is, the belief that one is in immediate danger (Eber, 1981: 928). Finally, the fact that almost half of the domestic homicide offenders had prior arrest histories, including 30 percent who had previously been arrested for violent crimes, belies a suggestion that they were either helpless or afraid of their victims.

In light of the above contradictions, it would appear that the women in this study did not kill because they were battered. Yet other factors could be interpreted otherwise. Compared to nondomestic female killers, women who killed sexual intimates differed significantly on two variables which could be construed as related to battering—motive and victim precipitation. Domestic killers claimed self-defense three times more frequently than nondomestic murderers, and victim precipitation was indicated in 83.7 percent of the domestic cases (see Table 4.7). Further, the victims in domestic murders were significantly more likely than their nondomestic counterparts to have prior arrest records and violent histories, and to have been drinking prior to their deaths. These are all possible contributing characteristics to abusive behavior. Finally, Table 7.3 reveals a number of significant differences in the criminal justice system processing of domestic and nondomestic offenders that might support the battered woman perspective. Female domestic killers were more likely to be released on bail, less likely to be charged with murder—both initially and finally—and less likely to be sentenced to prison or probation than the nondomestic killers. It is conceivable that the criminal courts were more lenient in cases of domestic lethal violence because the defendants' claims of self-defense and victim precipitation were seen as valid.

6. *Are ecological factors—season, weather, time, day of week—influential in murders committed by females?*

Time, day, and place are consistent factors in female-perpetrated lethal violence. As noted above, women usually kill in residences, at night, and on weekends—especially Saturdays. On the other hand, season and weather did not appear to be influential. Since only a few of the six cities listed the temperature and weather conditions at the time of a

Table 7.3

Criminal Justice History and Processing by Offender Type (in percentages)[1]

| | Offender Type | | |
Category	Domestic	Nondomestic	Significance
Prior arrests			
Yes	49.2	58.8	
No	50.8	41.2	
Violent history			
Yes	30.0	37.5	
No	70.0	62.5	
Bail			
Released	32.9	17.7	p = .04
Bond set	67.1	82.3	X^2 = 4.21; 1 df
Initial charge			
Murder	89.6	95.9	p = .01
Voluntary manslaughter	5.6	—	X^2 = 8.65; 2 df
All other	4.9	4.1	
Final charge			
Murder	28.1	33.6	p = .01
Voluntary manslaughter	52.8	37.4	X^2 = 8.34; 2 df
All other	19.1	29.0	
Sentence			
None[2]	49.6	33.6	p = .01
Prison	37.0	48.9	X^2 = 7.03; 2 df
Probation	13.3	17.6	
Prison time			
Under 10 yrs.	74.5	60.9	
10 yrs.–life	25.5	39.1	

1. Does not include missing cases.
2. Includes no bill, acquitted, dismissed, nolle prosequi.

homicide, weather was difficult to define. The only available measure of weather—months when the homicides were committed—is viewed as questionable because of the weather variations between the cities, but in any event, no significant differences were revealed.

7. *Are minority women who murder treated more punitively by the criminal justice system than nonminority women?*

There is ample evidence to suggest that men of color who kill, particularly African American men, are treated more punitively by the criminal justice system than their white counterparts (see Mann, 1993). However, the findings of this study generally do not support a notion of more severe criminal justice treatment of *women* of color who kill, particularly of African American women murderers. The only significant differences found between the criminal justice processing of white and nonwhite female homicide offenders were in the charges brought against them. Nonwhites, especially African Americans, were more frequently assigned the most serious initial and final murder charges than white female killers. Thereafter, neither sentences to prison nor the number of years of the sentences significantly differentiated whites and nonwhites.

While it could be argued that by levying the most serious charges, the criminal justice system effectively labeled nonwhite female homicide offenders as murderers, and this appellation might have deleterious effects on the defendants' cases as they progressed through the stages of the judicial system, such a speculation cannot be supported by the statistical evidence of the study.

8. *Does the race of the victim influence the sentencing process?*

Critics who view the criminal justice system as racist argue that it is especially harsh when African Americans murder whites. Statistical significance based on race/ethnicity was again found only in the final charge, but in the *opposite* direction from what was expected. The female killers of nonwhites, especially those with African American victims, were most likely to be given the more serious final charge of murder. Although women who killed whites received prison sentences more often and were given longer prison terms than women who killed nonwhites, these differences did not attain statistical significance (see Table 6.8).

9. *Are there city/"regional" differences in the criminal court processing of women who kill?*

There was tremendous diversity in the criminal justice processing across the six study cities. Since the practices of assigning bail, charging, and sentencing exhibit no consistent patterns, one wonders how justice is carried out in most of these cities (see Table 6.4). Only Chicago and New York City demonstrated processes that seemed to conform to an appropriate model of justice.

Compared to nonsouthern cities, cities in the South were more punitive toward female homicide offenders in all but one of the statistically significant measures of criminal justice system processing. While nonsouthern city courts did assign higher bond amounts, the southern courts were significantly more likely to extend the more serious final charge of murder/manslaughter and longer prison and probation times to women who killed. The South is clearly not the place for a woman to be arrested for murder.

STUDY LIMITATIONS AND CAVEATS

For the most part, obtaining a profile of women who kill was rather straightforward. There was a vexing amount of missing data on some of the variables, for example, on education and employment, but criminal justice data and characteristics of the homicides were fairly well recorded. On the question of missing data, it is reassuring to note that in their

Arizona study, Winn, Haugen, and Jurik (1988) found that women's homicide records were far more complete than those of men. Winn et al. did not offer an explanation for this gender difference, but it is possible that the relative rarity of female cases led to more careful scrutiny than in the more frequent cases involving male offenders.

An especially serious problem of definition and interpretation was encountered immediately during the preliminary examinations of the homicide records. Three crucial variables determined in previous research as those most influential in sentencing decisions—motive, premeditation of the murder, and victim precipitation—were the most difficult to define. A conservative approach and the extreme caution used in the definition and examination of these variables are believed to validate the interpretations found in the analyses.

The Rationales of Female Murderers

Often an in-depth reading of a specific case led to a different interpretation of the motive recorded in the homicide report. Thus, the difficulty of defining *motive* is viewed as the major limitation in the study. Fourteen possible homicide motives, plus an "unknown" category that includes cases in which the motive was not determined, were identified in the study. The fourteen motive variables were collapsed into two groupings for statistical analysis: *not responsible* (innocent, self-defense, accident, other's fault, defense of others, under the influence, physiological, psychological, and justifiable) and *responsible* for the murder (emotional, economic, argument/fight, senseless, and multiple reasons). A further refinement differentiated *psychological* motives from *emotional* ones. In the first instance, only offenders demonstrated to be mentally ill were seen as having psychological motives. Emotional motives included rage, jealousy, anger, and revenge. Although difficult to define, *senseless* murders were easily identified and distinguished from those in which the motive was classified as either psychological or emotional. "Senseless" homicides can probably be most closely described as involving simple meanness or sociopathic behavior.

Not surprisingly, the most frequent motives given by female homicide offenders were self-defense (38.9 percent), innocent (14.7 percent), accident (11.6 percent), and emotional (10.9 percent). Collectively, these rationales account for 76.1 percent of the identified motives. In light of other research findings on motives in female-perpetrated homicide, these self-explanations seemed questionable. Weisheit (1984: 485), for example, found the following ordering of the primary motives among female homicide offenders incarcerated in the 1940–1966 period: revenge (37 percent), response to abuse (22 percent), robbery (18 percent), and "other" (23 percent). By the 1981–1983 period, robbery (42 percent) had replaced revenge as the primary homicide motive, response to abuse had decreased to 17 percent, revenge declined to 12 percent, and all other motives made up the remaining 29 percent (ibid., p. 486).

While the data in the present study were being coded, it was observed that the motives recorded in the homicide files were based on statements made by the female killers as to why they committed the murders. But they did not necessarily represent *substantiated* motives. In many of the cases, the suspects' given reasons for the killings were not particularly convincing. In response, a variable, *motivan*, was created to compare analyses of the declared motives given by the female murderers from the "facts" of the case located in various official reports of the homicides. The frequencies for the motivan variable yielded a striking new ordering of the primary motives which together totaled 79 percent of the possible motives: argument/fight (48.6 percent), emotional (19.3 percent), and economic (11.1 percent). Both self-defense and emotional motives could be implied when there is an argument or fight with a victim, but curiously, the offenders did not admit to these possible determinants in their recorded statements. Since the motivan variable was derived solely by the researcher and lacked other coder verification, motivan was not used in the analyses reported throughout this volume. Its development and the partial findings on this variable are reported here as guidelines for future research efforts.

Premeditation of the Murders

Closely related to defining motive was the problem of determining *premeditation* of a murder. In many ways deciding wehther a murder was preplanned is even more complex than defining motive. In a number of cases the homicide reports indicated that premeditation had occurred. However, such official conclusions are often as fraught with subjectivity as interpretations made by researchers. To resolve the dilemma, only cases with clear indications of planning—for example, buying a gun; stashing a knife; or the offender's telling another person that she was going to kill the victim—were viewed as evidence of premeditation. Despite these precautions, the finding that more than half of the murders were premeditated does not coincide with results reported in similar research. For example, Winn, Haugen, and Jurik (1988) indicate that only 27 percent of the women in their study preplanned their homicides. This is about half of the proportion reported here.

Victim Precipitation

Defining *victim precipitation* presented another dilemma. Since police and homicide records rarely contain the term, clarification of the possible contribution of the victim to his/her homicide relies to a certain extent upon subjective assessments of the facts in each case.

In light of the recent proliferation of diverse opinions concerning the battered woman syndrome and its connection to female-perpetrated homicide, the issue of victim provocation is particularly sensitive. To conclude that victim precipitation had indeed occurred, it was necessary to minutely examine the victim/offender interaction both prior to as well as in relation to the homicide event. When this careful and rigorous examination was hampered by a lack of detail in some of the files, any attempt to determine victim precipitation was abandoned.

CONCLUSIONS AND RECOMMENDATIONS FOR FUTURE RESEARCH

Little support was found in this study for the notion that women are becoming more violent, at least as measured by the commission of homicide. Total arrest trends by sex from 1983 to 1987 reveal an 8.1 percent *decrease* in female arrests for murder and nonnegligent manslaughter, but an *increase* of 16.4 percent in arrests for all violent crimes by females (U.S. Department of Justice, 1988: 171). The most recent Uniform Crime Reports (1993: 224) continue to reflect these trends. While female arrests for murder and nonnegligent manslaughter decreased 9.6 percent from 1988 to 1992, female arrests for violent crimes increased 32.5 percent during this time period. Also, between 1979 and 1983, the years of this study, female arrests for murder decreased 19.5 percent for the total sample of female homicide offenders. Women who kill have historically been viewed as poisoners or slayers of their infants and children, either distancing themselves from their victims or preying upon helpless victims. In more recent years, a majority of the women sentenced to death row have committed heinous murders. Yet, the results reported in this volume do not produce a profile of monstrous female killers. One standard measure of cold-blooded murder is the felony killing of strangers or acquaintances for economic benefit. But the subgroup of females who killed strangers and acquaintances differed little from the other female homicide offenders in the sample. Studies of female homicide offenders over long periods of time, such as Weisheit's forty-four-year research span (1984), show little change in the proportions of those who kill strangers, while the number of women who kill acquaintances is increasing and appears to fluctuate (see Table 1.1).

Almost two decades ago, in her seminal work *Sisters in Crime*, Freda Adler stated, "Women are indeed committing more crimes than ever before. Those crimes involve a greater degree of violence" (1975: 3). Adler later qualified her initial statement by noting, "Murder and aggravated assault, curiously, remain the exception" (ibid., p. 16). The findings on women murderers in this study reinforce Adler's position by suggesting that women remain the exception and are *not* the deadliest of the species.

Recommendations

Exploratory research often generates substantially more questions than were initially proposed. This study is no exception. Its design now appears woefully inadequate to address the problem of violence, specifically homicide and, more important, its prevention. The following recommendations are an amalgam of thoughts stimulated by this research and concerns expressed by others.

Data collection should include more accurate, operationally defined descriptions of motive, premeditation, and victim precipitation. The height and weight of both offenders and victims should be obtained in order to determine whether female offenders, particulary in domestic homicide cases, really are at a physical disadvantage that requires "equalization" through the use of a weapon that often culminates in homicide. We also need to devote "special attention to the number of wounds inflicted on the victim" (Mann, 1988: 50). In 57 percent of the cases studied, only a single wound was inflicted, yet the victim died. More information is needed on the deployment and quality of medical and emergency services involved in the homicide incident. In urban minority communities there is a paucity of most social services and a history of poor police, ambulance, and medical/hospital services. With timely ambulance service and proper and prompt medical care, perhaps homicides would have been only assaults.

While police and homicide records may be more detailed than some data sources, a reliance on them can be a handicap. Larger and more comprehensive samples should be drawn to include both male and female homicide offenders. As Wilbanks has said, "The attempt to gain greater 'depth' of information . . . should be matched by efforts to obtain 'breadth'—that is, data obtained in one jurisdiction should be compared with those found in other jurisdictions" (1982: 177). Future homicide studies should ensure that every state is represented, and rural, suburban, and urban areas must be included appropriately.

In order to tap the changes in women's lifestyles and life circumstances and include "a method that captures the micro-level interactional dynamics of the situations in which women kill as well as the structural-historical forces that form the context in which such interactions and events occur" (Gregware and Jurik, n.d.: 2), future homicide research efforts should also be longitudinal. For example, to more fully understand the dynamics of "learned helplessness," we need to know the level of an offender's economic dependence, if any, on the victim. Gregware and

Jurik suggests that methods of acquiring such data might include "psycho-logical profiles and an analysis of the interactions surrounding the homi-cide event" (p. 32), "documentary study with indepth interviews of defendants, third parties, and witnesses" (p. 32), and "broader social, political, economic, and historical contexts" (p. 33).

In addition to these research methods, court observations and the collection of detailed court data—for example, presentence investigation reports (PSIs)—could provide a valuable source of frequently omitted data. Qualitative court data are especially needed in the study of female homicide offenders, who are believed to be favorably treated by the courts because of their gender. In contrast, peoples of color have been found to be discriminated against by the courts in the deliberations of their homicide cases. Also, we should know what subtleties exist in the courtroom setting that impact decisions and the roles that courtroom actors (judges, attorneys, probation officers) play in murder cases. Actual observations of trials can answer such questions. Only through the use of more comprehensive, eclectic methods of information gathering can we obtain the necessary knowledge to approach the intervention and preven-tion of violence, and the ultimate violence, homicide.

Appendix A: Research Protocol

Data Collection Form

Female Homicide Offenders

I. General Information

Case #_____ City: ATL___ CHGO___ HOU___ NYC___ Balt___ LA___
Year: 1979___ 1983___ Arrest Date: Month___ Day___
Change: Murder 1___ Murder 2___ Mansl___

II. Offender Characteristics

Ethnicity: Afro___ Cau___ Hisp___ Native___ Asian___ Other___
Age:___ Birthday: Month___ Day___ Year___
Birthplace: (state)_____
Marital Status: Single___ Mar___ Sep___ Div___ Wid___
No. Children:___ Ages: 1___ 2___ 3___ 4___ 5___ 6___
        7___ 8___ 9___ 10___ 11___ 12___
Education (years):___ Diploma: Yes___ No___ GED: Yes___ No___
College (years):___ Degree: AA___ BA/BS___ MA/MS___ Doctorate___
Employed: Yes___ No___   On Welfare: Yes___ No___
Type Employment:_____

III. Victim Characteristics

Ethnicity: Afro___ Cau___ Hisp___ Native___ Asian___ Other___
Age:___ Birthday: Month___ Day___ Year___   Sex: Male___ Female___
Victim Occupation:_____
Victim/Offender Relationship:
Married___ Divorced___ Common-law___ Lovers___ Friends___ Acquaintances___
Strangers___ Child___ Parent___ Other relative___ Commercial personnel___
Other___ Not known___

IV. Offense Characteristics

Premeditation: Yes___ No___ Not known___
Time of Offense: Month___ Day___ Year___ Time___ AM___ PM___ Not Known___
Location: Offender's Neighborhood:___   Offender's Residence:___
        Victim's Residence:___   Other Residence:___
Location in residence: Living Room:___ Dining Room:___ Bedroom:___ Kitchen:___
Bath:___ Foyer/Hall:___ Porch:___ Yard:___ Basement:___ Driveway:___ Street:___
Other:___ Not Known___
Away from Residence (location):_____
Offender's Role: Sole Perpetrator___ Conspirator___ Accessory___ Partner___
Not-Known___
If Crime Partner, Relation to Offender:
Husband___ Lover___ Friend___ Acquaintance___ Relative___ Other___
Offender's Rationale/Motive: Innocent___ Self Defense___ Fighting/Argument___
Defense of other(s)___ Justifiable___ Under Influence___ Accident___ Senseless___

Other's Fault___ Economic Reasons___ Psychological Reasons___ Emotional___
Physical Reasons (e.g. PMS)___ Multiple Reasons___ Other (List)___ No Information___
Sex of Crime Partner: Male___ Female___
Race of Crime Partner: Afro___ Cau___ Hisp___ Native___ Asian___ Other___
Weapon/Method Used: Gun___ Knife___ Household tool___ Poison (lye, etc.)___
Clubbing weapon (bat. bottle, etc.)___ Hands/Feet___ Strangulation___ Drowning___
Other___
Alcohol Involvement: Offender: Yes___ No___ Victim: Yes___ No___
Narcotics Involvement: Offender: Yes___ No___ Victim: Yes___ No___
Victim's Condition: Helpless (child)___ Ill___ Asleep___ Drunk___ Infirm (adult)___
Not Incapacitated___ Incapacitated___ No info___

V. *Criminal History*

Offender:
Previous Misdemeanor Arrests: None___
    Number/Charge 1___ 3___ 5___
               2___ 4___ 6___
Previous Misdemeanor Convictions: None___
    Number/Charge 1___ 3___ 5___
               2___ 4___ 6___
Previous Felony Arrests: None___
    Number/Charge 1___ 3___ 5___
               2___ 4___ 6___
Previous Felony Convictions: None___
    Number/Charge 1___ 3___ 5___
               2___ 4___ 6___
Unknown___
Victim:
Previous Misdemeanor Arrests: None___
    Number/Charge 1___ 3___ 5___
               2___ 4___ 6___
Previous Misdemeanor Convictions: None___
    Number/Charge 1___ 3___ 5___
               2___ 4___ 6___
Previous Felony Arrests: None___
    Number/Charge 1___ 3___ 5___
               2___ 4___ 6___
Previous Felony Convictions: None___
    Number/Charge 1___ 3___ 5___
               2___ 4___ 6___
Unknown___

VI. *Court Disposition*

Guilty Plea: Yes___ No___ Mistrial___ Acquitted___ Dismissed___
*PSI recommendation*_____ Trial: Bench___ Jury___
First Offender Treatment: Yes___ No___
*Original Charge(s):*_____ *Convicted Charge(s)*_____
*Number:*_____
Prison:
Up to 1 year___ 1–5 years___ 5–10 years___ 10–15 years___ 15–20 years___
20± years___ Life___ Death___ Years to serve___
Probation:
Up to 1 year___ 1–5 years___ 5± years___ Halfway HSE___ Drug Treatment___
Other___
Name of Recorder_____
Notes/*Comments:*

Appendix B: Female Homicide Offender

Code Book

Variable Name	Column	Variable Description	Code
CITY	1	City studied	1 = Chicago 2 = Houston 3 = Atlanta 4 = Los Angeles 5 = New York City 6 = Baltimore
YEAR	2	Year studied	1 = 1979 2 = 1983
CASNUMB	3–4	Case number	01–50

OFFENSE DATA

Variable Name	Column	Variable Description	Code
ARSTDATE	5–10	Arrest date actual	MMDDYY 888888 = Not applicable 999999 = Missing data
CHARGE	11	Charge (original)	1 = Murder 1 2 = Murder 2 3 = Murder 4 = Vol. Mansl. 5 = Invol. Mansl. 6 = other 7 = Justifiable Homicide 8 = Negligent Homicide 9 = Missing data
AMTBOND	12–16	Amount of bond set	00000 = none 00001 = bond denied 00002 = ROR (Release on own Recognizance) 88888 = Not applicable 99998 = 100,000 (and plus) 99999 = Missing Data
DISPDAY	17–22	Day of final disposition	MMDDYY 888888 = Not applicable 999999 = Missing data
DISP	23	Final disposition	0 = prison and probation 1 = no bill 2 = acquittal 3 = dismissed

181

Variable Name	Column	Variable Description	Code
			4 = prison
			5 = probation
			6 = other (nolle prosse, mistrial, dead docket, etc.), juvenile
			7 = NPGJ. (no grand jury); justifiable
			8 = Not applicable
			9 = Missing data
PRITIME	24–25	Prison time; actual years	00 = less than one year
			88 = Not Applicable
			98 = Life
			99 = Missing Data
PROTIME	26–27	Probation time	actual years
			00 = less than one year
			88 = Not applicable
			99 = Missing data
PREMISAR	28–29	Previous misdemeanor arrests	actual number
			00 = None
			99 = Missing data
MISCON	30–31	Previous misdemeanor convictions	actual number
			00 = None
			99 = Missing data
PREFELAR	32–33	Previous felony arrests	actual number
			00 = None
			99 = Missing data
FELCON	34–35	Previous felony convictions	actual number
			00 = None
			99 = Missing data

OFFENDER CHARACTERISTICS

Variable Name	Column	Variable Description	Code
AGE	36–37	Age (as given)	99 = Missing data
BIRTHDATE	38–43	Birthday (as given) (date of birth)	MMDDYY
			999999 = Missing data
MARSTAT	44	Marital status	1 = single
			2 = married
			3 = common-law married
			4 = divorced
			5 = separated
			6 = widowed (not by the crime)
			9 = Missing data
RACE	45	Race of offender	1 = Afro-American
			2 = Caucasian
			3 = Hispanic
			4 = Asian
			5 = Native American
			6 = other
			9 = Missing data

Variable Name	Column	Variable Description	Code
EDUCATN	46–47	Actual years of education	Actual years 99 = Missing data
EMPLOY	48	Employment status	1 = Yes 2 = No 8 = Not applicable 9 = Missing data
MOTHER	49	Maternal status	1 = Yes 2 = No 8 = Not applicable 9 = Missing data
CHILDRN	50–51	Actual number of children	actual number 00 = None 88 = Not applicable 99 = Missing data

VICTIM CHARACTERISTICS

Variable Name	Column	Variable Description	Code
VAGE	52–53	Age of victim as given	actual years 00 = Less than one year 99 = Missing data
VBRTHDAY	54–59	Victim's date of birth	MMDDYY 999999 = Missing data
VRACE	60	Race of victim	1 = Afro-American 2 = Caucasian 3 = Hispanic 4 = Asian 5 = Native American 6 = Other 9 = Missing data
VREC	61	Victim's previous record	1 = Yes 2 = No 8 = Not applicable 9 = Missing data
VPREVMS	62	Victim's previous misdemeanor arrests	1 = Yes 2 = No 8 = Not applicable 9 = Missing data
VPREMCN	63	Victim's previous misdemeanor convictions	1 = Yes 2 = No 8 = Not applicable 9 = Missing data
VPREVFL	64	Victim's previous felony arrests	1 = Yes 2 = No 8 = Not applicable 9 = Missing data
VPREFCN	65	Victim's previous felony convictions	1 = Yes 2 = No 8 = Not applicable 9 = Missing data

Variable Name	Column	Variable Description	Code

VICTIM-OFFENDER RELATIONSHIP

Variable Name	Column	Variable Description	Code
VORELSP	66–67	Victim-offender relationship	01 = married 02 = common-law married 03 = lovers (boy/girlfriend) 04 = living together (not common-law) 05 = divorced 06 = separated 07 = friends 08 = homosexual relationship 09 = acquaintances 10 = strangers 11 = victim is child of offender 12 = victim is parent of offender 13 = victim is other relative of offender 14 = brother 15 = sister 16 = victim is step-parent of offender 17 = victim is step-child of offender 18 = in-laws 19 = ex-lovers 20 = offender's employer 99 = Missing data

OFFENSE CHARACTERISTICS

Variable Name	Column	Variable Description	Code
OFFDATE	68–73	Date of offense	MMDDYY 000000 = unknown 99999 = Missing data
OFFDAY	74	Day of week of offense	1 = Sun 2 = Mon 3 = Tues 4 = Wed 5 = Thurs 6 = Fri 7 = Sat 9 = Missing data
OFFTIME	75–78	Time of offense (military)	Actual time 0000 = unknown 9999 = Missing data
OFFLOC	79–80	OFFLOC (location of offense)	01 = Offender's residence 02 = Residence of both 03 = Victim's residence 04 = Other residence 05 = In Tavern/Lounge 06 = Out Tavern/Lounge 07 = Street, alley, parking lot 08 = Offender's neighborhood 09 = Other 10 = Place of business

Variable Name	Column	Variable Description	Code
			11 = In car
			99 = Missing data

Card #2

Variable Name	Column	Variable Description	Code
PREMED	1	Murder was premeditated	1 = Yes
			2 = No
			3 = Unknown
OFFROLE	2	Offender's role in the murder	1 = alone
			2 = with others
			8 = not applicable
			9 = Missing data
MOTIVE	3–4	Motive of the offender	01 = innocent
			02 = self defense
			03 = defense of others
			04 = accident
			05 = under influence
			06 = other(s) fault
			07 = physical reasons (e.g. PMS)
			08 = psychological reasons
			09 = multiple reasons
			10 = emotional reasons (e.g. anger, jealousy)
			11 = economic reasons (e.g. robbery, insurance, money, etc.)
			12 = fighting/argument/domestic quarrel
			13 = senseless
			14 = justifiable
			15 = unknown
			99 = Missing data
METHOD	5	Method used in murder	0 = neglect, starvation
			1 = gun
			2 = knife
			3 = household tool
			4 = poison, lye, etc.
			5 = clubbing weapon
			6 = hands/feet
			7 = strangulation/suffocation/ scalding/burning
			8 = drowning
			9 = Missing data
GUNTYPE	6	Type of firearm used	1 = pistol (handgun)
			2 = rifle
			3 = shot gun
			8 = NA
			9 = Missing data
OFFALC	7	Offender-alcohol use prior to homicide	1 = Yes
			2 = No
			8 = NA
			9 = Missing data

Variable Name	Column	Variable Description	Code
OFFNARC	8	Offender-narcotics use prior to homicide	1 = Yes 2 = No 8 = NA 9 = Missing data
VICALC	9	Victim-alcohol use prior to homicide	1 = Yes 2 = No 8 = NA 9 = Missing data
VICNARC	10	Victim-narcotics use prior to homicide	1 = Yes 2 = No 8 = NA 9 = Missing data
VICCOND	11	Condition of victim	1 = Helpless (child) 2 = Ill 3 = Asleep 4 = Drunk 5 = Infirm (adult) 6 = Not incapacitated 7 = Incapacitated (e.g. bound or tied) 8 = unknown
VICSEX	12	sex of victim	1 = male 2 = female 9 = Missing data
RESLOC	13–14	Location of homicide	01 = living room, family room, den 02 = dining room 03 = bed room 04 = kitchen 05 = bathroom 06 = foyer/hall 07 = basement 08 = porch 09 = yard 10 = driveway 11 = street, parking lot 88 = Not applicable 99 = Missing data
FINDISP	15–15	Final Disposition Charge	01 = Murder 1 02 = Murder 2 03 = Vol. Mansl. 04 = Invol. Mansl. 05 = Aggravated Assault 06 = Aggravated Battery 07 = Unlawful Restraint 08 = Negligent Homicide 09 = Offender died 10 = Offender suicide 11 = CCW 12 = Aggravated Robbery 13 = Armed Robbery 14 = Robbery 15 = Juvenile-unavailable

Variable Name	Column	Variable Description	Code
			16 = Juvenile incarceration
			17 = Robbery with injury
			18 = Accessory to murder
			19 = Cruelty to children
			20 = Attempted murder
			21 = Endangering welfare of a child
			22 = Sealed; purged
			88 = Not Applicable
			99 = Missing Data
VIOHIST	17	Offender/previous violent arrest history	1 = Yes 2 = No 8 = Not applicable 9 = Missing data
VVIOHIST	18	Victim's violent arrest history	1 = Yes 2 = No 8 = Not applicable 9 = Missing data
MOTIVAN	19–20	Interpretation and analysis of motive; not offender's rationale for the murder	01 = innocent 02 = self defense 03 = defense of others 04 = accident 05 = under influence 06 = other(s) fault 07 = physical reasons (e.g. PMS) 08 = psychological reasons 09 = multiple reasons 10 = emotional reasons (e.g. anger, jealousy) 11 = economic reasons (e.g. robbery, insurance money, etc.) 12 = fighting/argument/domestic quarrel 13 = senseless 14 = justifiable 15 = unknown 99 = Missing data
VICPREC	21	Victim precipitation of own death	1 = Yes 2 = No 9 = Missing data
OFFSUN	22–23	Offender's sun sign (zodiac)	1 = Aries 2 = Taurus 3 = Gemini 4 = Cancer 5 = Leo 6 = Virgo 7 = Libra 8 = Scorpio 9 = Sagittarius 10 = Capricorn 11 = Aquarius 12 = Pisces 99 = Missing data

Variable Name	Column	Variable Description	Code
OFFELEM	24	Offender's element (zodiac)	1 = air 2 = fire 3 = earth 4 = water 9 = Missing data
VICSUN	25–26	Victim's sum sign (zodiac)	1 = Aries 2 = Taurus 3 = Gemini 4 = Cancer 5 = Leo 6 = Virgo 7 = Libra 8 = Scorpio 9 = Sagittarius 10 = Capricorn 11 = Aquarius 12 = Pisces 99 = Missing data
VICELEM	27	Victim's element (zodiac)	1 = air 2 = fire 3 = earth 4 = water 9 = Missing data
OPRIORS	28	Offender has previous arrest record	1 = Yes 2 = No 3 = Missing data
CHILDTX	29	Child abuse history of offender	1 = Yes 2 = No 8 = Not applicable 9 = Missing data
WOUND	30	Number of wounds inflicted in the homicide	1 = one 2 = multiple 9 = Missing data

Appendix C: Offender Previous Arrests and Convictions by Selected Variables[1]

| | Total | | Year | | | | City | | | | Race/Ethnicity | | | | | |
| | | | 1979 | | 1983 | | South | | Nonsouth | | White | | African-American | | Hispanic-American | |
	N	%	N	%	N	%	N	%	N	%	N	%	N	%	N	%
Misdemeanor arrests																
	Range = 1 to 30		Range = 1 to 18		Range = 1 to 30		Range = 1 to 12		Range = 1 to 30		Range = 1 to 9		Range = 1 to 30		Range = 1 to 9	
	Mean = 1.8		Mean = 1.6		Mean = 2.0		Mean = 1.5		Mean = 2.0		Mean = 1.6		Mean = 1.9		Mean = 1.2	
None	142	55.3	84	57.5	58	52.3	66	53.7	76	56.7	16	47.1	112	55.4	14	66.7
1–5	82	31.9	44	30.2	38	34.2	43	34.9	39	29.1	14	41.1	63	31.2	5	23.8
5–10	22	8.5	12	8.2	11	9.0	12	9.8	10	7.5	4	11.8	16	8.0	2	9.5
10+	11	4.3	6	4.1	4	4.5	2	1.6	9	6.7	—	—	11	5.4	—	—
Totals	257	100.0	146	100.0	111	100.0	123	100.0	134	100.0	34	100.0	202	100.0	21	100.0
Misdemeanor convictions																
	Range = 1 to 10		Range = 1 to 10		Range = 1 to 4		Range = 1 to 10		Range = 1 to 8		Range = 1 to 3		Range = 1 to 10		Range = 1 to 4	
	Mean = 0.65		Mean = 0.61		Mean = 0.69		Mean = 0.58		Mean = 0.71		Mean = 0.40		Mean = 0.68		Mean = 0.74	
None	170	70.8	100	73.5	70	67.3	84	74.3	86	67.7	22	73.3	134	70.2	14	73.7
1–5	64	26.7	30	22.1	34	32.7	26	23.0	38	29.9	8	26.7	51	26.7	5	26.3
5–10	5	2.1	5	3.7	—	—	2	1.8	3	2.4	—	—	5	2.6	—	—
10+	1	0.4	1	0.7	—	—	1	0.9	—	—	—	—	1	0.5	—	—
Totals	240	100.0	136	100.0	104	100.0	114	100.0	127	100.0	30	100.0	191	100.0	19	100.0

Appendix C (Continued)

| | Total | | Year | | | | City | | | | Race/Ethnicity | | | | | |
| | | | 1979 | | 1983 | | South | | Nonsouth | | White | | African-American | | Hispanic-American | |
	N	%	N	%	N	%	N	%	N	%	N	%	N	%	N	%
Felony arrests	Range = 1 to 18 Mean = 1.3		Range = 1 to 14 Mean = 1.3		Range = 1 to 18 Mean = 1.3		Range = 1 to 14 Mean = 1.4		Range = 1 to 18 Mean = 1.3		Range = 1 to 5 Mean = 0.79		Range = 1 to 14 Mean = 1.4		Range = 1 to 18 Mean = 1.9	
None	159	62.1	92	63.0	67	60.9	73	60.8	86	63.2	21	63.6	126	62.4	12	57.1
1–5	71	27.7	37	25.4	34	30.9	34	28.4	37	27.2	10	30.3	54	26.7	7	33.4
5–10	20	7.9	14	9.5	6	5.5	10	8.3	10	7.4	2	6.1	18	8.9	—	—
10+	6	2.3	3	2.1	3	2.7	3	2.5	3	2.2	—	—	4	2.0	2	9.5
Totals	256	100.0	146	100.0	110	100.0	120	100.0	136	100.0	33	100.0	202	100.0	21	100.0
Felony conviction	Range = 1 to 7 Mean = 0.48		Range = 1 to 6 Mean = 0.46		Range = 1 to 7 Mean = 0.52		Range = 1 to 7 Mean = 0.47		Range = 1 to 5 Mean = 0.50		Range = 1 to 2 Mean = 0.19		Range = 1 to 7 Mean = 0.51		Range = 1 to 5 Mean = 0.78	
None	191	79.6	112	80.0	79	79.0	90	80.4	101	78.9	27	84.4	151	79.5	13	72.2
1–5	40	16.6	23	16.4	17	17.0	18	16.0	22	17.2	5	15.6	31	16.3	4	22.2
5–10	9	3.8	5	3.6	4	4.0	4	3.6	5	3.9	—	—	8	4.2	1	5.6
10+	—	—	—	—	—	—	—	—	—	—	—	—	—	—	—	—
Totals	240	100.0	140	100.0	100	100.0	112	100.0	128	100.0	32	100.0	190	100.0	18	100.0

1. Does not include missing cases.

Appendix D: Variables in the Regression Analysis of Prison Time

Variable	Coding
Dependent	
Prison time (PRITIME)	Actual numbers
Independent	
City	0 = Nonsouthern
	1 = Southern
Offender's total previous arrests (OPRIORS)	0 = Prior arrests
	1 = No prior arrests
Motive of offender (MOTIVE)	0 = Responsible
	1 = Not Responsible
Murder was premeditated (PREMED)	0 = No
	1 = Yes
Race of offender (RACE)	0 = White
	1 = Nonwhite (Black & Hispanic)
Race of victim (VRACE)	0 = White
	1 = Nonwhite (Black & Hispanic)
Number of wounds (WOUND)	0 = Single wound
	1 = Multiple wounds
Age of victim (VAGE)	Actual numbers
Offender's employment status (EMPLOY)	0 = Employed
	1 = Unemployed
Method used in murder (METHOD)	0 = Other
	1 = Gun
Age of offender (AGE)	Actual numbers
Offender's maternal status (MOTHER)	0 = Not a mother
	1 = A mother
Victim precipitation (VICPREC)	0 = No
	1 = Yes
Offender alcohol involvement (OFFALC)	0 = No
	1 = Yes
Offender narcotics involvement (OFFNARC)	0 = No
	1 = Yes
Gender of victim (VICSEX)	0 = Female
	1 = Male

Variable	Coding
Victim-offender relationship (VORELSP)	0 = Nonfamily 1 = "Family"
Offender's role in murder (OFFROLE)	0 = With others 1 = Alone
Condition of victim (VICCOND)	0 = Incapacitated[2] 1 = Not incapacitated

1. Common-law married, lovers, and in-laws included.
2. Helpless (child), ill or infirm (adult), asleep, drunk, bound or tied.

Bibliography

Abel, E. L. (1986). "Childhood Homicide in Erie County, New York." *Pediatrics* 77 (5) May: 709–713.

Abel, E. L. and P. Zeidenberg. (1986). "Alcohol and Homicide: A Comparison Between Erie County, New York, and Los Angeles County, California." *Am. J. Drug Alcohol Abuse* 12 (1 & 2): 121–129.

Adler, F. (1975). *Sisters in Crime: The Rise of the New Female Criminal.* New York: McGraw-Hill.

Archer, D. and R. Gartner. (1984). *Violence and Crime in Cross-National Perspective.* New Haven, Conn.: Yale University Press.

Arnold, R. A., P. J. Goldstein, H. H. Brownstein, & P. J. Ryan. (1988). "Women, Drugs, and Violence: Female Homicide Victims and Perpetrators." Unpublished paper.

Bailey, W. C. (1984). "Poverty, Inequality, and City Homicide Rates." *Criminology* 22 (4): 531–550.

Baron, L. "Gender Inequality and Child Homicide: A State-Level Analysis." In A. V. Wilson (ed.) *Homicide: The Victim/Offender Connection.* Cincinnati, Ohio: Anderson Publishing Company.

Bernstein, I. N., J. Cardascia, and C. E. Ross (1979). "Defendant's Sex and Criminal Court Decisions." In R. Alvarez and K. G. Lutterman and Associates (eds.), *Discrimination in Organizations.* San Francisco: Josey-Bass.

Biggers, T. A. (1979). "Death By Murder: A Study of Women Murderers." *Death Education* 3: 1–9.

Blackburne, Brian D. (1984). "Women Victims of Homicidal Violence." Unpublished paper.

Blau, J. R. and P. M. Blau. (1982). "The Cost of Inequality: Metropolitan Structure and Violent Crime." *American Sociological Review* 47: 114–129.

Block, C. R. (1985). *Lethal Violence in Chicago Over Seventeen Years: Homicides Known to the Police, 1965–1981.* (Chicago, Ill.: Criminal Justice Information Authority).

——— (1987). "Lethal Violence at Home: Racial/Ethnic Differences in Domestic Homicide Chicago, 1965 to 1981." Paper presented at the annual meeting of the American Society of Criminology.

——— and R. Block. (1991). "Beginning With Wolfgang: An Agenda for Homicide Research." *J. of Crime and Justice* XIV (2): 31–70.

Block, K. J. (1986). "Life Stages, Routine Activities and Homicides: Women in Baltimore, 1974–1984." Paper presented at the annual meeting of the American Society of Criminology, Atlanta.

Browne, A. (1986). *When Battered Women Kill.* New York: Free Press.

Browne, A. and K. R. Williams. (1993). "Gender, Intimacy, and Lethal Violence: Trends from 1976 through 1987." *Gender and Society* 7 (1): 78–98.

Bullock, H. A. (1955). "Urban Homicide in Theory and Fact." *J. of Criminal Law, Criminology and Police Science* 45: 565–575.

Bunch, B. J., L. A. Foley, & S. P. Urbina. (1983). "The Psychology of Violent Female Offenders: A Sex-Role Perspective." *The Prison Journal* 63 (2): 66–79.

Carpenter, A. and C. Provorse. (1992). *Facts About the Cities.* New York: H. W. Wilson Co.

Champion, D. J. (1990). *Criminal Justice in the United States.* Columbus, Ohio: Merrill Publishing Company.

Cheatwood, D. (1991). "Doing the Work of Research: Wolfgang's Foundation and Beyond." *J. of Crime and Justice* XIV (2): 3–15.

Christensen, F. (n.d.). "Balancing the Approach to Spouse Abuse." Unpublished paper sent to author.

Cole, K. E., G. Fisher and S. R. Cole (1968). "Women Who Kill." *Archives of General Psychiatry* 19: 1–8.

Curran, D. and C. Renzetti. (1994). *Theories of Crime.* Boston: Allyn and Bacon.

Daly, K. (1987). "Structure and Practice of Familial-Based Justice in a Criminal Court." *Law & Society Review* 21 (2): 267–290.

——— (1989). "Neither Conflict Nor Labeling Nor Paternalism Will Suffice: Intersections of Race, Ethnicity, Gender, and Family in Criminal Court Decisions." *Crime and Delinquency* 35 (1): 136–168.

Daly, M. and M. Wilson. (1988) *Homicide.* Hawthorne, N.Y.: Aldine de Gruyter.

De Witt, C. B. (1990). *DUF-Drug Use Forecasting.* Washington, D.C.: U.S. Government Printing Office.

Decker, S. (1993). "Exploring Victim-Offender Relationships in Homicide: The Role of Individual and Event Characteristics." *Justice Quarterly* 10 (4): 585–612.

Dixon, J. and A. J. Lizotte. (1987). "Gun Ownership and the 'Southern Subculture of Violence.' " *American J. of Sociology* 93 (2): 383–405.

Dodge, R. W. & H. R. Lentzer, (1980). *Crime and Seasonality.* Washington, D.C.: U.S. Department of Justice.

Dodge, R. W. (1988). *The Seasonality of Crime Victimization.* Washington, D.C.: U.S. Department of Justice.

Doerner, W. G. (1983). "Why Does Johnny Reb Die When Shot? The Impact of Medical Resources Upon Lethality." *Sociological Inquiry* 53 (1): 1–15.

Eber, L. P. (1981). "The Battered Wife's Dilemma: To Kill or To Be Killed." *The Hastings Law Journal* 32: 895–931.

Empey, L. T. (1978). *American Delinquency.* Homewood, Ill.: Dorsey Press.

Fenster, C. (1979). "Females as Partners in Crime: The Adjudication of Criminal Co-Defendants." Paper presented at annual meeting of the American Society of Criminology.

Flanagan, T. J., D. J. van Alstyne, & M. R. Gottfredson. (1982). *Sourcebook of Criminal Justice Statistics–1981.* Washington, D.C.: U.S. Government Printing Office.

Foley, L. A. & C. E. Rasche (1979). "The Effect of Race on Sentence, Actual Time Served and Final Disposition of Female Offenders." In J. A. Conley (ed.), *Theory and Research in Criminal Justice.* Cincinnati: Anderson.

Formby, W. A. (1986). "Homicides in a Semi-Rural Southern Environment." *J. of Criminal Justice* 9: 138–151.

Frazier, C. E., E. W. Bock, & J. C. Henretta. (1983). "The Role of Probation Officers in Determining Gender Differences in Sentencing Severity." *Sociological Quarterly* 24 (Spring): 305–318.

Gastil, Raymond D. (1971). "Homicide and a Regional Culture of Violence." *American Sociological Review* 36 (June): 412–427.

Gibbs, D. L., I. J. Silverman, and M. Vega (1977). "Homicides Committed by Females in the State of Florida." Paper presented at the annual meeting of the American Society of Criminology.

Goetting, A. (1987). "Homicidal Wives: A Profile." *Journal of Family Issues* 8 (3): 332–341.

——— (1988a). "Patterns of Homicide Among Women." *Journal of Interpersonal Violence* 3 (1): 3–20.

——— (1988b). "When Females Kill One Another." *Criminal Justice and Behavior* 15 (2): 179–189.

——— (1989). "Patterns of Marital Homicide: A Comparison of Husbands and Wives." *Journal of Comparative Family Studies* XX (3): 341–354.

Giordano, N. V. (1982). Unpublished doctoral dissertation sent to author.

Goldstein, P. J. (1985). "The Drugs-Violence Nexus: A Tripartite Conceptual Framework." *Journal of Drug Issues* 15 (4): 493–506.

———, P. A. Bellucci, B. J. Spunt, & T. Miller (1991). "Volume of Cocaine Use and Violence: A Comparison Between Men and Women." *J. of Drug Issues* 21 (2): 345–367.

Greenfield, L. A. and S. Minor-Harper. (1991). *Women in Prison.* Washington, D.C.: U.S. Department of Justice.

Gregware, P. and N. Jurik. (n.d.). "A Method for Murder: The Study of Female Homicide." Unpublished paper.

Hackney, S. (1969). "Southern Violence." *American Historical Review* 74: 906–925.

Hagan, F. E. (1982). *Research Methods in Criminal Justice and Criminology.* New York: Macmillan Publishing Co., Inc.

Hanke, P. J. and A. J. Shields, (1992). "Sentencing Variations of Women Convicted of Homicide in Alabama: 1929–1985." Paper presented at annual meeting of American Society of Criminology.

Harries, K. D. (1980). *Crime and the Environment.* Springfield, Ill.: Charles C. Thomas.

Hawkins, D. F. (1986). "Black and White Homicide Differentials: Alternatives to an Inadequate Theory." In Darnell F. Hawkins (ed.), *Homicide Among Black Americans.* (Lanham, Md.: University Press of America).

Hazlett, M. H. and T. C. Tomlinson, (1988). "Females Involved in Homicides: Victims and Offenders in Three U.S. States." Paper presented at the annual meeting of the American Society of Criminology, Chicago.

Hewitt, J. D. and G. A. Rivers. (1986). "The Victim-Offender Relationship in Convicted Homicide Cases: 1960–1984." Paper presented at the annual meeting of the Academy of Criminal Justice Sciences.

HRWG. (1994). Annual meeting of the Homicide Research Working Group, June 12–15, 1994, Emory University, Atlanta, Georgia.

Jason, J. and N. D. Andereck (1983). "Fatal Child Abuse in Georgia: The Epidemiology of Severe Physical Child Abuse." *Child Abuse and Neglect* 7: 1–9.

Johann, S. L. & F. Osanka. (1989). *Representing . . . Battered Women Who Kill.* Springfield, Ill.: Charles C. Thomas.

Jones, A. (1980). *Women Who Kill.* New York: Holt, Rinehart, and Winston.

Jose-Kampfner, C. (1990). "Coming to Terms with Existential Death: An Analysis of Women's Adaptation to Life in Prison." *Social Justice* 17 (2): 110–125.

Jurik, N. C. and R. Winn. (1990). "Gender and Homicide: A Comparison of Men and Women Who Kill." *Violence and Victims* 5 (4): 227–241.

Kaplan, S. J. (1960). "Climatic Factors and Crime." *The Professional Geographer* XII (6): 1–4.

Kaplun, D. and R. Reich (1976). "The Murdered Child and His Killers." *American Journal of Psychiatry* 133 (7), July: 809–813.

Kellermann, A. L. and J. A. Mercy. (1992). "Men, Women, and Murder: Gender-Specific Differences in Rates of Fatal Violence and Victimization." *The Journal of Trauma* 33 (1): 27–32.

Kempinen, C. (1983). "Changes in the Sentencing Patterns of Male and Female Criminal Defendants." *The Prison Journal* 63 (2): 3–11.

Kowalski, G. S., A. J. Shields and D. G. Wilson (1985). "The Female Murderer: Alabama 1929–1971." *Amer. J. Criminal Justice* 10 (1) Fall: 75–90.

Kruttschnitt, C. (1984). Sex and Criminal Court Dispositions: The Unresolved Controversy." *Research in Crime and Delinquency* 21 (3): 213–232.

―――― & D. E. Green. (1984). "The Sex-Sanctioning Issue: Is it History?" *American Sociological Review* 49 (4): 541–551.

Lab, S. P. & J. D. Hirschel. (1988). "Climatological Conditions and Crime; The Forecast is. . . ?" *Justice Quarterly* 5 (2): 288–299.

Langevin, R. & L. Handy (1987). Stranger Homicide in Canada: A National Sample and a Psychiatric Sample. *Journal of Criminal Law & Criminology*, 78, (2), 398–429.

Liska, A. E. and M. B. Chamlin. (1984). "Social Structure and Crime Control Among Macrosocial Units." *American Journal of Sociology* 90 (2): 383–395.

Loftin, C. K., S. L. Norris, & B. Wiersema (1987). An Attribute Approach to Relationships Between Offenders and Victims in Homicide. *Journal of Criminal Law & Criminology*, 78, (2), 259–271.

Loya, F., P. Garcia, and J. Sullivan. (1985). "Homicide in Los Angeles: Demographic Factors Related to Changes in the Rate of Violent Deaths: 1970–1979." Unpublished paper.

Loya, F. and J. Mercy. (1985). *The Epidemiology of Homicide in Los Angeles, 1970–1979*. Department of Health and Human Services, Public Health Service, Center for Diseases Control. Washington, D.C.: U.S. Government Printing Office.

Luckenbill, D. F. (1977). "Criminal Homicide as a Situated Transaction." *Social Problems* 25: 176–186.

―――― and D. P. Doyle. (1989). "Structural Position and Violence: Developing a Cultural Explanation." *Criminology* 27 (3): 419–436.

Lundsgaarde, H. P. (1977). *Murder in Space City*. New York: Oxford University Press.

Mann, C. R. (1984a). *Female Crime and Delinquency*. University, Ala.: University of Alabama Press.

―――― (1984b). "Race and Sentencing of Women Felons: A Field Study." *International Journal of Women's Studies* 7 (2): 160–172.

——— (1986). "The Black Female Criminal Homicide Offender in the United States." In Report of the Secretary's Task Force on Black and Minority Health. Vol. V.: Homicide, Suicide, and Unintentional Injuries. Washington, D.C.: U.S. Government Printing Office.

——— (1988). "Getting Even: Women Who Kill in Domestic Encounters." Justice Quarterly 5 (1): 33–51.

——— (1989). "Respondent Comments to: 'Are Women As Violent As Men?'" Paper presented at the annual meeting of the American Society of Criminology.

——— (1990). "Black Female Homicide in the United States." J. of Interpersonal Violence 5 (2): 176–201.

——— (1993). Unequal Justice: A Question of Color. Bloomington, Ind.: Indiana University Press.

Marsh, K. L. and D. D. Simpson. (1986). "Sex Differences in Opiod Addiction Careers." American J. of Drug and Alcohol Abuse 12 (4): 309–329.

McClain, P. D. (1981). In Harold M. Rose. Black Homicide and the Urban Environment. Washington, D.C.: National Institute of Mental Health.

——— (1982). "Black Female Homicide Offenders and Victims: Are They From the Same Population?" Death Education 6: 265–278.

———. (1982–83). "Black Females and Lethal Violence: Has Time Changed the Circumstances Under Which They Kill?" Omega 13 (1): 13–25.

McGarrell, E. F. & T. J. Flanagan. (1985). Sourcebook of Criminal Justice Statistics–1984. Washington, D.C.: U.S. Government Printing Office.

McLeod, M. (1984). "Women Against Men: An Examination of Domestic Violence Based on An Analysis of Official Data and National Victimization Data. Justice Quarterly 1 (2): 171–193.

McNeely, R. L. and C. R. Mann. (1990). "Domestic Violence Is a Human Issue." J. of Interpersonal Violence 5 (1): 129–132.

Messner, S. F. (1982). "Poverty, Inequality, and the Urban Homicide Rate." Criminology 20 (1): 103–114.

——— (1983). "Regional Differences in the Economic Correlates of the Urban Homicide Rate: Some Evidence on the Importance of Cultural Context." Criminology 21 (4): 477–488.

———— and Kenneth Tardiff. (1985). "The Social Ecology of Urban Homicide: An Application of the 'Routine Activities' Approach." *Criminology* 23 (2): 241–26.

———— and Kenneth Tardiff. (1986). "Economic Inequality and Levels of Homicide: An Analysis of Urban Neighborhoods." *Criminology* 24 (2): 297–317.

Miller, W. H. (1968). "Santa Ana Winds and Crime." *The Professional Geographer* XX (1): 23–27.

Moulds, E. T. (1978). "Chivalry and Paternalism: Disparities in the Criminal Justice System." *Western Political Quarterly* 31: 415–430.

Munford, R. S., Ross S. Kazer, Roger A. Feldman, and Robert R. Stivers. (1976). "Homicide Trends in Atlanta." *Criminology* 14 (2): 213–232.

NAACP Legal Defense Fund. (1992). *Death Row, U.S.A.* New York.

Nagel, S. & L. Weitzman. (1972). "The Double Standard of American Justice." *Society*: 18–25, 62–63.

New York City Police Department (NYCPD). (1977). *Homicide Analysis Report: New York City 1977.* New York: Crime Analysis Section, Office of Management Analysis.

Perkins, C. (1992). *National Corrections Reporting Program, 1989.* Washington, D.C.: U.S. Government Printing Office.

Pierce, R. L. and R. Trotta. (1986). "Abused Parents: A Hidden Family Problem." *J. of Family Violence* 1 (1): 99–110.

Pokorny, A. D. (1965). "A Comparison of Homicides in Two Cities." *J. of Criminal Law, Criminology and Police Science* 56 (December): 479–487.

Pollak, O. (1950). *The Criminality of Women.* Philadelphia: University of Pennsylvania Press.

Rasche, C. E. (1990). "Early Models for Contemporary Thought on Domestic Violence and Women Who Kill Their Mates: A Review of the Literature from 1895 to 1970." *Women and Criminal Justice* 1 (12): 31–53.

———— (1993). "Given Reasons for Violence in Intimate Relationships." In A. V. Wilson (ed.) *Homicide: The Victim/Offender Connection.* Cincinnati, Ohio: Anderson Publishing Company.

Raskó, G. (1976). "The Victim of the Female Killer." *Victimology* 1 (3): 396–402.

Renshaw III, B. H. (1980). *Crime and Seasonality.* Washington, D.C.: U.S. Government Printing Office.

Renzetti, C. (1992). *Violent Betrayal: Partner Abuse in Lesbian Relationships.* Newbury Park, Calif.: Sage.

Resnick, P. J. (1969). "Child Murder by Parents." *American Journal of Psychiatry* 126 (3) September: 325–334.

―――― (1970). "Murder of the Newborn: A Psychiatric Review of Neonaticide." *American Journal of Psychiatry* 126 (10) April: 1414–1420.

Riedel, M. (1987). Stranger Violence: Perspectives, Issues, and Problems. *Journal of Criminal Law & Criminology,* 78, (2), 223–258.

―――― and R. K. Przybylski. (1993). "Stranger Murders and Assault: A Study of a Neglected Form of Stranger Violence." In A. V. Wilson (ed.) Homicide: *The Victim/Offender Connection.* Cincinnati, Ohio: Anderson Publishing Company.

Rose, H. M. and P. D. McClain. (1990). *Race, Place, and Risk: Black Homicide in Urban America.* Albany, N.Y.: State University of New York Press.

Rose, L. (1986). *Massacre of the Innocents: Infanticide in Great Britain: 1800–1939.* London, U.K.: Routledge and Kegan Paul.

Rosenblatt, A. & C. Greenland. (1974). "Female Crimes of Violence." *Canadian J. of Criminology and Corrections* 16: 173–180.

Rosenfeld, A. (1983). "When Women Rape Men: The Body." *Omni:* 28, 194.

Saltzman, L. E. & J. A. Mercy. (1993). "Assaults Between Intimates: The Range of Relationships Involved." In A. V. Wilson (ed.) Homicide: *The Victim/Offender Connection.* Cincinnati, Ohio: Anderson Publishing Company.

Sampson, R. J. (1987). Personal Violence by Strangers: An Extension and Test of the Opportunity Model of Predatory Victimization. *Journal of Criminal Law & Criminology,* 78, (2), 327–356.

Sarrel, P. M. & W. H. Masters. (1982). "Sexual Molestation of Men by women." *Archives of Sexual Behavior* 11 (2): 117–131.

Sarri, R. C. (1986). "Gender and Race Differences in Criminal Justice Processing." *Women's Studies Int. Forum* 9 (1): 89–99.

Schneider, E. M. (1989). "Describing and Changing: Women's Self-Defense Work and the Problem of Expert Testimony on Battering." In S. L. Johann and F. Osanka (eds.) *Representing . . . Battered Women Who Kill.* Springfield, Ill.: Charles C. Thomas.

Segall, W. E. & A. V. Wilson. (1993). "Who is at Greatest Risk in Homicides?: A Comparison of Victimization Rates by Geographic Region." In A. V. Wilson (ed.) *Homicide: The Victim/Offender Connection.* Cincinnati, Ohio: Anderson Publishing Company.

Shield, A. J. (1987). "Female Homicide: Alabama 1930–1986." Unpublished paper.

Shin, Y., D. Jedlicka, and E. S. Lee. (1977). "Homicide Among Blacks." *Phylon* 38 (4): 398–407.

Silverman, R. A. & L. W. Kennedy. (1987). *The Female Perpetrator of Homicide in Canada.* Edmonton, Alberta: Centre for Criminological Research.

––––––– (1988). "Women Who Kill Their Children." *Violence and Victims* 3 (2): 113–127.

Silverman, I. J., M. Vega, and T. A. Danner. (1993). "The Female Murderer." In A. V. Wilson (ed.) *Homicide: The Victim/Offender Connection.* Cincinnati, Ohio: Anderson Publishing Company.

Simon, R. J. (1975). *The Contemporary Woman and Crime.* Washington, D.C.: U.S. Government Printing Office.

Snell, T. L. and D. C. Morton. (1994). *Women in Prison: Survey of State Prison Inmates, 1991.* Washington, D. C.: U.S. Department of Justice.

Spohn, S., J. Gruhl, and S. Welch (1985). "Women Defendants in Court: The Interaction Between Sex and Race in Convicting and Sentencing." *Social Science Quarterly* 66: 178–185.

Spunt, B. (1992). "Female Drug Relationships in Murder." A preliminary proposal shared with the author.

Steffensmeier, D. J. (1980). Sex Differences in Patterns of Adult Crime: A Review and Assessment. *Crime and Delinquency,* 26, 344–57.

––––––– and J. H. Kramer. (1982). "Sex-Based Differences in the Sentencing of Adult Criminal Defendants." *Sociology and Social Research* 66 (3): 289–304.

Straus, M. L. (1986). "Domestic Violence and Homicide Antecedents." *Bulletin of the N.Y. Academy of Medicine* 62 (5): 446–465.

—— (1989a). "Gender Differences in Assault in Intimate Relationships: Implications For Primary Prevention of Spousal Violence." Paper presented at the annual meeting of the American Society of Criminology.

—— (1989b). "Assaults By Wives on Husbands: Implications for Primary Prevention of Marital Violence." Paper presented at the annual meeting of the American Society of Criminology.

—— & R. J. Gelles. (1986). "Societal Change and Change in Family Violence from 1975 to 1985 as Revealed by Two National Surveys." *J. of Marriage and the Family* 48 (August): 465–479.

Straus, M. L., R. J. Gelles, & S. Steinmetz. (1980). *Behind Closed Doors: Violence in the American Family.* Newbury Park, Calif.: Sage Publications.

Steinmetz, S. K. (1978). "The Battered Husband Syndrome." *Victimology* 2 (3–4): 499–509.

Suval, E. M. and R. C. Brisson. (1974). "Neither Beauty Nor Beast: Female Homicide Offenders." *Intl. J. of Crime and Penology* 2 (1): 23–24.

Swersey, A. J. and E. Enloe. (1975). *Homicide in Harlem.* New York: The Rand Institute.

Temin, C. E. (1973). "Discriminatory Sentencing of Women Offenders: The Argument for ERA in a Nutshell." *American Criminal Law Review* 11: 355–372.

Thar, A. E. (1982). "The Admissibility of Expert Testimony on Battered Wife Syndrome: An Evidentiary Analysis." *Northwestern University Law Review* 77 (3): 348–373.

Thibault, E. A. & J. Rossier. (1992). "Misframed Family Violence Issues." Paper presented at the annual meeting of the American Society of Criminology.

Timrots, A. D. and M. R. Rand. (1987). *Violent Crime by Strangers and Non-strangers.* Washington, D.C.: U.S. Department of Justice.

Totman, J. (1978). *The Murderers: A Psychosocial Study of Criminal Homicide.* San Francisco, Calif.: R and E Research Associates.

U.S. Department of Health and Human Services. (1986). *Black and Minority Health, Vol. 5: Homicide, Suicide, and Unintentional Injuries.* Washington, D.C.: U.S. Government Printing Office.

U.S. Department of Justice. (1980). *Crime in the United States, 1979.* Washington, D.C.: U.S. Government Printing Office.

—— (1984). *Crime in the United States, 1983.* Washington, D.C.: U.S. Government Printing Office.

—— (1986). *Criminal Victimization in the United States, 1984: A National Crime Survey Report.* Washington, D.C.: U.S. Government Printing Office.

—— (1988). *Crime in the United States, 1987.* Washington, D.C.: U.S. Government Printing Office.

—— (1993). *Crime in the United States, 1992.* Washington, D.C.: U.S. Government Printing Office.

Walker, L. E. (1984). *The Battered Woman Syndrome.* New York: Springer.

Ward, D. A., M. Jackson, & R. E. Ward. (1969). "Crimes of Violence by Women." In D. Mulvihill & M. Tomin (eds.) *Crimes of Violence.* Washington, D.C.: U.S. Government Printing Office.

Weisheit, R. (1984). "Female Homicide Offenders: Trends Over Time in an Institutionalized Population." *Justice Quarterly* 1 (4): 471–489.

—— (1986). "When Mothers Kill Their Children." *The Social Science Journal* 23 (4): 439–448.

Wilbanks, W. (1982). "Murdered Women and Women Who Murder: A Critique of the Literature." In N. H. Rafter and E. A. Stanko (eds.) *Judge, Lawyer, Victim, Thief: Women, Gender Roles, and Criminal Justice.* Boston: Northeastern University Press.

—— (1983a). "The Female Homicide Offender in Dade County, Florida." *Criminal Justice Review* 8 (2): 9–14.

—— (1983b). "Female Homicide Offenders in the U.S." *International J. of Women's Studies* 6 (4): 302–310.

Wilson, M. I. and M. Daly. (1992). "Who Kills Whom in Spouse Killings? On the Exceptional Ratio of Spousal Homicides in the United States." *Criminology* 30 (2): 189–215.

Wilson, N. K. (1993). "Gendered Interaction in Criminal Homicide." In A. V. Wilson (ed.) *Homicide: The Victim/Offender Connection.* Cincinnati, Ohio: Anderson Publishing Company.

Wiltz, C. J. (1985). "Poverty, Family Structure and Black Homicide." Paper presented at annual meeting of the Academy of Criminal Justice Sciences.

Winn, R. G., L. M. Haugen, and N. Jurik. (1988). "A Comparison of the Situational Determinants of Males and Females Convicted of Murder." Paper presented at the annual meeting of the Academy of Criminal Justice Sciences.

Wolfgang, M. E. (1958). *Patterns in Criminal Homicide.* Philadelphia: University of Pennsylvania Press.

———— and F. Ferracuti. (1967). *The Subculture of Violence.* Beverly Hills: Sage.

Zahn, M. A. (1991). "The Wolfgang Model: Lessons for Homicide Research in the 1990s." *J. of Crime and Justice* XIV (2): 17–30.

———— and P. C. Sagi. (1987). Stranger Homicides in Nine American Cities. *Journal of Criminal Law & Criminology,* 78, (2). 377–397.

Zimring, F. E., S. K. Mukherjee, & B. Van Winkle. (1983). "Intimate Violence: A Study of Intersexual Homicide in Chicago." *U. of Chicago Law Review* 50: 910–930.

Index

whites
  elder abuse of, 6
  homicide victim of, 165, 173
    African American, 122
    friends, 113
    infant, 70, 72, 73, 94
    domestic, 79–80, 81–82
    drug use, and, 124
    in other studies, 84, 86, 87, 88,
      98, 99
    southern, 90
  lesbian homicide and, 91
  intragender homicide and, 100
  female homicide offender, 118, 120,
    164, 166, 172
  comparisons by race, 139–146
  life sentences of, 158

prior arrests of, 161
as battered women, 170
wife-husband homicide, *see* domestic
  homicide
Wilbanks, William, 4, 9, 10, 15, 16,
  20n. 9, 22, 40, 41, 46, 64, 71,
  83, 86, 89, 99, 177
Wilson, Margo, 4, 36–38, 39, 40, 43n.
  16, 79, 97
Wolfgang, Marvin, 7, 10, 14, 15, 16,
  21n. 11, 25, 29, 38, 40, 41, 46,
  49, 54, 60, 61, 63, 79, 84, 86,
  88, 89, 99, 107, 108, 109, 169
wounds, number of, 46, 65–66
  in filicide, 76–77
  in lesbian cases, 91
  multiple, 54, 65–66, 154
  single, 65, 154